ANCIENT
CHRISTIAN
TEXTS

COMMENTARY ON THE GOSPEL OF JOHN

Theodore of Mopsuestia

TRANSLATED WITH AN
INTRODUCTION AND NOTES BY
MARCO CONTI

EDITED BY
JOEL C. ELOWSKY

SERIES EDITORS
THOMAS C. ODEN AND GERALD L. BRAY

IVP Academic
An imprint of InterVarsity Press
Downers Grove, Illinois

InterVarsity Press
P.O. Box 1400, Downers Grove, IL 60515-1426
World Wide Web: www.ivpress.com
E-mail: email@ivpress.com

InterVarsity Press® is the book-publishing division of InterVarsity Christian Fellowship/USA®, a movement of students and faculty active on campus at hundreds of universities, colleges and schools of nursing in the United States of America, and a member movement of the International Fellowship of Evangelical Students. For information about local and regional activities, write Public Relations Dept., InterVarsity Christian Fellowship/USA, 6400 Schroeder Rd., P.O. Box 7895, Madison, WI 53707-7895, or visit the IVCF website at <www.intervarsity.org>.

Design: Cindy Kiple

Images: Saints Peter and Paul by Carlo Crivelli at Accademia, Venice/Art Resource, NY

ISBN 978-0-8308-2906-4

Printed in the United States of America ∞

 InterVarsity Press is committed to protecting the environment and to the responsible use of natural resources. As a member of Green Press Initiative we use recycled paper whenever possible. To learn more about the Green Press Initiative, visit <www.greenpressinitiative.org>.

Library of Congress Cataloging-in-Publication Data

Theodore, Bishop of Mopsuestia, ca. 350-428 or 9.
  Commentary on the Gospel of John / Theodore of Mopsuestia;
translated by Marco Conti; edited by Joel C. Elowsky.
      p. cm.—(Ancient Christian texts)
  Includes bibliographical references and index.
  ISBN 978-0-8308-2906-4 (cloth: alk. paper)
  1. Bible. N.T. John—Commentaries I. Elowsky, Joel C., 1963- II.
Title.
  BS2615.53.T4913 2010
  226.5'07—dc22

                                                                                                    2009042067

| **P** | 24 | 23 | 22 | 21 | 20 | 19 | 18 | 17 | 16 | 15 | 14 | 13 | 12 | 11 | 10 | 9 | 8 | 7 | 6 | 5 | 4 | 3 | 2 | 1 |
| **Y** | 31 | 30 | 29 | 28 | 27 | 26 | 25 | 24 | 23 | 22 | 21 | 20 | 19 | 18 | 17 | 16 | 15 | 14 | 13 | 12 | 11 | 10 | | |

CONTENTS

GENERAL INTRODUCTION

The Ancient Christian Texts series (hereafter ACT) presents the full text of ancient Christian commentaries on Scripture that have remained so unnoticed that they have not yet been translated into English.

The patristic period (A.D. 95-750) is the time of the fathers of the church, when the exegesis of Scripture texts was in its primitive formation. This period spans from Clement of Rome to John of Damascus, embracing seven centuries of biblical interpretation, from the end of the New Testament to the mid-eighth century, including the Venerable Bede.

This series extends but does not reduplicate texts of the Ancient Christian Commentary on Scripture (ACCS). It presents full-length translations of texts that appear only as brief extracts in the ACCS. The ACCS began years ago authorizing full-length translations of key patristic texts on Scripture in order to provide fresh sources of valuable commentary that previously was not available in English. It is from these translations that the ACT Series has emerged.

A multiyear project such as this requires a well-defined objective. The task is straightforward: *to introduce full-length translations of key texts of early Christian teaching, homilies and commentaries on a particular book of Scripture.* These are seminal documents that have decisively shaped the entire subsequent history of biblical exegesis, but in our time have been largely ignored.

To carry out this mission the Ancient Christian Texts series has four aspirations:

1. To show the approach of one of the early Christian writers in dealing with the problems of understanding, reading and conveying the meaning of a particular book of Scripture.

2. To make more fully available the whole argument of the ancient Christian interpreter of Scripture to all who wish to think with the early church about a particular canonical text.

3. To broaden the base of biblical studies, Christian teaching and preaching to include classical Christian exegesis.

4. To stimulate Christian historical, biblical, theological and pastoral scholarship toward deeper inquiry into early classic practitioners of scriptural interpretation.

For Whom Is This Series Designed?

We have selected and translated these texts primarily for general and nonprofessional use by an audience of persons who study the Bible regularly.

In varied cultural settings around the world, contemporary readers are asking how they might grasp the meaning of sacred texts under the instruction of the great minds of the ancient church. They often study books of the Bible verse by verse, book by book, in groups and workshops, sometimes with a modern commentary in hand. But many who study the Bible intensively hunger to have available to them as well the thoughts of some reliable classic Christian commentator on this same text. This series will give the modern commentators a classical text for comparison and amplification. Readers will judge for themselves as to how valuable or complementary are their insights and guidance.

The classic texts we are translating were originally written for anyone (lay or clergy, believers and seekers) who would wish to reflect and meditate with the great minds of the early church. They sought to illuminate the plain sense, theological wisdom, and moral and spiritual meaning of an individual book of Scripture. They were not written for an academic audience, but for a community of faith shaped by the sacred text.

Yet in serving this general audience, the editors remain determined not to neglect the rigorous requirements and needs of academic readers who until recently have had few full translations available to them in the history of exegesis. So this series is designed also to serve public libraries, universities, academic classes, homiletic preparation and historical interests worldwide in Christian scholarship and interpretation.

Hence our expected audience is not limited to the highly technical and specialized scholarly field of patristic studies, with its strong bent toward detailed word studies and explorations of cultural contexts. Though all of our editors and translators are patristic and linguistic scholars, they also are scholars who search for the meanings and implications of the texts. The audience is not primarily the university scholar concentrating on the study of the history of the transmission of the text or those with highly focused interests in textual morphology or historical-critical issues. If we succeed in serving our wider readers practically and well, we hope to serve as well college and seminary courses in Bible, church history, historical theology, hermeneutics and homiletics. These texts have not until now been available to these classes.

Readiness for Classic Spiritual Formation

Today global Christians are being steadily drawn toward these biblical and patristic sources for daily meditation and spiritual formation. They are on the outlook for primary classic sources of spiritual formation and biblical interpretation, presented in accessible form and grounded in reliable scholarship.

These crucial texts have had an extended epoch of sustained influence on Scripture interpretation, but virtually no influence in the modern period. They also deserve a hearing among modern readers and scholars. There is a growing awareness of the speculative excesses and spiritual and homiletic limitations of much post-Enlightenment criticism. Meanwhile the motifs, methods and approaches of ancient exegetes have remained unfamiliar not only to historians but to otherwise highly literate biblical scholars, trained exhaustively in the methods of historical and scientific criticism.

It is ironic that our times, which claim to be so fully furnished with historical insight and research methods, have neglected these texts more than scholars in previous centuries who could read them in their original languages.

This series provides indisputable evidence of the modern neglect of classic Christian exegesis: it remains a fact that extensive and once authoritative classic commentaries on Scripture still remain untranslated into any modern language. Even in China such a high level of neglect has not befallen classic Buddhist, Taoist and Confucian commentaries.

Ecumenical Scholarship

This series, like its two companion series, the ACCS and Ancient Christian Doctrine (ACD), are expressions of unceasing ecumenical efforts that have enjoyed the wide cooperation of distinguished scholars of many differing academic communities. Under this classic textual umbrella, it has brought together in common spirit Christians who have long distanced themselves from each other by competing church memories. But all of these traditions have an equal right to appeal to the early history of Christian exegesis. All of these traditions can, without a sacrifice of principle or intellect, come together to study texts common to them all. This is its ecumenical significance.

This series of translations is respectful of a distinctively theological reading of Scripture that cannot be reduced to historical, philosophical, scientific, or sociological insights or methods alone. It takes seriously the venerable tradition of ecumenical reflection concerning the premises of revelation, providence, apostolicity, canon and consensuality. A high respect is here granted, despite modern assumptions, to uniquely Christian theological forms of reasoning, such as classical consensual christological and triune reasoning, as distinguishing premises of classic Christian textual interpretation. These cannot be acquired by empirical methods alone. This approach does not pit theology against critical theory; instead, it incorporates critical historical methods and brings them into coordinate accountability within its larger purpose of listening to Scripture.

The internationally diverse character of our editors and translators corresponds with the global range of our audience, which bridges many major communions of Christianity. We have sought to bring together a distinguished international network of Protestant, Catholic and Orthodox scholars, editors, and translators of the highest quality and reputation to accomplish this design.

But why just now at this historical moment is this need for patristic wisdom felt particularly by so many readers of Scripture? Part of the reason is that these readers have been long deprived of significant contact with many of these vital sources of classic Christian exegesis.

The Ancient Commentary Tradition

This series focuses on texts that comment on Scripture and teach its meaning. We define a commentary in its plain-sense definition as a series of illustrative or explanatory notes on any work of enduring significance. The word *commentary* is an Anglicized form of the Latin *commentarius* (or "annotation" or "memoranda" on a subject or text or series of events). In its theological meaning it is a work that explains, analyzes or expounds a biblical book or portion of Scripture. Tertullian, Origen, John Chrysostom, Jerome, Augustine and Clement of Alexandria all revealed their familiarity with both the secular and religious commentators available to them as they unpacked the meanings of the sacred text at hand.

The commentary in ancient times typically began with a general introduction covering such questions as authorship, date, purpose and audience. It commented as needed on grammatical or lexical problems in the text and provided explanations of difficulties in the text. It typically moved verse by verse through a Scripture text, seeking to make its meaning clear and its import understood.

The general western literary genre of commentary has been definitively shaped by the history of early Christian commentaries on Scripture. It is from Origen, Hilary, the *Opus imperfectum in Matthaeum*, John Chrysostom and Cyril of Alexandria that we learn what a commentary is—far more so than in the case of classic medical or philosophical or poetic commentaries. It leaves too much unsaid simply to assume that the Christian biblical commentary took a previously extant literary genre and reshaped it for Christian texts. Rather it is more accurate to say that *the Western literary genre of the commentary (and especially the biblical commentary) has patristic commentaries as its decisive pattern and prototype.*

It is only in the last two centuries, since the development of modern historicist methods of criticism, that modern writers have sought more strictly to delimit the definition of a commentary so as to include only certain limited interests focusing largely on historical-critical method, philological and grammatical observations, literary analysis, and socio-political or economic circumstances impinging on the text. While respecting all these approaches, the ACT editors do not hesitate to use the classic word *commentary* to define more broadly the genre of this series. These are commentaries in their classic sense.

The ACT editors freely take the assumption that the Christian canon is to be respected as the church's sacred text. The reading and preaching of Scripture are vital to religious life. The central hope of this endeavor is that it might contribute in some small way to the revitalization of religious faith and community through a renewed discovery of the earliest readings of the church's Scriptures.

An Appeal to Allow the Text to Speak for Itself

This prompts two appeals:

1. For those who begin by assuming as normative for a commentary only the norms considered typical for modern expressions of what a commentary is, we ask: Please allow the ancient commentators to define *commentarius* according to their own lights. Those who assume the preemptive authority and truthfulness of modern critical methods alone will always tend to view the classic Christian exegetes as dated, quaint, premodern, hence inadequate, and in some instances comic or even mean-spirited, prejudiced, unjust and oppressive. So in the interest of hermeneutical fairness, it is recommended that the modern reader not impose on ancient Christian exegetes modern assumptions about valid readings of Scripture. The ancient Christian writers constantly challenge these unspoken, hidden and indeed often camouflaged assumptions that have become commonplace in our time.

We leave it to others to discuss the merits of ancient versus modern methods of exegesis. But even this cannot be done honestly without a serious examination of the texts of ancient exegesis. Ancient commentaries may be disqualified as commentaries by modern standards. But they remain commentaries by the standards of those who anteceded and formed the basis of the modern commentary.

The attempt to read a Scripture text while ruling out all theological and moral assumptions—as well as ecclesial, sacramental and dogmatic assumptions that have prevailed generally in the community of faith out of which it emerged—is a very thin enterprise indeed. Those who tendentiously may read a single page of patristic exegesis, gasp and toss it away because it does not conform adequately to the canons of modern exegesis and historicist commentary are surely not exhibiting a valid model for critical inquiry today.

2. In ancient Christian exegesis, chains of biblical references were often very important in thinking about the text in relation to the whole testimony of sacred Scripture, by the analogy of faith, comparing text with text, on the premise that *scripturam ex scriptura explicandam esse*. When ancient exegesis weaves many Scriptures together, it does not limit its focus to a single text as much modern exegesis prefers, but constantly relates it to other texts, by analogy, intensively using typological reasoning, as did the rabbinic tradition.

Since the principle prevails in ancient Christian exegesis that each text is illumined by other texts and by the whole narrative of the history of revelation, we find in patristic comments on a given text many other subtexts interwoven in order to illumine that text. In these ways the models of exegesis often do not correspond with modern commentary assumptions, which tend to resist or rule out chains of scriptural reference. We implore the reader not to force the assumptions of twentieth-century hermeneutics on the ancient Christian writers, who themselves knew nothing of what we now call hermeneutics.

The Complementarity of Research Methods in this Series

The Ancient Christian Texts series will employ several interrelated methods of research, which the editors and translators seek to bring together in a working integration. Principal among these methods are the following:

1. The editors, translators and annotators will bring to bear the best resources of *textual criticism* in preparation for their volumes. This series is not intended to produce a new critical edition of the original-language text. The best Urtext in the original language will be used. Significant variants in the earliest manuscript sources of the text may be commented on as needed in the annotations. But it will be assumed that the editors and translators will be familiar with the textual ambiguities of a particular text and be able to state their conclusions about significant differences among scholars. Since we are working with ancient texts that have, in some cases, problematic or ambiguous passages, we are obliged to employ all methods of historical, philological and textual inquiry appropriate to the study of ancient texts. To that end, we will appeal to the most reliable text-critical scholarship of both biblical and patristic studies. We will assume that our editors and translators have reviewed the international literature of textual critics regarding their text so as to provide the reader with a translation of the most authoritative and reliable form of the ancient text. We will leave it to the volume editors and translators, under the supervision of the general editors, to make these assessments. This will include the challenge of considering which variants within the biblical text itself might impinge on the patristic text, and which forms or stemma of the biblical text the patristic writer was employing. The annotator will supply explanatory footnotes where these textual challenges may raise potential confusions for the reader.

2. Our editors and translators will seek to understand the *historical context* (including socioeconomic, political and psychological aspects as needed) of the text. These understandings are often vital to right discernment of the writer's intention. Yet we do not see our primary mission as that of discussing in detail these contexts. They are to be factored into the translation and commented on as needed in the annotations, but are not to become the primary focus of this series. Our central interest is less in the social location of the text or the philological history of particular words than in authorial intent and accurate translation. Assuming a proper social-historical contextualization of the text, the main focus of this series will be on a dispassionate and fair translation and analysis of the text itself.

3. The main task is to set forth the meaning of the biblical text itself as understood by the patristic writer. The intention of our volume editors and translators is to help the

reader see clearly into the meanings which patristic commentators have discovered in the biblical text. *Exegesis* in its classic sense implies an effort to explain, interpret and comment on a text, its meaning, its sources and its connections with other texts. It implies a close reading of the text, utilizing whatever linguistic, historical, literary or theological resources are available to explain the text. It is contrasted with *eisegesis*, which implies that interpreters have imposed their own personal opinions or assumptions on the text. The patristic writers actively practiced intratextual exegesis, which seeks to define and identify the exact wording of the text, its grammatical structure and the interconnectedness of its parts. They also practiced extratextual exegesis, seeking to discern the geographical, historical or cultural context in which the text was written. Our editors and annotators will also be attentive as needed to the ways in which the ancient Christian writer described his own interpreting process or hermeneutic assumptions.

4. The underlying philosophy of translation that we employ in this series, like that of the Ancient Christian Commentary on Scripture, is termed *dynamic equivalency*. We wish to avoid the pitfalls of either too loose a paraphrase or too rigid a literal translation. We seek language that is literary but not purely literal. Whenever possible we have opted for the metaphors and terms that are normally in use in everyday English-speaking culture. Our purpose is to allow the ancient Christian writers to speak for themselves to ordinary readers in the present generation. We want to make it easier for the Bible reader to gain ready access to the deepest reflection of the ancient Christian community of faith on a particular book of Scripture. We seek a thought-for-thought translation rather than a formal equivalence or word-for-word style. This requires the words to be first translated accurately and then rendered in understandable idiom. We seek to present the same thoughts, feelings, connotations and effects of the original text in everyday English language. We have used vocabulary and language structures commonly used by the average person. We do not leave the quality of translation only to the primary translator, but pass it through several levels of editorial review before confirming it.

The Function of the ACT Introductions, Annotations and Translations

In writing the introduction for a particular volume of the ACT series, the translator or volume editor will discuss, where possible, the opinion of the writer regarding authorship of the text, the importance of the biblical book for other patristic interpreters, the availability or paucity of patristic comment, any salient points of debate between the Fathers, and any special challenges involved in translating and editing the particular volume. The introduction affords the opportunity to frame the entire commentary in a manner that will help the general reader understand the nature and significance of patristic comment on the biblical texts under consideration and to help readers find their critical bearings so as to read and use the commentary in an informed way.

The footnotes will assist the reader with obscurities and potential confusions. In the annotations the volume editors have identified Scripture allusions and historical references embedded within the texts. Their purpose is to help the reader move easily from passage to passage without losing a sense of the whole.

The ACT general editors seek to be circumspect and meticulous in commissioning volume editors and translators. We strive for a high level of consistency and literary quality throughout the course of this series. We have sought out as volume editors and translators those patristic and biblical scholars who are thoroughly familiar with their original language sources, who are informed historically, and who are sympathetic to the needs of ordinary nonprofessional readers who may not have professional language skills.

Thomas C. Oden and Gerald L. Bray

ABBREVIATIONS

Aug	*Augustinianum*
CCSL	Corpus Christianorum: Series latina
CPG	*Clavis patrum graecorum*
CSCO	Corpus scriptorum christianorum orientalium
CSEL	Corpus scriptorum ecclesiasticorum latinorum
GCS	Die griechischen christlichen Schriftsteller der ersten [drei] Jahrhunderte
HSem	Horae Semiticae
ITQ	*Irish Theological Quarterly*
PG	Patrologia graeca
PL	Patrologia latina
RB	*Revue biblique*
RSO	*Rivista degli studi orientali*
RSR	*Recherches de science religieuse*
SC	Sources chrétiennes
Vat. Syr.	Vatican Syriac manuscripts

TRANSLATOR'S INTRODUCTION

The only reliable historical information about Theodore's life is based on the testimonies of three writers who published their works shortly after his death: Socrates,[1] Sozomen[2] and Theodoret of Cyr.[3] They all agree that he was born in Antioch[4] and had a traditional literary and rhetorical education at the school of the sophist Libanius.[5] It was there that he met John Chrysostom and began a lifelong friendship with him that crucially influenced his life and religious career. After completing his studies, Theodore was invited by Chrysostom to embrace the monastic life under the spiritual guidance of Diodore of Tarsus.[6] However, after a few years Theodore decided to go back to his secular activities and to marry. Chrysostom intervened by way of two letters, which he sent to Theodore openly condemning his decision.[7] Theodore was persuaded by his friend and dissuaded from following his plans for life in the secular world.

In 383 he was ordained into the priesthood by Flavian, the bishop of Antioch, and in 392 was elected bishop of Mopsuestia in Cilicia. Throughout these years he kept close ties with Diodore of Tarsus, who strongly influenced his activity as a theologian and interpreter of Scripture. After Diodore's death, just before 394, Theodore succeeded him as the key interpreter of Scripture among the Antiochenes. He gained much popularity for his profound theological insights, which contributed to the success of his work in Mop-

---

[1] Cf. Socrates *Ecclesiastical History* 6.3 (PG 67:665-68).

[2] Cf. Sozomen *Ecclesiastical History* 8.2 (PG 67:1516).

[3] Cf. Theodoret of Cyr *Ecclesiastical History* 5.39 (PG 82:1277). See also R. Devreesse, *Essai sur Théodore de Mopsueste*, Studi e Testi 141 (Vatican City: Biblioteca Apostolica Vaticana, 1948), pp. 1-4.

[4] There is no precise indication of when he was born. Scholars place his birth around the middle of the fourth century (ca. 350), allowing roughly thirty years to the time when he would have been ordained a priest, which occurred in 383.

[5] Libanius was a pagan rhetorician and sophist who studied in Athens with Basil the Great and Gregory of Nazianzus. Later he opened his own school, first in Constantinople, and then in Nicomedia and Antioch. He was a close friend and supporter of the emperor Julian, and tried with his help to restore paganism and Hellenism in the Roman Empire.

[6] Diodore is acknowledged as one of the most important representatives of the theological and exegetical school of Antioch. He had an extremely strong influence on his contemporaries, and began the interpretative line which was later developed and perfected by Theodore of Mopsuestia and Nestorius.

[7] John Chrysostom *Ad Theodorum lapsum* 1-2 (PG 47:277-316).

suestia and the See of Antioch and its environs.[8] Both Nestorius[9] and Theodoret of Cyr[10] may have been among his pupils. He died in 428 before the outbreak of the controversy between Nestorius and Cyril of Alexandria. But this did not spare him a posthumous participation in that controversy.

More than one hundred years after his death, Theodore's writings were included in Justinian's campaign against Nestorius and were condemned by the emperor, along with those of Theodoret of Cyr and Ibas of Edessa.[11] Although obviously not present to defend himself, Theodore was nonetheless accused and then condemned as one of the originators of Nestorianism.[12] His writings were branded as heretical in the edict of the Three Chapters (543-544),[13] and again ten years later at the Second Council of Constantinople (553).

The Works of Theodore of Mopsuestia

Once Theodore's writings were condemned as Nestorian, a large portion of them were destroyed or lost. In fact, at present many of his works are only known by title, having not survived the purge of the sixth-century condemnations. It is possible to read an almost complete list of his works in two catalogs of books dating from the end of the medieval period. The first, in Arabic, dates from the early thirteenth century and is included in the so-called Chronicle of Seert.[14] The second is in Syriac and is part of the "Catalog of Syriac Books" compiled by Ebedjesu at the beginning of the fourteenth century.[15] On the basis of the extant works and fragments and the two medieval catalogs, Theodore's works

---

[8]See also J.-M. Vosté, "La chronologie de l'activité littéraire de Théodore de Mopsuestia," *RB* 34 (1925): 54-81; G. Kalantzis, "Theodore of Mopsuestia's 'Commentarius in evangelium Iohannis Apostoli': Text and Transmission," *Aug* 43, no. 2 (2003): 473-93.

[9]Nestorius (ca. 390-451), originally from Syria, studied in a monastery in Antioch, probably under the direction of Theodore of Mopsuestia. He soon became one of the most brilliant representatives of this theological school. After being elected bishop of Constantinople in 428, his theological views, which are the basis of the Nestorian heresy, were condemned by Cyril, bishop of Alexandria, so that he was deposed from his see in 431. It is extremely difficult to reconstruct with certainty the theory of Nestorius concerning the two natures of Christ, and it is even more difficult to determine exactly what aspects of his teaching could be accused of heresy. According to Nestorius's opponents, he not only taught that there were two separate natures (human and divine) in Christ, but two separate persons (a divine Christ and a human Christ). This accusation was based primarily on the fact that Nestorius opposed the term *Theotokos* ("Mother of God" or, more literally, "God-bearer") as an epithet of the Virgin Mary.

[10]Theodoret of Cyr (ca. 393-466) is another extremely important representative of the Antiochene school. He supported Nestorius's christological views and opposed Cyril of Alexandria. It is possible that he abandoned the Nestorian party in the last years of his life, that is, after 451.

[11]Ibas of Edessa (ca. 400-460) held a more moderate position in comparison with Theodoret and tried to find a compromise between Cyril's and Nestorius's doctrine.

[12]Cf. n. 9.

[13]The "Three Chapters," as it was called, was an edict pronounced by the emperor Justinian in 543-44, in which he condemned Theodore of Mopsuestia, Theodoret of Cyrus and Ibas of Edessa as Nestorians. This same edict was confirmed in the Second Council of Constantinople of 553.

[14]Cf. Addai Scher, ed., *Histoire Nestorienne (Cronique de Séert)*, Première Partie (II), Patrologia Orientalis 5 (Paris: Firmin-Didot, 1910), pp. 217-344 (289-90). Seert (Siirt) is a town in Kurdistan (presently in southeast Turkey). Its important library was unfortunately destroyed in the course of World War I.

[15]Cf. J.-S. Assemani, ed., *Catalogus Librorum Syrorum Ebedjesu*, Bibliotheca Orientalis 3, no. 1 (Rome: Typis Sacrae Congregationis de Propaganda Fide, 1725), pp. 30-35.

---

can be easily grouped into two main categories: exegetical and theological.[16]

According to the Chronicle of Seert and Ebedjesu's Catalog, Theodore wrote a commentary on Genesis and the Pentateuch. Fragments found in catenae, however, demonstrate that he also analyzed the entire Octateuch. Unfortunately, only fragments covering small sections of Genesis, Exodus, Joshua and Judges are extant. The largest are those commenting on the first chapters of Genesis (known as the *Hexaemeron*), in which Theodore uses the literal approach typical of his exegesis and openly opposes the theories of Basil the Great, who conceived a sort of precreation world reserved for the spiritual powers.[17] We know from the two medieval catalogs and other testimonies that Theodore also wrote commentaries on nearly all the other books of the Old Testament.[18] Of this extremely large and important exegetical activity only the commentaries on the Psalms and the twelve Minor Prophets are extant.

The commentary on the Psalms, as Theodore tells his readers in a fragment from one of his lost writings,[19] was a work he had hurriedly composed in his early twenties.[20] Despite its limitations, the commentary, of which the catenae have preserved many fragments,[21] appears to be extremely important among Theodore's works. Based on these fragments, Devreesse constructed a critical edition of Theodore's commentary on the Psalms from which the late Robert C. Hill has provided us an English translation of Theodore's *Commentary on Psalms 1–81* in the series Writings from the Greco-Roman World.[22] Already at this early stage of his writing, the main characteristics of his literal exegesis and Christology are evident. The importance of this work is also confirmed by the frequent references that Theodore himself makes to this commentary in other works.

The commentary on the twelve Minor Prophets did not suffer the same fate as his Psalms commentary. It has been preserved in its entirety and was first published in the nineteenth century by Angelo Mai, whose edition was later included in Migne's Patrologia graeca.[23] A more critical edition was published in 1977.[24] In this work Theodore's exegetical approach appears to be more focused and, again, completely in line with that of the Antiochene school. A sound literal analysis and a constant attention to the historical context characterize this commentary. Allegorical and typological interpretations

---

[16]Theodore is also the author of three ascetical treatises and an epistolary, which are almost entirely lost. See below.

[17]Devreesse, *Essai sur Théodore de Mopsueste*, pp. 5-27.

[18]See CPG 2:3827-38; Supplementum 3827-36.

[19]The passage is quoted in a Latin translation by Facundus: cf. Facundus of Hermiane *Pro defensione trium capitulorum* 3.6 (PL 67:602B-C; CCSL 90A:96, 104-15).

[20]See also Vosté, "La chronologie de l'activité littéraire de Théodore de Mopsuestia," pp. 54-81.

[21]See PG 66:648-96; R. Devreesse, *Le commentaire de Théodore de Mopsuestia sur le Psaumes*, Studi e Testi 93 (Vatican City: Biblioteca Apostolica Vaticana, 1939).

[22]For the English translation, see *Theodore of Mopsuestia: Commentary on Psalms 1–81*, translated with an introduction by Robert Hill, Writings from the Greco-Roman World (Atlanta: Society of Biblical Literature, 2006).

[23]Angelo Mai, *Scriptorum veterum nova collectio*, vol. 7.1 (Rome: Typis Vaticanis, 1832), pp. 1-298; *Nova Patrum Bibliotheca*, vol. 7.1 (Rome: Typis Sacri Consilii Propagando Christiano Nomini, 1854), pp. 1-389 = PG 66:124-632.

[24]H. N. von Sprenger, *Theodori Mopsuesteni commentarius in XII Prophetas, Einleitung und Ausgabe*, Göttinger Orientforschungen, V. Reihe: Biblica et Patristica 1 (Wiesbaden: Harrassowitz, 1977).

are limited to a small number of passages. Theodore does not discount all typological interpretations of the Old Testament. He does, however, choose to confine such interpretations to those episodes for which an actual correspondence to events found in the New Testament can be demonstrated. And then, the interpreter must be careful not to deny the historical significance of the original events, although he may acknowledge their inferiority in comparison to the New Testament episodes they prefigured.[25] Therefore Theodore's use of allegory is framed in a precise and rigorous system which opposes what he viewed as the frequent excesses of the Alexandrian school.

Besides the commentary on the Gospel of John, which we will discuss in detail in the next section, Theodore wrote commentaries on other books of the New Testament, including commentaries on Matthew, Luke,[26] the Acts of the Apostles[27] and the letters of Paul. Of this extended exegetical material only the commentary on John is extant in its entirety in a Syriac translation, while all the others are lost with the exception of the commentary on Paul's minor epistles (Galatians, Ephesians, Philippians, Colossians, 1-2 Thessalonians, 1-2 Timothy, Titus, Philemon) preserved in a Latin translation, along with numerous Greek fragments of the commentary on Romans, 1-2 Corinthians and Hebrews.[28] In his exegesis on the New Testament, Theodore, even more than in his commentaries on the Old Testament, makes use of a strictly literal interpretation. The words of Jesus are analyzed only to the extent that the immediate literal and historical context in which they are found will allow. Jesus' words are often interpreted by Theodore in opposition to Judaic legalism or as that which leads the dying paganism of the Gentiles to its natural destruction. This is further confirmed by Theodore's emphasis, in his analysis of Pauline doctrine, on the sharp division between the Judaism of the Old Testament and the Christianity of the New Testament, without however allowing any possible affinity with Gnosticism or Marcionism,[29] which he consistently and openly opposes in many of his works.

Of the numerous theological works of Theodore[30] only the Catechetical Homilies[31] and the Discourses against the Macedonians[32] are extant in a Syriac translation. Most

---

[25]See M. Simonetti, "Note sull'esegesi veterotestamentaria di Teodoro di Mopsuestia," *Vetera Christianorum* 14 (1977): 69-102.

[26]See PG 66:703-28; J. Reuss, "Matthäuskommentare aus der griechischen Kirche," *Texte und Untersuchungen zur Geschichte der altchristlichen Literatur*, GCS 61:96-135.

[27]See PG 66:785-86; E. von Dobschütz, "A Hitherto Unpublished Prologue to the Acts of the Apostles (Probably by Theodore of Mopsuestia)," *American Journal of Theology* 2 (1898): 353-87.

[28]See H. B. Swete, *Theodori Episcopi Mopsuesteni in epistolas beati Pauli commentarii*, 2 vols. (Cambridge: Cambridge University Press, 1880, 1882); K. Staab, *Pauluskommentare aus der griechischen Kirche* (Münster: Aschendorff, 1933), 113-72; U. Wickert, *Studien zu den Pauluskommentaren Theodors von Mopsuestia* (Berlin: A. Töpelmann, 1962).

[29]Since the Gnostics and especially Marcion believed that the God of the Old Testament was different from that of the New Testament, and was actually a sort of inferior God (a "Demiurge" according to the Platonic definition), the church fathers of the third and fourth centuries tended to emphasize the continuity between the two Testaments and diminish their differences.

[30]See CPG 2:3854, 3861-62, 3864; Supplementum 3861, 3865.

[31]R. Tonneau and R. Devreesse, *Les Homélies catéchétiques de Théodore de Mopsueste*, Studi e Testi 145 (Vatican City: Biblioteca Apostolica Vaticana), 1949.

[32]F. Nau, *Théodore de Mopsueste: Controverse avec les Macédoniens*, Patrologia Orientalis 9 (Paris: Firmin-Didot, 1913), pp. 637-

unfortunate for our purposes is the loss of the *De Incarnatione* (*On the Incarnation*), of which only fragments survive.[33] This extremely important work, extant in a complete Syriac translation, was discovered in the library of Seert[34] in 1905 by Addai Scher, who described the manuscript in an article published in 1909.[35] Unfortunately, before an edition of the work could be prepared, the manuscript perished during the course of the tragic events of World War I. Scher also did not survive the ravages of the war. From the extant fragments preserved in the works of Theodore's opponents, or supporters, it is difficult to make any definitive hypothesis on the specific contents and tenor of this work. Other lost theological works[36] of Theodore are described by Photius in his "Library."[37] These are primarily concerned with the Arian and Apollinarian[38] controversies and with the debate on free will and original sin.[39]

The *Catechetical Homilies*, which comprise Theodore's most important extant theological work, provide us with one of the clearest pictures of his Christology. He is a typical representative of the Antiochene school and as a result is critical of the positions of Apollinaris on Christology.[40] In Theodore's view, the humanity assumed by God the Word, the Logos, must be held fully intact, having its own capacity to operate autonomously. It represents, as it were, a subject of its own, which Theodore calls the "Son of David" in correlation with the "Son of God," the Logos.[41] This conception is developed and often amplified in his commentary on the Gospel of John.

I would be remiss at the end of this brief description of Theodore's works not to mention his ascetical writings—*On the Priesthood*[42] and *On the Perfection of the Way of*

---

67. The name "Macedonians" generally indicated the heretics who denied the divinity of the Holy Spirit. This was the case even though, it seems, there is no definite proof that Macedonius (ca. 320-370), a moderate Arian (homoiousian), was the initiator of the debate about the Holy Spirit or the first to deny its divinity.

[33]PG 66:969-94; E. Sachau, *Theodori Mopsuesteni fragmenta syriaca* [translation only] (Leipzig: Sumptibus Guilelmi Engelmann, 1869), pp. 28-57; L. Abramowski, "On the Fragments of Theodore of Mopsuestia in the Syriac Ms. Brit. Library Add. 12156 and the Christological Fragment in Double Tradition," *The Harp: A Review of Syriac and Oriental Studies* 6 (1993): 199-206; fragments of this work are also in Swete, *Theodori Episcopi Mopsuesteni in epistolas beati Pauli commentarii*, 2:290-312.

[34]Cf. n. 14 on Addai Scher.

[35]Addai Scher, "Joseph Hazzaya, écrivain syriaque du VIIIe siècle," *Comptes-rendus de l'Académie des Inscriptions et Belles-Lettres* (Paris: A. Picard, 1909), pp. 306-7; reprinted in *RSO* 3 (1910): 62-63.

[36]See *CPG* 2:3858-60; Supplementum 3859.

[37]Cf. Photius *Bibliotheca* 4, 81, 177.

[38]Apollinaris of Laodicea supported and developed the so-called *Logos-sarx* theology, according to which the *Logos* (God the Word, the Son of God, in Theodore's terminology) had assumed a human body and had replaced the human soul in it. Later Apollinaris developed this doctrine by maintaining that God the Word had only replaced the rational part of the human soul (the so-called *nous*), while the lower functions of the human soul remained unchanged. Apollinaris's theory is generally considered to be the basis of the later heresy of the Monophysites.

[39]Theodore accepted aspects of Pelagius's theology and actually provided hospitality for Julian of Aeclanum, a moderate Pelagian and adversary of Augustine, when he was exiled from Italy. Pelagius and the Pelagians believed that human beings are able to make the most important steps toward salvation with their own effort, without the intervention of divine grace. See Joanne McWilliam Dewart, *The Theology of Grace of Theodore of Mopsuestia* (Washington, D.C.: Catholic University of America Press, 1971).

[40]See n. 38 on Apollinaris.

[41]Cf. M. Simonetti, "Teodoro di Mopsuestia," *Dizionario Patristico di Antichità Cristiane*, vol. 2 (G-Z) (Genoa: Marietti, 1984), col. 3384.

[42]See A. Mingana, *Early Christian Mystics*, Woodbrooke Studies 7 (Cambridge: W. Heffer, 1934); Fragments of this work are in

Life[43]—which demonstrate his concern that theology and exegesis inform the life of the church. This is also evidenced in his collection of letters, generally known under the title *The Book of Pearls*,[44] of which only a few fragments survive. These writings round out a picture of an interpreter who wrote for the church, seeking to ground the church in the clear Word and words of Scripture, following an Antiochene approach he had learned from Diodore that strayed little, if at all, from the text, even in theological and ascetical ruminations.

The Commentary on the Gospel of John
Reconstruction of the Text

Latin and Greek fragments. Both the Chronicle of Seert and Ebedjesu's Catalog, respectively published in the thirteenth and fourteenth centuries,[45] mention among Theodore's works a commentary on the Gospel of John. However, in the first two centuries following the publication of these medieval lists, it seemed that the work had perished almost entirely. The extremely scarce surviving fragments were only available in a Latin translation and were part of the dossier of the Second Council of Constantinople (553).[46] In 1630 P. Cordier published a certain number of Greek fragments from a catena that he had discovered in a manuscript of Cues.[47] New fragments from different catenae were published in the mid-nineteenth century by I. A. Cramer[48] and Cardinal Mai[49] and, together with the fragments published by Cordier, were gathered by J. P. Migne in his *Patrologia*.[50] In 1927 R. Devreesse provided a detailed examination of this material deriving from different sources and began to eliminate a portion of the fragments mistakenly attributed to Theodore.[51] In 1948 he presented the Greek fragments in a very precise critical edition, establishing the number of fragments at 140.[52] Very recently George Kalantzis has

---

R. Draguet, *Commentaire du livre d'Abba Isaïe par Dadisho Qatraya*, CSCO 326-27 (Scriptores Syri 144-45) (Louvain: Secrétariat du CorpusSCO, 1972).

[43]Fragments of this work are in Draguet, *Commentaire du livre d'Abba Isaïe*; F. Graffin, "Une page retrouvée de Théodore de Mopsueste," in *A Tribute to Arthur Vööbus: Studies in Early Christian Literature and its Environment, primarily in the Syrian East*, ed. R. H. Fischer (Chicago: Lutheran School of Theology at Chicago, 1977), pp. 29-34.

[44]PG 66:1011-13; fragments of this work are also in Draguet, *Commentaire du livre d'Abba Isaïe*.

[45]Cf. above nn. 14-15.

[46]The fragments were included in the Acts of the Second Council of Constantinople (only extant in a Latin translation): see J. Straub, ed., *Acta Conciliorum Oecumenicorum (Acta Concil. Constantinop. II)*, vol. 4.1 (Berlin: de Gruyter, 1971), pp. 49, 50, 55, 58, 59; in the so-called *Constitutum Vigili*, a Latin translation of the council acts ordered by the Pope Vigilius: see O. Günther, ed., *Imperatorum Pontificum aliorum inde ab a. CCCLXVII usque ad a. DLIII datae Avellana quae dicitur collectio*, Pars I, CSEL 35 (Vienna: F. Tempsky, 1895), pp. 248-50; and in the defense of Theodore, Theodoret and Ibas by Facundus of Hermiane; see *Pro defensione trium capitulorum* 9.3.5-6 (PL 67:746D-747A; CCSL 90A:lines 273ff.; see also above n. 13.

[47]B. Corderius, *Catena Patruum Graecorum in Sanctum Iohannem ex Antiquissimo Graeco Codice MS nunc primum in lucem edita* (Antwerp, 1630); cf. also J. Marx, *Verzeichnis der Handschriften-Sammlung des Hospitales zu Cues* (Trier: Selbstverlag des Hospitals, 1905), p. 13.

[48]I. A. Cramer, *Catenae Graecorum Patrum in Novum Testamentum* (Oxford: E Typographeo Academico, 1844), 2:175-413.

[49]Angelo Mai, *Novae Patrum Bibliothecae*, vol. 7.1 (Rome: Typis Vaticanis, 1854), pp. 396-407.

[50]PG 66:728-85.

[51]See R. Devreesse, "Notes sur le chaînes grecques de saint Jean," *RB* 36 (1927): 203-15.

[52]Devreesse, *Essai sur Théodore de Mopsueste*, pp. 305-419.

reexamined the Greek fragments and presented them in a new translation with a full introduction and notes.[53]

The Syriac version. The quite limited knowledge of Theodore's commentary, which previously had been based exclusively on a series of fragments, was radically increased in 1868 when a complete Syriac translation was discovered by Mar G. E. Khayyatt in a manuscript of the Chaldean monastery of Saint George near Telkef.[54] The manuscript, named A by the editors,[55] appears to be fairly recent, as it dates, according to the inscription of the copyist, from the year 2015 of the reign of king Macedonius, equivalent to A.D. 1704. Four copies of this manuscript were made just after its discovery and are presently preserved in the Vatican Library (B = Borgianus syriacus 77), in the Royal Library of Berlin (Berolinensis syriacus 80), in the National Library of Paris (P = Parisinus syriacus 308) and in the Mingana Collection (Mingana syriacus 52).[56]

Even though G. E. Khayyatt announced that soon an edition and a translation of this extremely important work would be produced, it actually remained unpublished until 1897, when the first critical edition was produced by I. B. Chabot.[57] About forty years later, in 1940, a definitive edition was published by J.-M. Vosté, who collated the archetypus A with the best copies, B and P, and with Chabot's edition, and then added a Latin translation.[58] Vosté's edition is particularly commendable because he also reconstructed those sections of the text that contained more lacunae or were defective. In order to accomplish this, he used some of the Greek fragments, which he then incorporated into his translation, while also utilizing some Syriac fragments of Theodore's commentary that were quoted by Isho'dad of Merv,[59] or were included in the Syriac catena Gannat Bussāmē.[60]

Date and authorship of the translation. According to the Catalog of Ebedjesu,[61] Ibas

---

[53]Theodore of Mopsuestia, *Commentary on the Gospel of John*, introduction and commentary by G. Kalantzis, Early Christian Studies 7 (Sydney: Saint Paul's Publications, 2004).

[54]Telkef is north of Mossoul in Iraq. The manuscript was later moved to the library of the monastery of Our Lady of the Seeds in Alkosh, which is north of Telkef; see Addai Scher, "Notice sur le mss. syriaques conserves dans la bibliothèque des Chaldéens de Notre-Dame des Semences," *Journal Asiatique* 10, no. 7 (1909): 479-512.

[55]See J.-M. Vosté, ed., *Theodori Mopsuesteni Commentarius In Evangelium Iohannis Apostoli*, CSCO, Scriptores Syri, Series 4, Tomus 3 (Paris: E Typographeo Reipublicae, 1940), Textus, pp. i-ii; idem, "Le Commentaire de Théodore de Mopsueste sur S. Jean, d'après la version syriaque," *RB* 32 (1923): 522-26.

[56]See Vosté, *Theodori Mopsuesteni Commentarius In Evangelium Iohannis Apostoli*, Textus, pp. ii-iv; idem, "Le Commentaire de Théodore de Mopsueste sur S. Jean," pp. 526-31.

[57]Jean Baptiste Chabot, *Commentarius Theodori Mopsuesteni in evangelium Iohannis* (Paris: Ernestum Leroux, 1897).

[58]J.-M. Vosté, ed., *Theodori Mopsuesteni Commentarius In Evangelium Iohannis Apostoli*, CSCO, Scriptores Syri, Series 4, Tomus 3, Textus et Versio (Paris: E Typographeo Reipublicae, 1940).

[59]*The Commentaries of Isho'dad on the Gospels*, English translation by M. Dunlop Gibson, introduction and notes by J. R. Harris, HSem 5 (Cambridge: Cambridge University Press, 1911), pp. xxxiii-xxxvi; *The Commentaries of Isho'dad in Syriac: Luke and John*, Syriac text edited by M. Dunlop Gibson, HSem 7 (Cambridge: Cambridge University Press, 1911), pp. 220-23; see also Book 7 n. 36 on the translation in this present volume.

[60]J.-M. Vosté, "Le Gannat Bussāmē," *RB* 37 (1928): 221-32, 386-419 (especially 394-96); see also Book 7 nn. 36 and 45 on the translation in this present volume.

[61]See Assemani, *Catalogus Librorum Syrorum Ebedjesu*, p. 85.

---

of Edessa[62] and his disciples Koumi and Probus translated from Greek into Syriac all the works of Theodore of Mopsuestia, together with those of Aristotle. However, since Theodore actually wrote a large number of works, it is difficult to believe that they were all translated by Ibas and his two disciples in such a relatively short period of time. It is more likely that the translations were produced in different places and over a longer period. According to the testimony of Barhebraeus,[63] the translation of Theodore's exegetical commentaries was made by Ma'na, who was exiled from Edessa after the death of Ibas (ca. 457) and later became the metropolitan of Rewardashir.[64] This is also confirmed by the Chronicle of Seert.[65] Therefore the translation of the commentary on the Gospel of John can be placed, with some reliability, in the years 460-465.[66]

Structure and Nature of the Work

The Syriac version of Theodore's commentary on the Gospel of John is divided into seven books, covering the following chapters of the biblical text: Book One 1:1–2:22; Book Two 2:23–5:47; Book Three 6:1–8:59; Book Four 9:1–10:42; Book Five 11:1–12:50; Book Six 13:1–17:26; Book Seven 18:1–21:25. According to Kalantzis,[67] the original Greek version actually consisted of eight books, which more or less coincided with the Syriac translation until the seventh book. The last section of the commentary, however, was divided in the Greek original into two books: Book Seven 18:1–19:42; Book Eight 20:1–21:25. These differences were due to the perceived need of the Syriac translator to adjust and adapt Theodore's commentary to the text of the Peshitta[68] and to the liturgical usage of the Syriac communities.[69] The seven books of the commentary are introduced by a preface in which Theodore explains the purposes and method of his work, and by an *Argumentum Libri* ("subject of the book"), in which he examines the Evangelist John in his historical and cultural context according to the typical style of Antiochene exegesis.

Since the length of each book of the Syriac version is essentially equal, it immediately becomes evident that certain sections of the Gospel text are analyzed more in detail than others. Theodore tends to concentrate his attention on those passages that lend themselves to more theological or philosophical discussion. Thus, for instance, he devotes most of Book One to John 1:1-18. In Book Six, covering John 13:1–17:26, Theodore again focuses his analysis on the theological issues of the text, and discusses in detail the

---

[62]Cf. above n. 11.

[63]Barhebraeus *Chronica Ecclesiastica* 2.19 (Jean Baptiste Abbeloos and Thomas Joseph Lamy, eds. *Gregorii Barhebraei Chronicon Ecclesiasticum* [Louvain: C. Peeters, 1872-1877], 2:54).

[64]In Persia (presently in northwest Iran, close to the border with Iraq).

[65]Addai Scher, ed., *Histoire Nestorienne (Cronique de Séert)*, Seconde Partie (I), Patrologia Orientalis 7 (Paris: Firmin-Didot, 1911), pp. 116-17.

[66]See Vosté, "Le Commentaire de Théodore de Mopsueste sur S. Jean," pp. 531-34.

[67]Kalantzis, "Theodore of Mopsuestia's 'Commentarius in evangelium Iohannis Apostoli,'" pp. 490-91; Theodore of Mopsuestia, *Commentary on the Gospel of John* (Kalantzis), p. 151.

[68]This is the name (meaning "simple") of the standard Syriac translation of the Bible.

[69]See Vosté, "Le Commentaire de Théodore de Mopsueste sur S. Jean," p. 545.

role and nature of the Son in his relationship with the Father, and the action of the Holy Spirit inside the economy of God's will. It becomes quite clear that Theodore's theological reflections are firmly grounded in the literal content of the Gospel, which he is constantly examining in light of its immediate context, and in the clear meaning of the words, without looking in the same passage or expression for different levels of interpretation, which he feels may lead to erroneous or unreliable conclusions. He also emphasizes, in his commentary, the sharp separation of Christ's message and doctrine from Judaism, without searching for any possible affinity between the two.

In Book Seven, where the events of the passion play the main role in the narrative and the space left to theological speculations is much smaller, Theodore displays his primary interest in a historical analysis of Scripture. He sets out to examine all those passages in the four Gospels' account of Christ's passion that may appear to be inconsistent with each other or with the Gospel of John in particular. By an accurate and historically sound comparison of the different passages, he is able to carry out what he sees as his primary task: refuting all heretical and dissenting interpretations[70] that might otherwise portray inconsistency in the Gospel narratives as a sign of the weakness of orthodox Christianity.

Although most recent scholarship has questioned the existence of a real Antiochene school of exegesis with a common definitive line of biblical interpretation,[71] in Theodore's commentary on John, at least two typical characteristics of Antiochene exegesis are evident: the constant attention to the letter of the text and the flow of the narrative, and the sound analysis of the work in its proper historical context. He can even sound almost like a modern day form critic when he notes, in the final verses of the Gospel, that these words are clearly not by John but by someone else.[72]

The Problem of Theodore's Christology

If we exclude the hostile and biased criticism expressed in the Acts of the Council of Constantinople and in the Three Chapters,[73] which openly regard Theodore's theological arguments as *ante litteram* examples of Nestorianism,[74] two main critical trends are noticeable in the interpretation of his Christology. The first trend[75] recognizes in his system

---

[70]Especially the Gnostics and Marcionites. See above.

[71]Cf. R. C. Hill, "Theodore of Mopsuestia, Interpreter of the Prophets," *Sacris Erudiri* 40 (2001): 107-29; idem, "Sartor Resartus: Theodore under Review by Theodoret," *Aug* 41, no. 2 (2001): 465-76; F. G. McLeod, *The Roles of Christ's Humanity in Salvation: Insights from Theodore of Mopsuestia* (Washington, D.C.: The Catholic University of America Press, 2005); idem, "Theodore of Mopsuestia Revisited," *Theological Studies* 61, no. 3 (2000): 447-80; J. O'Keefe, "A Letter that Killeth: Toward a Reassessment of Antiochene Exegesis," *Journal of Early Christian Studies* 8, no. 1 (2000): 83-104; F. M. Young, *Biblical Exegesis and the Formation of Christian Culture* (Cambridge: Cambridge University Press, 1997); B. Nassif, "Spiritual Exegesis in the School of Antioch," in *New Perspectives on Historical Theology: Essays in Memory of John Meyendorff*, ed. B. Nassif (Grand Rapids: Eerdmans, 1996).

[72]CSCO 4 3:364.

[73]For a detailed examination of these accusations, see McLeod, *Roles of Christ's Humanity in Salvation*, 205-14.

[74]Cf. n. 9 on Nestorius.

[75]For this trend see Facundus of Hermiane, *Défense des Trois Chapitres (à Justinien)*, Texte critique par J. M. Clément et R. Vander Plaetse; introduction, traduction et notes par A. Fraïsse-Bétoulières, SC 471, 478-79, 484, 499 (Paris: Cerf, 2002-

an excessive separation between Christ's human and divine natures, which is due, on the one hand, to the fact that an accurate definition of the unity of Christ's natures was established only after Theodore's death; on the other, to the fact that in his polemic against the Apollinarists[76] he exaggerated the separation of the two natures of Christ. Therefore, according to this trend, Theodore's Christology appears to be typically Antiochene, because the excessive attention to the humanity of Christ leads him to separate the Son's human nature from the divine.[77] R. A. Norris has summarized Theodore's Christology with these words:

[Its] most obvious mark is its dualism. Individual scholars have offered widely varying evaluations and interpretations of this phenomenon: but the fact remains for all to see. It is manifested in Theodore's systematic development of a doctrine of "two natures" in Christ. It appears in his exegetical practice of "dividing the sayings": of assigning epithets applied to Christ, or sayings of Christ, some to his human nature and others to his divine nature. It reveals itself in his assertion that the Incarnation took place by the "inhabitation" of the divine Son in a whole and perfect Man.[78]

The second trend, which is prevalent in some very recent studies, sets out to demonstrate that Theodore's views of Christ's natures and person are largely orthodox. According to this trend the dispute concerning the correctness of Theodore's Christology is mostly unjustified and is due, on the one hand, to an erroneous and hostile interpretation of his theological terminology;[79] and on the other, to the fact that his works are largely lost in their Greek original version, and are often only available in Syriac translations which appear to be interpolated and manipulated in a Nestorian sense.[80]

The purpose of this introduction is by no means that of analyzing in detail the *vexata quaestio* of Theodore's christological orthodoxy. I personally think that the serious and historically sound reappraisal of Theodore's theological thought in Galtier's article[81] and in McLeod's recent monograph[82] is essential to understanding the Christology of the

---

2006); K. McNamara, "Theodore of Mopsuestia and the Nestorian Heresy," *ITQ* 19 (1952): 254-78; and 20 (1953): 172-91; F. A. Sullivan, *The Christology of Theodore of Mopsuestia*, Analecta Gregoriana 82 (Rome: Universitatis Gregorianae, 1956); R. A. Norris, *Manhood and Christ: A Study in the Christology of Theodore of Mopsuestia* (Oxford: Clarendon, 1963).

[76]See above n. 38 on Apollinaris.

[77]See Facundus of Hermiane, *Défense des Trois Chapitres (à Justinien)*, SC 471 (2002), pp. 29-30.

[78]Norris, *Manhood and Christ*, p. 190. See also McNamara, "Theodore of Mopsuestia and the Nestorian Heresy," *ITQ* 19 (1952): 254-78, and 20 (1953): 172-91; Sullivan, *The Christology of Theodore of Mopsuestia*, pp. 203-28; McLeod, *Roles of Christ's Humanity in Salvation*, pp. 252-66.

[79]See especially P. Galtier, "Théodore de Mopsueste: Sa vraie pensée sur l'incarnation," *RSR* 45 (1957): part one, pp. 161-86; part two, pp. 338-60; R. A. Greer, *Theodore of Mopsuestia: Exegete and Theologian* (London: Faith Press, 1961); McLeod, *The Roles of Christ's Humanity in Salvation*, pp. 252-66; idem, "Theodore of Mopsuestia Revisited," pp. 447-80.

[80]M. Richard, "La tradition des fragments du traité *Peri tēs anthrōpēseōs* de Théodore de Mopsueste," *Le Muséon* 46 (1943): 55-75; Devreesse, *Essai sur Théodore de Mopsueste*, pp. 287-304; Kalantzis, "Theodore of Mopsuestia's 'Commentarius in evangelium Iohannis Apostoli,'" pp. 473-93; Theodore of Mopsuestia, *Commentary on the Gospel of John* (Kalantzis), pp. 16-18, 23-37.

[81]Galtier, "Théodore de Mopsueste: Sa vraie pensée sur l'incarnation."

[82]McLeod, *The Roles of Christ's Humanity in Salvation*, pp. 252-66.

---

bishop of Mopsuestia and to remove many unjustified accusations of unorthodoxy. However, it does not seem to me that these works completely explain and solve the problem of the evident dualism of Theodore's Christology. I still believe that Norris's definition is mostly correct and faithful in describing the main character of Theodore's views on the nature of Christ and his person.

The commentary on the Gospel of John, which is presented here in a complete English translation of the Syriac text, confirms Norris's definition in many passages, and even though it is not possible to define Theodore's Christology as unorthodox, as Galtier and McLeod have amply demonstrated,[83] at the same time, its dualism is undeniable.

In his article and recent monograph on Theodore's commentary, which also includes a complete English translation of all the Greek fragments, George Kalantzis suggests that the presence of this apparent dualism in Theodore's Christology is due to the fact that the Syriac translator evidently manipulated the original Greek text of Theodore's commentary: "It becomes clear, therefore, that the liberty with which the Syriac translator(s) edited the works of the *Mephasqana*[84] was not limited to the substitution of the Greek version of the New Testament which Theodore used with their familiar Peshitta,[85] but extended to the reshaping and adaptation of his original text to meet the theological needs and expectations of the Nestorian, eastern Syriac Churches."[86] He bases his theory on two main arguments: the evident difference in some parallel passages between the Greek and the Syriac version, and the fact that the expression *lēphthēs anthrōpos (homo assumptus)*[87] never appears in any of the 140 surviving Greek fragments.[88]

In order to support his first argument Kalantzis quotes the two parallel passages on John 17:11 that read in Syriac:

In regard to his nature, the divine Logos is connected with the Father. Moreover, by means of the connection with him, the *homo assumptus* (assumed man) is also connected with the Father. In addition to our similarity with the natural connection we have with Christ in the flesh, as great as it happens to be, we receive spiritual participation with him, and we are his body, each of us is truly a member.

And in Greek:

In regards to his nature, Christ was connected to the Father as divine Logos and to us as a human; and we, therefore, are united with Christ as parts of his flesh, as his

---

[83]See above nn. 79 and 80.

[84]The "Interpreter." This is the title of excellence usually given by the Nestorian Syriac Church to Theodore.

[85]Cf. above n. 67.

[86]Kalantzis, "Theodore of Mopsuestia's 'Commentarius in evangelium Iohannis Apostoli,'" p. 492; Theodore of Mopsuestia, *Commentary on the Gospel of John* (Kalantzis), pp. 152-53.

[87]"The assumed man," that is, the man assumed by the Logos, the God Word.

[88]See Kalantzis, "Theodore of Mopsuestia's 'Commentarius in evangelium Iohannis Apostoli,'" pp. 491-92; Theodore of Mopsuestia, *Commentary on the Gospel of John* (Kalantzis), p. 152.

members, receiving spiritual communion through faith.[89]

Then Kalantzis concludes: "It is apparent that the two versions are quite different. The Syriac version places great emphasis on identifying the *homo assumptus* (assumed man) as a separate and autonomous center of attribution from that of the *Deus Verbum* (God the Word). The Greek version, on the other hand, does not justify such a distinction."

This argument relies on the assumption that the text of the Greek fragment is undoubtedly the genuine one: a text that has suffered no manipulation. But how can we be sure about this? At first sight, the Greek text seems to be a summary or abridged version of the Syriac one. Is it really possible that the Syriac translator took the liberty to expand and manipulate the Greek text to such an extent? Theodore was a cult figure in the Syriac Church and it seems far from certain that his writings could actually be submitted to such manipulation. In addition, it must be carefully considered that all the Greek fragments of Theodore's commentary are taken from Greek catenae. Those familiar with catenae know well that their quotations are very often manipulated and reduced. Should we not consider the possibility that the Greek text is an abridged version of the one preserved in its full form in the Syriac translation?

Kalantzis proceeds to support his theory by asserting that the expression *lēphthēs anthrōpos* (*homo assumptus*) is never attested in any of the 140 extant Greek fragments. However, in a fragment of the *De Incarnatione (On the Incarnation)*, quoted in Latin by Facundus of Hermiane we read:

> Whoever distinguishes the natures necessarily finds one and another; I think that not even the adversaries[90] refuse to accept it, because it must be conceded that, by nature, one is God the Word, and another he who is assumed, whatever it may be. Therefore he finds himself to be the same according to the person, not at all because of the confusion of the natures, but through the union of the assumed which is accomplished towards the one who assumes.[91]

How can we explain the presence of the expression "assumed man" in this fragment? Kalantzis says that the presence of this expression is a consequence of the manipulations of the Syriac Nestorians. Should we think that Facundus, who lived about one hundred years after Theodore's death, read the *De Incarnatione* in a Syriac version which had been already interpolated and manipulated by the Syriac Nestorians instead of simply reading it in Greek? Or is it possible that Theodore amply used the expression "assumed man" in some of his works, and then decided not to use it anymore in his commentary on the Gospel of John? Kalantzis's second argument judges Theodore's Christology by only considering the Greek fragments of a single work instead of examining the extant writings

---

[89]Cf. above n. 86.
[90]That is, those who oppose Theodore's Christology.
[91]Facundus of Hermiane *Pro defensione trium capitulorum* 9.3.5-6 (PL 67:747C-748A; CCSL 90A:273, 275-81).

of Theodore as a whole. While we are appreciative of Kalantzis's work in making these Greek fragments available to a wider audience, we believe we have demonstrated that there is sufficient room for disagreement regarding whether the Greek or the Syriac text more closely reflects Theodore's original commentary on John. Thus we offer the present translation, which we believe represents the earlier and more authentic tradition. We might also add that we understand Theodore's Christology to be largely orthodox in its specific historical context, as Galtier and McLeod have accurately demonstrated. At the same time, however, one cannot deny the presence of the apparent christological dualism which is typical of Antiochene theology.

Note on the Present Translation
This translation is based on the critical text of the Syriac version established by Vosté: J.-M. Vosté, ed., *Theodori Mopsuesteni Commentarius In Evangelium Iohannis Apostoli*, CSCO, Scriptores Syri, Series 4, Tomus 3, Textus et Versio (Paris: E Typographeo Reipublicae, 1940). I have included in the translation the passages reconstructed on the text of the Greek fragments which the editor has incorporated in his Latin translation of the Syriac text. I have also emended a few readings of the Syriac text, which are indicated in the notes to the translation.

THEODORE OF MOPSUESTIA
Commentary on the Gospel of John

Preface

In your strength which strengthens those who are weak, my weakness begins to transcribe (into Syriac) the commentary on the Evangelist John, written by the holy Theodore, Bishop of Mopsuestia, interpreter of the divine Scripture.

We begin with the preface addressed to the one who asked Theodore to write this commentary.

God help us. Amen.

As is already well known to you, O Porphyry, admirable and most glorious among the bishops, I was about to write about other topics. I certainly intended to say something in defense of Basil's discourse against the iniquitous Eunomius, especially because I see that many want to hear the speeches which that deceiver wrote. No one who devotes himself to speaking about divine matters without a preliminary examination will receive any praise from me. I believe that it is necessary to face any subject with an investigation and examination so that if what we are inquiring into should appear to be harmful, it might also raise awareness in those who want to guard against it. But if it turns out to be the contrary after an examination, that is, it appears to be good and is demonstrated to be so on the basis of a sound argument, then it will be most lovingly accepted by those who possess it.

Since your invitation [to write this commentary] is prior to the project I wanted to begin—I presume, in fact, that what you command is not without divine grace since you are a man whose life is filled with power and discipline—I have abandoned what I intended to do and immediately acquiesce to your request. I am prepared to explain the book as you ordered us to do. You ordered us—it is necessary that this is said openly so that what you did may be known—you ordered us to explain the sense of the blessed Evangelist John because, as you said, the comprehension of his thought is more useful than that of the other Evangelists.

Therefore this work will be advantageous to many, if God so wills. We truly believe that it can be accomplished only though your prayers. We already are confident that you will not forget us but instead will ensure that the work may be worthy of what you ordered us to do so that it may be evident to you that your order was not given in vain. I will not allow you to stop praying now because it is through the assistance of your prayers that some hidden strength may be sent to us by God. For this reason we more willingly begin this book than others.

Concerning this book, our intention, with the help of Almighty God, is the following: we intend not to omit, in our explanation, any of those questions that appear to be difficult to readers and, at the same time, not to linger on those questions which are clear to anyone after reading them just once. We certainly are not envious of the sophist Asterius,[1] nor will

---

[1] Asterius was one of the most prominent personalities among the Arians of the first generation. He was, from the beginning, a very close collaborator of Arius, and even though the information about his activities in the course of this phase of the Arian controversy is quite scarce, we know with certainty that he attended the main councils of the period until Antioch 341. The work by Asterius on the Gospel

we imitate that man. Indeed, in examining the work he wrote about this Gospel, it seems to me that he looked more for glory than edification. The extended volume compiled by him about this subject only caused the reader to miss anything that was truly useful for the comprehension of the Gospel, because he only lingers on those questions that are obvious, and fraudulently strives to express his useless arguments with many words.

On the contrary, in any of our commentaries on the Scriptures, we are quite attentive that we not include superfluous words in our exposition. And now we will attempt to do the same with this task, as far as it is possible. Indeed we think that the duty of the interpreter is to explain those words which are difficult to many, while the duty of the preacher is to speak about those topics which are already clear enough. Even superfluous topics can sometimes be useful to a preacher, but the interpreter must explain and say things concisely. However, when it is the case that an explanation cannot be clear unless we use many words—and this happens when we come upon verses which have been corrupted by the deceit of the heretics[2] because of the disease of their impiety—then we will not avoid discussing them in detail, so that what is needed [in order to understand the verses] may be clearly evident. We will take special care to do this. Indeed this is also the duty of the interpreter—especially of one who expounds a text accurately—not only to discuss questions with authority but also to refute those who oppose his arguments.

I will first express my opinion about this book in its entirety. This is useful indeed. Then I will make preparations to explain the individual texts, with the help of God.

End of the preface.

The Subject of the Book

John the evangelist was one of the Twelve and undoubtedly the youngest of all the disciples. He was honest and far removed from any search for subtlety. Therefore he enjoyed great confidence from our Lord, who loved John more than the others, even though we find that the blessed Simon was often first. But about this question anyone is free to judge according to his own opinion. Indeed I think this is not a human question that must be judged by us. However, it is said that the Lord loved John more than the others.[3]

After the ascension of the Lord into heaven, the disciples lived for a long time in Jerusalem, traveling to the nearby cities and speaking with those Jews who had believed the word that had been preached to them until the great Paul was elected and clearly reserved for the preaching to the Gentiles.[4] With the passing of the years, since divine grace did not allow her preachers to be confined to a small country, she sent them by various arrangements to faraway places. The case of Simon the magician provided the blessed Peter the occasion to leave for Rome,[5] while others moved for other reasons. But this is not the place to rehearse all these events. And so the blessed John, in his turn, came to Ephesus

---

of John, at which Theodore hints here, is entirely lost. Unfortunately only a fragment from his *Syntagmation* and the newly discovered homilies on the Psalms are his sole surviving writings. In general, the Arians maintained that Christ was not generated, but created by the Father; therefore, even though the Son was a divine being, his divinity was somehow inferior to that of the Father, and his substance was only similar (and, according to some extreme forms of Arianism, different) to that of the Father.   [2]Here Theodore is alluding again to the Arians, but probably also to the apocryphal writings of the Gnostics and the Manichaeans, who maintained, in general, that the God of the Old Testament was an inferior divine being (a demiurge), or even a cruel deity who had formed the world with the darkness of evil, and that Christ was an envoy whose task was to enlighten humankind with the revelation of this truth.   [3]See Jn 13:23. [4]See Acts 13:2; Gal 2:7-9. [5]Here Theodore is alluding to an apocryphal writing the *Acts of Peter*. See *Acta Petri* 5.1-2. Simon the Magician is the first known founder of a Gnostic sect, and in a sense, the inventor of Gnosticism. His ideas are the basis for all the Gnostic systems that came after him. See also Acts 8:1-8; Irenaeus *Against Heresies* 1.23.1-2; 1.24.1-2.

and lived there, wandering throughout Asia and greatly benefiting the inhabitants of that region through his preaching.[6]

At that time the books of the other Evangelists were published: Matthew, Mark and Luke, who wrote their own Gospels. Therefore the gospel became widespread all over the world. All the faithful ardently studied it in order to know about the life and deeds of the Lord on earth. We find that similar things are described in the books of the three Evangelists with only this one difference. While one of them believed that it was necessary to write about the birth of our Lord in the flesh and about the events that happened at that time,[7] the other immediately started from the baptism of John.[8] The blessed Luke actually started from the events which occurred at the time of the birth of John [the Baptist], and then passing to the birth of our Lord, came to the baptism of John.

Now, since the Asian faithful believed that the blessed John would be superior to the others in authority and faith as an Evangelist—indeed he had lived with the Lord from the beginning and had been endowed with a greater grace for his love—they brought him the books of the Gospels in order to hear his opinion about the things that were written in them. He certainly praised the writers for their consistency and truth. He said, however, that some details had been neglected by them—especially certain miracles that needed to be related—and that doctrine was almost entirely absent from their books. He also added that, since they had mostly discussed in detail the advent of the Lord in the flesh, the question of his divinity could not be omitted; otherwise, with the passing of time, people having grown accustomed to their testimony, might think of the Lord only as he appeared from their accounts.

Therefore he was requested by all his brothers to write down all the things that he judged to be absolutely necessary and that appeared to have been omitted by the others. He immediately began his work. Indeed he thought it would be shameful if, for the slothfulness of one, many would suffer loss.

For this reason, John set about to write his Gospel. And so he immediately started from the beginning with the doctrine about the divinity [of Christ], because he thought that the teaching of the gospel necessarily had to start from there. Then after passing to the event of the incarnation, he arrived at the baptism of John, because he had a deep understanding of the things that were done and said after the advent of Christ in the flesh, and he thought that this was the only proper way to begin. However, when he reached this stage of the narrative, he also believed that he had to include those things that had been omitted by the others. This was his intention from the beginning, and this is the subject of the book to be written. Therefore he reports the words that the Jews spoke to John after they sent officers to question him and the answers that he gave to those who questioned him. But he also was extremely precise in weaving his narrative in an orderly way, indicating which events happened on the [first] day and where. For instance, he says, "These things were done in Bethany beyond the Jordan."[9] Then he relates the events of the second day, that is, about the disciples who followed him. In a word, if one examines this section attentively, he will find that with regard to John the Baptist he mentions in agreement with the other Evangelists only those events that the logical succession of the facts required, and whose omission appeared to be unsuitable to him.

He continues in an orderly way by relating the events omitted by the others. He is also

---

[6]See Eusebius *Ecclesiastical History* 3.23.2-6; Irenaeus *Against Heresies* 2.22.5; Clement of Alexandria *Salvation of the Rich* 42; Egeria *Pilgrimage* 23.10.   [7]Matthew.   [8]Mark.   [9]Jn 1:28.

the only one who mentions the presence of Christ at the wedding party in Cana. And he clearly says that event was the beginning of his miracles.[10] The speeches that he reports were mostly omitted by the others. The same thing happens concerning the miracles. If in some passage he mentions a sign already related by the others, he undoubtedly does this for a specific purpose. For example he reports the miracle of the loaves in which by means of five loaves the Lord satisfied the hunger of five thousand men without including the women and children.[11] The others also related this miracle.[12] But he necessarily reported this event for the speech connected to it in which [the Lord] also spoke about the mysteries.[13] The occasion for these words was the accomplished miracle. The Evangelist could not have included these words without reporting the occasion in which they were spoken. In a word, if one said that the Gospel of the blessed John is the complement of all the things that were missing and had been omitted by the others, he would not be speaking out of turn. Therefore he wrote his Gospel as those Asians requested, that is, by mentioning the facts that the others had omitted and had not included in their narratives.

For the same reason, he was also very accurate with regard to the order of the events because the others had taken no care in this regard. Now there is no time to discuss why they made that choice. But they certainly reported in advance many facts that only happened later, and they also reported other facts as occurring later that actually had happened earlier. And whoever carefully reads their books can see this. But since we have already described their purpose, we need not rehearse the individual wording of each of them. The blessed John, on the other hand, was very accurate in this regard. He placed the events that had happened in the beginning first, and then

included those which happened later together with the rest of the events that actually happened in sequence. And even though he left out many things in the middle, since they had already been related by the others, and even though he passes from a previous event to a subsequent event—even if that event does not happen immediately but only a long time afterward—he still does not invert the order of the events because he does not place in the beginning events that happened later, nor does he move events that happened in the beginning to a place after other events. And so, for instance, this is what he did with the episode of John the Baptist, as we have said. There he kept the order and sequence of the events. And you will find that the order is preserved in other sections as well. This is why in this book you will frequently find phrases such as "After this," which occur at the beginning of episodes. For instance, "*After this*, there was a feast of the Jews;"[14] or, "*After this* Jesus went over to the sea,"[15] and so forth. Indeed, as we have already said, the events that had happened in the meantime were omitted by the author because they had already been related by the others, or were superfluous. In this way he could concisely focus on the necessary facts.

The explanation we are about to write with the help of God will provide precise comprehension of the words to those who carefully read this book.

It seems to me that because of his great love for Christ, John was driven to gather those events that had been omitted by the others. His words about the divinity of Christ sufficiently demonstrate his greatness, but the words of humility, not being consistent with the Lord's majesty, cause a greater confusion among the Jews resulting in their cruelty against him. Nor did they really have any excuse when they thought that he must be crucified in order to defend the name of the Father,

[10]Jn 2:1-11, esp. v. 11. [11]Jn 6:1-15. [12]Mt 14:13-21; Mk 6:30-44; Lk 9:10-17. [13]That is, the Eucharist, see Jn 6:25-70. [14]Jn 5:1. [15]Jn 6:1.

because he referred all of his actions and words to the Father, as he testifies by saying that the things that he does or says are not his.[16] And this will clearly appear from the words of the Lord to the one who attentively examines what was said.

Therefore immediately from the beginning, after he has spoken about his divinity, he says that John [the Baptist] had also come to testify to his greatness. And in order to show that this is his purpose in this book, that is, to reproach those who did not believe or receive him, he says, "He was not that light, but was sent to bear witness to that Light."[17] This statement blames those who seemed to obey John but did not receive him to whom John testified. And so, by intensifying his accusation, he says, "He came to his own and his own did not receive him";[18] and a little below, "John testified to him and cried and said. . . ."[19] When [the Evangelist] adds that the Jews sent men from Jerusalem who were renowned among them so that they might ask and know who he was and whether he was to be regarded as the Messiah, [the Baptist] openly answered that he was not the Christ, but that he had come to make known the one who was to come, according to the word of the prophet. He confirms this with the words that follow and with many others, especially with those which he reports our Lord said to the Jews.

If one attentively considers the words of our Lord, he will find that many of them are varied in their meaning. Some show his greatness, others his weakness and evidently, after a thorough examination, cannot be suitable to him.[20] But those words that the Evangelist wrote at the beginning of his book about the divinity of the Only Begotten are certainly an exception.

John reports these words, not as the words of the Lord, but as his own. Indeed these words do not diminish the Lord in any way. The words of Christ too, when he preached to the faithful, were quite suitable to the greatness of the Only Begotten, but not when he spoke to his enemies.[21]

Here begins the commentary.

Book One (John 1:1–2:22)

[1:1] *In the beginning was the Word.* In my opinion we must not criticize one who says that when the blessed John pronounced these words, he was not immediately able to understand all their strength, but understood it later, after further considering their meaning. In fact, it seems to me that the use and meaning of these words is not only far removed from human ingenuity, but completely overwhelms human nature itself. John was not only able to understand the essence of that [Word][1]—that which pertained to its own nature—but also to express what he understood. He could speak about the inscrutable essence of God the Word so concisely that another would not have been able to show what he had understood even if he had used six hundred words. Every time I consider these words, I am astonished by the heretics[2] and wonder how they can fight against such a lofty concept. The one who stubbornly contradicts these words, I believe, is no different than those Greek philosophers who intend to destroy all the doctrines and religions accepted among human beings. They have even asserted that the sun does not shine, promising to demonstrate their assertion through suitable examples.

In fact, if something did exist before the beginning, we would have to admit that the

---

[16]Jn 14:24. [17]Jn 1:8. [18]Jn 1:11. [19]Jn 1:15. [20]Here we notice a typical and recurring aspect of Theodore's Christology, that is, a clear distinction between what actually belongs to Christ the man and what belongs to Christ the Word. The two natures of Christ, the human and the divine, are sharply separated into two different entities. See also the translator's introduction, esp. the quotation from Norris, p. xxvi. [21]Theodore's point is that when Christ spoke to his enemies, he did not reveal his divinity to them, and therefore what he said would not have revealed his greatness. **Book One** [1]Theodore is saying that John was able to understand the essence of "Christ the Word." [2]Theodore is referring to the Arians. See also n. 1 of the previous section.

Son is not the first substance. If, in any ordering, the beginning is said to be first, either it is not the beginning, if something existed before it, or it necessarily is—understand that this is our opinion—the beginning among the things that appear.

The Evangelist clearly indicated that God the Word was in the beginning. If someone wants to investigate what the meaning of this word *beginning* is—both according to the use of philosophers and the use of Scripture— he will find out that the two of them equally indicate the divine essence of the Only Begotten. And in addition, if one examines carefully the use of this word among the philosophers, he will realize that it does not differ from the use made by Scripture. For the difference in religious doctrine does not cause diversity in the understanding of the words. Even though [the philosophers] erred in many respects, the common meaning still obliged them not to adulterate the sense of the words. And divine Scripture, therefore, also treated those words the same way according to their obvious value and meaning.[3]

But let us examine this word *beginning* in a different way. And before examining it let us describe how the word is normally used among human beings. We call "beginning" anything that is first among them; whereas we do not call anything that is second "beginning." In fact, if it is *after* something, it is not first; and if it is not first, then it necessarily is not the beginning. If someone wants to consider this more carefully, he will find that this term *beginning* means something more than "first." It may happen that something is first, but is not called "beginning" because this designation is not appropriate in this instance. The notion of first is necessarily connected with the notion of beginning—unless one calls "beginning" what is first by making an inappropriate use

of this designation. Through the idea of "first" the idea of "beginning" also becomes known; therefore the idea of first appears to be fully connected with the idea of beginning. An example would be if someone wants to remove in different stages a certain number of stones from a heap and says, "Remove that stone first among them." Here the reference is to what is first, whereas what the beginning is is not shown at all because the similarity among the stones gathered together does not allow for it; unless someone says, "The beginning of their removal is to be that stone." In this case the connected concept, "Remove that stone," receives the name "beginning." However, it does not indicate the beginning of the stones, but of their removal.

What else can I say? Through this investigation which we are carefully considering, I must show that in the name *beginning* there is more than the [concept of] first. "First," we understand, has to be followed by something. "Beginning" is actually the beginning of something, but it is evident that it has not received the qualification of being the first by the order of those following. Rather, it is already a "beginning" even when those following it do not exist yet who then become the descendants of what is called "beginning." "First," on the other hand, is always something followed by something. The "beginning" is therefore called "first"; but at the same time it certainly existed before those things that follow it whose beginning it is said to be.

Because of this accuracy of terms the blessed Moses intentionally did not say, "There was evening, and there was morning, the *first* day," but, "There was evening, and there was morning, *one* day."[4] Therefore he called that day "one" because, as there was no other day before it, he did not believe it would be correct to call it "first" because there was

---

[3]Theodore is asserting here that Scripture uses words consistently according to their context and their intrinsic meaning.   [4]Gen 1:5. This is most clearly seen in the LXX translation.

---

still no day after this one in existence which would necessitate calling this one "first," even though later the day was created that was second to it.

In a similar way we call the beginning of a house its foundation because they start building the house from no other place than the foundation. A house cannot be built if it has no foundation. Even though the foundation exists because of the house, it nevertheless existed before the house was built. In a similar way we also say that Adam was the beginning of man, because before him no man existed—in truth, Adam existed before any other man was created. Therefore according to the usual custom of those who make use of a sane mind, *beginning* refers to what is first in itself and not at all to what is first according to order or mere appellation.

The pagans who wrote about the use of names followed the same method. When they faced this question with natural arguments, they transmitted a very beautiful definition of the name *beginning*. They said, "Beginning is the first cause of the things that follow." And, thinking to clarify this further, they called the "first cause" that which is before everything. Therefore they would call "beginning" "that which is before everything." And others said that God himself was the cause and the beginning of all existing things since he was the one who existed before everything and nothing existed before him. Others thought that there were certain visible things that were eternal: the earth or the air or the water or the fire or the four elements together—according to the opinion of each[5]—so that all the other things were made with them. In a word, they have shown in their use of names and their doctrines that they called beginning that which existed before everything.

And you will not find that the divine Scriptures say anything different from that.

Even among common people the word *beginning* is used with this same sense. And now, after omitting all other examples, let me provide you with a single, suitable one: the blessed Moses, intending to instruct the Jewish nation about both God and created things—how it was certainly God alone who existed while those things were made [by him]—as well as desiring to explain to us the order of the creation of what was made, said as follows, "In the beginning God created the heavens and earth."[6] He did not say that they were in the beginning. Moses did not think that such a designation was suitable for things that did not exist by themselves and were created, since he was not ignorant of the fact that their creator, God, existed before them. Nor did he dare to say that they were made "in the beginning." Because he thought that it would be best to mention their creator first, he said, "In the beginning God created," and then mentioned what was created in the beginning. He first mentioned their creator—God—in order to raise the mind of his audience first toward him; then he reported the things which had been made.

In the beginning he indicated those things [the heavens and the earth] which had been made, and evidently through them he also designated those things which were made with them. Actually, since all the other things were contained in them, he thought it was sufficient to mention [these two] to indicate the other things included in them as well. I am speaking about the air and water, the mountains and hills, and all the other things on heaven and earth whose creation does not appear to be related in any passage. On the other hand, Moses immediately mentioned the light that was made afterward, together with all the other things that were created on the second and third day until he arrived at the creation of man. In this way he teaches us that in the

---

[5]Here Theodore appears to allude to the pre-Socratic naturalist philosophers, and then to Plato, Aristotle and the Stoics.   [6]Gen 1:1.

divine Scriptures "beginning" is called that which is before everything.

It is incredible how these heretics[7] have overlooked all these things—even the common custom and usage of all the teachers, if we must say so. And, what is worse than anything else, they have abandoned the customary usage which Scripture itself practices. They also deceive many with their deceptively simple argument, saying the phrase, *In the beginning was . . .* stands for "in *his* beginning." In other words, the Word had a beginning. But they have no idea what a difference there is between "was" and "had," that is, how opposed these are to each other. If the Word *had* a beginning, he *was not* in the beginning; if he actually *was* in the beginning, then he did not *have* a beginning. It is not difficult to understand the magnitude of the nonsense of what they are saying since none of the things which did not exist at one time but were made could be said to be present at their own beginning.

And even if we could say this, it would be something found to be common to all created things. In fact, when all these things began to exist, it is possible, according to their theory,[8] that the Son because he was not and was made, could be said to have existed in his own beginning. This would put him in the same category with all the things that were made. It would seem then that the Evangelist John, who was explaining the divinity of the Only Begotten to be something new, had written in vain the sentence, *In the beginning was . . .* Such a phrase is suitable neither to angels and archangels, nor to any other heavenly powers—not even to frogs or ugly reptiles. In fact, when referring to those things which did not exist before and began to be, we would say, "In the beginning they were," that is, "In their beginning they were," as was also the case with [the Only Begotten]. If according to their madness this is referred to

the assertion of John about God the Word— since [all the other creatures] also began to exist later—such an assertion would be quite suitable to them as well.

But they must tell us why, even though these other things have a beginning, the phrase *In the beginning was,* is only acceptable for him[9] and not for these other things. In fact, if through these words we understand (according to what we are saying) that he is the first cause as Creator of everything, such [words] are only suitable to the dignity of the Only Begotten, and to none of the things which were created. It is therefore clear that the Evangelist in this sense said, *In the beginning was . . .*

Since it is difficult for the human mind to consider that another is cause of the cause through which everything was made, the Evangelist, intending to [temporarily] resolve this ambiguity for the faithful, did not call him "Son," in order that the parallel with the time of our generation might not obfuscate the incomprehensible instantaneousness of the divine generation and therefore it might be thought, by not admitting the eternity of the Son, that it was impossible that he always was with the Father, even though he is with him from the beginning. He is called the cause of everything as well as the beginning, not because he is superior to the Father, nor because, like his Father, he is devoid of beginning, but because he coexists with him from eternity. He most certainly proceeds from him but does not take his origin from him afterward. Therefore [the Evangelist] did not call him Son, but Word, so that he might designate him through this name by analogy.

This is the custom of divine Scripture: when it wants to show something about the divine nature, it gives it a name taken from our things which is suitable to describe it, as this sentence of the apostle confirms, "Our God is

---

[7]Again Theodore is referring to the theories of the Arians, who maintained that the Son had a beginning, so that there had been a time in which he did not exist. [8]That is, the heretics. [9]That is, the Word.

a consuming fire."[10] The apostle thought that the judgment proceeding from God could be described sufficiently only by using an analogy with our things. Therefore he did not hesitate to call him "fire." In a similar way the blessed John called him *Word* in order to remove any doubts from our mind by means of this analogy. He did not call him "Word," as some think, to indicate the one who reveals the will of the Father, because we humans express through words the intention of our soul.

Otherwise [the heretics] should tell us how they want the will of the Father to be expressed to men through the Son. Perhaps through a word? But this is foolish. On one occasion only, namely, during his incarnation, [the Son] was seen while he talked to men. But maybe they will reply that he appeared many times in different guises to righteous people and talked to them. But it seems that this happened to them by means of angels. An angel appeared to Balaam on the way, clearly showing him the will of God. And because of his advice Balaam walked that way.[11] We always see the prophet Zechariah saying, "The angel who spoke with me said to me."[12] It is evident that the angel only said what God wanted him to say.

Even if the heretics said that [the Word] shows the will of God through his works, we would find that this is not extraneous to angels either. "Bless the Lord, O you his angels, you mighty ones who do his bidding, obedient to his spoken word."[13] The apostle spoke in a similar way about all the angelic powers, "Are not all angels spirits in the divine service, sent to serve for the sake of those who inherit salvation?"[14] It is evident that the angelic powers, sent for this purpose, perfectly fulfill God's will. If they say that [the Son] reveals the will of God through a "word," the angels appear to do this as well; [if they say he reveals the will

of God] through works, it cannot be denied the angels do the same, as is evident. Therefore the designation "word" appears to be suitable to angels as well. And John, who intended to expound the divine nature, seems to have employed in vain then such a designation that is appropriate to so many others.

If this is so, why is he nowhere called "Word" in other passages of the divine books except for this one? In fact, it would have been very appropriate to have been called this by John the Baptist when he said, "No one has ever seen God. It is God the only Son who is close to the Father's heart who has made him known,"[15]—if he was supposed to be referred to by this name because he demonstrated the will of the Father.

Employing great accuracy, the Evangelist did not say "Word of God," but simply "Word." He knew perfectly well that "Word of God" both indicated his command and carried out the work according to the will of God, as is said about the prophets, "The Word of God was upon this or that person"; that is, it was a revelation made to them according to the will of God in order that they might proclaim their prophecies. The apostle says something similar to this, "The Word of God that was proclaimed through us to you,"[16] which indicates preaching. And again in another passage, "The message about the cross is foolishness to those who are perishing,"[17] that is, the preaching about the cross. And so also the blessed David said, "Fire and hail, snow and frost, the work of his word,"[18] that is, those things which happen and are set into motion according to his command and will. Again the blessed Peter says, "You know the word he sent to the people of Israel, preaching peace and tranquility by Jesus Christ—he is Lord of all."[19] Through these [words] he meant to say that through Jesus

---

[10]Heb 12:29. [11]See Num 22–24. [12]Zech 1:9. [13]Ps 103:20. [14]Heb 1:14. [15]Jn 1:18. [16]2 Cor 1:19. [17]1 Cor 1:18. [18]Ps 148:8. [19]Acts 10:36.

the Messiah, [God] sent this doctrine to be preached to the Jews so that they might learn that he is the Lord of all. And when the apostle says, "The word of God is living and sharp,"[20] he does not mean anything but this: the command of God and his judgment are powerful and sharp because he examines and sees everything, and therefore is able to bring his punishment on sinners.

When in other places Scripture mentions the word of God, it does not speak in an indefinite way. In fact, it says "word of God," or "word of the Lord," or "word of the cross," or "word that he sent," by specifying [the term *word*] with some additions. Here, the blessed John called him "Word" in an absolute sense.

Therefore we respond briefly to those who ask and say: Why did he call him Word? The holy book does not always use *word* according to *hypostasis*;[21] but here [the Evangelist] does actually call the Son "Word" according to *hypostasis* without any addition or specification, thus naming him so absolutely and singularly.

[The heretics] also suggest that he was called "word" figuratively when they try to explain why he was called with this name. But we have shown above, with the help of God, that he was not designated so in the sense that they intend.

So what do we say? The meaning of *word* is twofold for us. It indicates what is uttered by the voice through our tongue as well as what is hidden in our mind that we say is located in our rational soul or is natural to it. We are not discussing the definition of this term. This "word" is from the soul and is known to be always with it.

Therefore we solve the doubt by means of analogy. Since we see that this "word" which is in the soul is not separated or divided from it, and that it never proceeds in time from it, but rather appears to exist always with it and in it—how much more must we not doubt that

the Son cannot proceed from the Father as if being divided or separated [from him]. Nor did he receive his nature in time; rather it is always with him and beside him. No [interval of time] ever existed between the Father and the Son because from eternity [the Son] is with the Father and only has the Father as a beginning. In substance, truly, he is with him as Son and is united to him.

Certainly, another argument of the heretics is entirely ridiculous: As everyone knows, [they say], the Son, he who is begotten, came into existence after the Father. For, [they say] if they can find his beginning from the Father, they can rightly say about him that he [the Son] came into existence later, seeing that he was begotten. And other arguments like these are just as ridiculous. In fact, since this begetting occurs faster than the blink of an eye, how can it be understood that the begotten comes into existence after the begetter? Among us those who are begotten come into existence after their begetters only because these begetters are not able to beget immediately. They only receive this power after a long time. And after receiving such ability, they still need another long period in which to conceive their offspring through marriage. And then the child has to be made and formed so that it may slowly come to birth.

Since we cannot apply such conceptions to God, how does the Father's being the cause of the Son's generation make [the Son] come into existence after him from whom he was born? In fact if the begetter is incomprehensible, how much more incomprehensible is it for the begotten one to have come into existence after him since, as we said, the birth of the begotten occurred in an instant. And the existence of the begotten one himself is also eternal. How can the Son be defined as having come into existence after the Father when the Father himself is infinite and the existence of him

---

[20]Heb 4:12.　[21]Latin *hypostasim* (accusative); in Syriac: *qnŭmo*; in Greek: *hypostasis*.

who was born from the Father occurred in an instant? Nor is [the Son] said to exist previous to the creatures because he is their Creator, for such anteriority is not suitable at all for the Creator because it suggests that he existed just prior to his creatures, that is, only for the requisite time it was needed for creation [to occur].

What else can we say except that he *was?* Nothing else can be said in addition to that. What can we say about the nature of one whose beginning in which he began to be we cannot find? The thought that he came into being is incompatible with who he is, and we can also attest that such a thought is a serious offense against him. We do say that the [creatures] were made later, but we cannot conceive how long after they were made. There is no temporal measure between the Creator and their creation. However, God did exist before them, although it cannot be measured, since there is no time that can measure his life. But after [the creatures] began to exist there followed a time after their birth and a limit to that time that could be measured.

For this reason, the blessed David also said about God, "He who is before ages,"[22] not because ages are entities themselves, but because they are stretches of time which measure those things which had a beginning. Therefore he said that God existed before ages because God exists apart from every age, nor does he have a beginning in which he was made from which it might be ascertained what stretch of time followed him.

The blessed Paul says the same thing about the Son: "He through whom he also made the ages."[23] He does not mean here that he made things that do not exist, but that he himself is the beginning of all things that began to exist since he exists above every age, and his life cannot be included between an end and a beginning. The blessed John refers to this as well.

And so, after he said, *In the beginning was,* by adding the designation *Word,* he wanted to prove by analogy that it is possible that something may proceed from something else without being separated from it by any stretch of time. In the same way the blessed Paul, after the words, "through whom he also made the ages," added, "who is the splendor of the glory of his [Father]."[24] Splendor is from the nature of sun and fire, and proceeds from them without being separated in time. Its nature is not divided from those from which it derives.

When the Evangelist said *In the beginning was the Word,* he sufficiently demonstrated the eternity of his nature. And after by analogy he called him *Word,* and resolved any ambiguity, he also established that he did not say *in the beginning was* in order to show that [the Word] was devoid of a beginning, but rather to show that he was coexistent from eternity with his beginning. He also explained and clarified this concept by saying *and the Word was with God;* that is, it was with him and beside him and united to him. Indeed when he puts forward the phrase *was with God,* he clearly shows that he had said, *In the beginning was [the Word],* not in the sense that he was devoid of a beginning, but that he was always coexistent with his beginning.

And when he said *was with God,* he added, *and the Word was God,* without saying *was God* before assuring us that he *was with God.* But after he had said, *was with God,* he then added, *and was God,* as if saying that he was nothing else but what the one whom he was with also was. A very similar passage occurs with the apostle who, after calling him, "the splendor of his glory," adds, "and the imprint of his substance,"[25] in order to indicate a perfect similarity while at the same cautiously staying away from the idea that there is no difference as well.

But the Evangelist did not stop here. Ex-

---

[22]Ps 55:19 (54:20 LXX).   [23]Heb 1:2.   [24]Heb 1:3.   [25]Heb 1:3.

plaining in a more profound way what he had said before through what he had said later, and intending to speak more clearly about the divinity of the Only Begotten, he set out to show the difference indicated by [the Son's] dignity, not only through a comparison with the created things, but also by demonstrating that he has no communion [of nature] with them.

[1:2-3] He says, *He was with God in the beginning*, and, *all things were made through him*. By saying *he* in a demonstrative sense, he has contrasted him with *all things made*. He was, he says, in the beginning with God, and all creatures were made through him. And clearly he made a comparison with *in the beginning was*, introducing in opposition the phrase *all things were made through him*. Therefore he was not made because he [already] existed in the beginning; whereas those things were made because they had not existed before. This is also the explanation of what was said before, because it shows what the Evangelist means by the words *In the beginning was*. Clearly, he is asserting his eternity.

And in order to confirm this even more he said, *and without him not one thing was made which was made*. He wanted to show through all these words that [the Son] was always with the Father and that he is of the same nature and a partner with him in creation since he created everything when it was time for those things to be made. This addition also explains what had been said previously. The phrase, *all things . . . through him* shows that this was not attributed to him because of his assistance [in creation], but because of his cooperation. Then, in order that none of the things that were made might be subtracted from his creation, he also added, *And without him not one thing was made which was made*.

Some have read this passage as follows,

"And without him not one thing was made which was made *in him*," that is, of those things that were made *through him*.[26] Would it not be ridiculous if, by speaking this way, the Evangelist intended to teach something new and unknown to humankind? Anyone could have said about anyone else, "not one of the things which were made through him was made without him." And anyone may say the same about anything when it is obvious that the only thing we can say about someone who makes things is, "of those things which were made through him, none was made without him."

Some have read *without him not one thing was made* in a different way, uniting [this phrase] with, *what was made in him was life*. This is even more ridiculous: not all the things he made were life. In fact, there are many things he made that have no life, such as the mountains, the earth, and many others which we cannot list in detail. All this combines and confirms what had been said before, and even clarifies it. After saying, *all things were made through him*, [the Evangelist] adds, *And without him not one thing which was made, was made*, that is, to put it briefly, not one of the things that was made, was made without him—if we exclude from his creation the Father alone, because he is always with the Father, and it is necessary that he accomplishes the creation of things together with him.

Some suggested that also the Spirit was included here[27] because [the Evangelist] said that *all things* were made through him. We need to say a number of things about this. It is the habit of the Holy Scriptures to use the word *everything*, without including all things. For instance, "All who came are thieves and bandits"[28] does not include Moses or Samuel or all the other prophets. And there are many

---

[26]Those who put forward this possibility add "in him" from the next verse in John, which they interpret as "through him." The implication is that there were things made by the Word, as well as things that were not made by him. Theodore's point (which he makes in what follows), however, is that such reasoning leads to tautology. [27]That is, in the things that were made. [28]Jn 10:8.

other examples of this usual way of doing things. In a similar way the Evangelist, when he said, *Without him not one thing which was made, was made*, shows that he is saying that all created things *were made through him*, but not the uncreated ones. How can it be so? Because it is self-evident; and it is also asserted by the Evangelist. In the first place it would be necessary to ask if the Holy Spirit had been made and to prove that it was included among those things mentioned above. But I simply dismiss this whole question.

On the other hand, I say the following succinctly: God certainly created all creatures diversely. He composed the entire creation in a single body—certainly the highest heaven and the earth and all the other visible and invisible things. All created things are connected, and visible things are moved by the invisible. God did not make a being among the spiritual ones who is only and unique in his kind, nor did he make a single angel or archangel or other spiritual power. Rather, he created the angelic orders in the greatest quantity and caused them to devote themselves to a single form of service. If the Holy Spirit were one of them, we should ask in which [angelic] order it might be included, and to which it might belong. If it were visible, it should be counted among those that are of such a nature that they are mutually constituted and subsist together in this way. But since its nature is invisible, it is necessary that we place it among something else. It is not, however, connected to any of those [angelic orders]. The Holy Spirit, in fact, is unique, and does not perform any service like that of an angel. Rather it is always and everywhere sufficient to itself—and therefore it is evident that it is distinct from them. How could it be enumerated among those in whose orders it is not included? It is one and united with the Father and the Son, as the Father is one and the Son is one.

I think that this is sufficient, in order not to go beyond the limits of this book with too many words. The questions which we have diffusely expounded above, O Porphyry, most glorious among the bishops, were written by us because we found that these testimonies had been adulterated a great deal by the malice of the heretics. We believe that it is the duty of the interpreter to disclose the real sense of a sentence, not only for the sake of the literal interpretation, but also in order to reject any contrary opinion. Since we said that those words needed a careful examination in case anyone wanted to attain to their comprehension through an attentive investigation, we made such an investigation for those who may run across this book. Know also, my lord, that with the help of God we could say many other things necessary to confirm these truths, but we have given up doing so because we only intended to say those things whose omission would be a detriment to a clear interpretation of the words.

[1:4] *In him was life*. He did not simply say *was life*, since this can also be suitable to living creatures; rather, he said, "*in him* was life." In other words, life-giving power springs forth from him so that he not only lives but gives life to others as well. And this is consistent with the phrase, *without him not one thing which was made, was made*. He made all things by supplying life; he does not produce mere natures. He is able to create *living* creatures. [The Evangelist] recalled this because, among the things that were made, this was the most important. By saying *in him was life*, he did not intend to indicate his nature but his power.

Therefore he adds, *and the life was the light of men*. In other words, this power of his was not only capable of enlivening the souls of people, but also of abundantly filling them with all knowledge. Since he had mentioned his role in creation, and that he was the creator of everything, he wanted to mention the most excellent aspect of his creation in order to testify to the excellence of his creative power. Therefore, first he said that he could create living creatures, which are the most excellent among created things. Then, because human beings stand out among the living creatures because they are endowed with reason, he adds, *and the life was the light of men*. With these words he testified to the excellence of his power, because he not only is able to create living creatures but also generously grants them reflective minds. In other words, he created spiritual beings. And this is what [the Evangelist] signified by saying, *and the life was the light of men*, namely, "this is their origin, this is the bestower of reason."

[1:5] *The light shines in the darkness, and the darkness did not grasp it.* It would be more fitting for him to say, "and the darkness will not grasp it," which is required by the context. But it is evident that in sacred texts different times are simply placed together without distinction. If anyone wants to investigate this further, he will find that this is usually the case, especially in the Old Testament.

What the text means is this: [Previously] all creatures had been subject to error and ignorance. But now, the one who created everything—the one who formed living creatures and created rational beings—this one has appeared in order to remedy all the things that had hold of them, and to lead them all to virtue. Error cannot approach him. Rather, like a shining light he dissolves and dispels all that darkness. This sentence[29] is prophetic. It would have been appropriate to the context if, instead of saying, "did not grasp it" he had said, "will not grasp it," as we also read in Isaiah, "like a lamb that was led to the slaughter,"[30] instead of "that will be led." And the facts which occur later demonstrate that this prophecy was indeed true. The Evangelist included them because he did believe in what our Lord promised, that when he was lifted up he would draw all to himself.[31]

And what else? After he had spoken words

appropriate to his divinity—saying that he was with the Father from eternity and shared with him the creation of things because he was endowed with such power that he was not only able to create but also to create living creatures, and even rational beings—in good order he added that he was also the generous giver of knowledge and reason to human beings. It was also appropriate that he now had made himself known for the salvation of everyone. From this point [the Evangelist] begins to relate how he appeared.

Since he had a number of things that could be put forward as testimonies in this regard—for these would serve as a confirmation of who he was, while confounding the unbelievers—he added immediately, [1:6] *There was a man sent from God whose name was John*. Indeed, passing to the manifestation of the Messiah, what more proper beginning could he find· than to begin from John? From him, in fact, we learn who the one is whom he welcomed at the beginning. What else does he say?

[1:7] *He came as a witness to testify to the light, so that all might believe through him.* Concerning John, he truly says, [1:8] *He was not the light.* The Evangelist is making it clear that John had come to the conclusion that his purpose was to confront the Jews. What else could he conceive of saying with the words: *He was not the light?* Simply that he wanted to accuse those who had thought that John had to be accepted, whereas they crucified the one about whom John had testified, because he had not come in order to testify about himself but to reveal Christ.

And since the Evangelist said, *He was not the light*, in order to avoid anything contrary that might appear to oppose that statement—in fact, if he is not the light perhaps one might conclude that he is the darkness—he adds as an explanation, [1:9] *The true light which enlightens everyone was coming into the world.*

---

[29]That is, Jn 1:5. [30]Is 53:7. [31]Jn 12:32.

[The Evangelist is, in effect, saying,] "I did not say that [John the Baptist] was the darkness but only that he was not the true light: for a short time he acted as a lamp shining in the darkness. [Christ], however, is the true light—he, I mean who came into the world and revealed himself and enlightened everyone. He has never stopped shining and continues to do so." At that time, people had to come to the knowledge of Christ through the words of John, but later they embraced the faith even without his preaching.

The phrase *coming into the world* is connected according to meaning with *he was the true light*. He meant: When he came into the world and appeared, he enlightened everyone. He does not say, *everyone*, as if everyone was to be converted, but because he will be the salvation of all those who want to be enlightened. He will not work for a short time, like John, but will always be able to give his help, even to the end of time, to those who want to live and believe.

After he had said that John *was not the light*, he added a comparison with Christ, *the true light that enlightens everyone who was coming into the world*. By this he meant that John was active for a short time and for few people since he only preached to the Jews. This is, in fact, the purpose of a lamp: to enlighten for a short time and then to be extinguished. Christ, on the other hand, like a perpetual light, never dies. The Evangelist expresses this when he says *he was the true light* that remains to the consummation of the world and that provides everyone with its help.

[1:10] *He was in the world, and the world was made through him; yet the world did not know him.* After having said, *coming into this world*,

he rightly added, *he was in the world*, with reference to the Lord Christ in order to declare that that *coming* referred to his manifestation in the flesh. In fact, according to his hypostasis[32] and his nature, he was in the world even before this. And as if this was not enough, he added, *and the world was made through him*. In other words, would it be strange if he were in the world which would have not existed at all if he did not want it so? But he was certainly in the world and before the world, and he himself also made the world, *and the world did not know him*. He rightly said, *and [the world] did not know him*, that is, it did not know its Lord.

[1:11] *He came to what was his own and his own people did not accept him.* He explains his argument more clearly here. It is clear that in all of this he is blaming the unbelievers.

[1:12] *But to all who received him who believed in his name, he gave power to become children of God,* [1:13] *who were born, not of blood or of the will of the flesh or the will of man, but of God.* For those, he says who accepted him, this situation was not useless. He gave them something great and excellent. Certainly, insofar as it is possible, he made them equal in honor by giving them the gift of adoptive sonship.[33] They take advantage of that grace, not by being reborn in the body according to the natural order of generation, but being born through divine power through a certain similarity and affinity with him.

After saying these things, it remained to be declared how his advent occurred so that the accusation against the unbelievers might be increased even more. Therefore, after he had demonstrated in the previous verses that there were many ways for them to believe if they had wanted to, he increased the accusation

---

[32]"Substance," or simply "person," in the technical language of Greek patristic theology. Theodore, however, had a different understanding of *hypostasis* than, for instance, Cyril of Alexandria. For Theodore, *hypostasis* could be understood as a concrete example of a nature, or *physis*. In this case it was his divine nature as God the Word that was manifest. Cyril of Alexandria spoke of *hypostasis* in terms of the entire person, human and divine. See the discussion of terminology in John McGuckin, *St Cyril of Alexandria: The Christological Controversy, Its History, Theology and Texts*, Supplements to Vigiliae Christianae 23 (New York: E. J. Brill, 1994), pp. 138-51. [33]Here Theodore alludes to the supreme principle of Christian mysticism, namely, the affiliation and assimilation with Christ.

against them. In the first place he describes the inherent dignity of the one who appeared to them. After this he utilizes the testimony of John who did not come for himself but to testify about him and to declare that he was the true light to which all those who want to be converted must look. And finally, there is the generous gift that he gave to believers by raising them to adoptive sonship. After he had exalted the Word by means of these three virtues, that is, the excellence of his nature, the truth of his actions and the gifts which his grace brought to believers, he added how his advent occurred by saying:

[1:14] *And the word became flesh.* He made use of this word in a conspicuous way. "See," he says, "he deigned to become flesh." Since this was the opinion of those who saw him— because he was so debased in his humanity that he was believed to be only a man by many according to how he appeared—in order to explain the word *was*, he added, καὶ ἐσκή νωσεν ἐν ἡμῖν, and *set up a tabernacle among us*; that is, in this sense he became flesh, insofar as he lived in our nature. For evidently the words καὶ ἐσκήνωσεν ἐν ἡμῖν stand for *he lived among us*, as also the apostle said about us human beings, "We who are still in this tab- ernacle groan,"[34] by calling our body a taber- nacle. And again, "We know that if the earthly tabernacle we live in is destroyed."[35] It is well known that in Scripture the whole human be- ing is usually indicated by flesh. For example, "To you all flesh shall come."[36] Therefore here too, in saying, *[the Word] became human*, he said, *became flesh.* But he did not say *became* as if he was changed but because he was believed

to be so according to his appearance.

He said this in order to emphasize those things which show his mercy and the fault of the unbelievers. It was very appropriate that he said, *[he] became flesh*, so that he underlined both aspects: the fault of those [unbelievers] and the manifestation of his own benevolence.

Now we think that enough words have been said to explain the text, and it does not seems appropriate for me to proceed further with this argument. In my opinion, in fact, we have opposed our adversaries with enough words. They either maintained that *became* means "was changed"—and this, I believe, can only be said by fools—or they understood those words like the majority of people do. The Evangelist explains it sufficiently by adding *lived among us* to the word *became.*

If you want to be more diligent in learning more about these questions, you can read the volume we wrote about the nature of Christ.[37] There you will be instructed about this verse and the subject under discussion.

In the meantime, the Evangelist returns to his train of thought. So that the phrases *became flesh* and *appeared so* do not obscure [the Word's] dignity, he added, *and we have seen his glory, the glory as of the Only Begotten who is from the Father, full of grace and truth.* In effect, he is saying here, "Not from the many things he did will I make known who he is. Nor did we agree to believe in him rashly, but accepted him as the true Only Begotten Son because of those things that we saw. And the things we saw are such that they demonstrated the greatness of him who appeared. They could not belong to anyone else but the Only

---

[34]2 Cor 5:4. [35]2 Cor 5:1. [36]Ps 65:2. [37]Theodore alludes here to his treatise *De incarnatione* (On the Incarnation). This extremely important work had been discovered in the library of Seert in a complete Syriac translation in 1905 by Addai Scher, who described the manuscript in an article published in 1909 and republished with additions in 1910: see Addai Scher, "Joseph Hazzaya, écrivain syriaque du VIIIe siècle," *RSO* 3 (1910): 62-63. Unfortunately, before an edition of the work could be prepared, the manuscript perished, as well as its discoverer, in the course of the tragic events of World War I. At the moment only a few fragments are extant in the form of quotations in the works of Theodore's opponents or supporters. On the basis of the available material it is extremely difficult to make any reliable hypothesis on the general contents and tenor of this work. See also M. Richard, "La tradition des fragments du traité *Peri tēs anthrōpēseōs* de Théodore de Mopsueste," *Le Muséon* 46 (1943): 55-75; R. Devreesse, *Essai sur Théodore de Mopsueste*, Studi e Testi 141 (Vatican City: Biblioteca Apostolica Vaticana, 1948), pp. 44-48.

Begotten, who possesses perfect likeness with the Father. Thus the works which were done through him were full of true grace." Therefore the Evangelist called the truth *grace* in comparison with that[38] of the Jews. He sets out to show through that comparison the greatness of [the Lord] in order to accuse the unbelievers, and reveals his intention with the words that follow.

He indicates *grace* with the name of truth, that is, true grace, because Christ pardoned the former transgressions and gave salvation and the remission of sins. In addition he also destroyed death which reigned because of sin, and gave us a sure hope of the resurrection by adopting us as sons—not only in word, as he did with the Jews, but in action through the power of the Spirit, as he regenerated us in the hope of resurrection so that death itself will never destroy. This is symbolized in baptism. Besides this he prepared for us the delights of the heavenly kingdom, if we preserve pure in our actions the honor of the adoptive sonship given to us through baptism.

But it is the height of madness that some have dared to press the fact that the Evangelist most certainly said, "*as* of an only Son" and not just "of an only Son." Who can ignore that the particle *as*, if used in a comparison, refers one thing to another but, if used as in our case, gives abundance and soundness to an expressed concept? This use is certainly frequent in Scripture.

If [the words] *as of an only Son* were said by way of comparison, they should show us to whom the Evangelist compares [Christ] by saying that he saw his glory "as of an only Son." If another term is not given, it is evident that he wants to indicate his dignity and confirm what he is saying. This is his purpose from the first to the last of these verses, namely, to express his praises that he speaks in truth and without any falsehood. He means: Through experience

we have obtained the things that we assert, and the works accomplished by him demonstrate his dignity so clearly that they are suitable to the Only Begotten Son in whom there is absolute likeness with the Father.

Further aggravating the accusation against the unbelievers and confirming the greatness of Christ, he says, [1:15] *John testified to him and cried out.* He says in effect: "These things that we are asserting, John never ceased from proclaiming with a loud voice." What did he say? *This was he of whom I said, he who comes after me was born before me because he was before me.* "These," he says, "are John's words which he often said before Christ came, and which he often repeated after his advent and through which he indicated him, saying: This is the one about whom I said many times to you: he is higher than me, he will rise and will be exalted—and with good reason—because he is greater than I."

The Baptist does not say *was born before me* about the birth of Christ, as the heretics assert, since they do not worry about the meaning of the words as long as they can make their astute observations. And these words, since they were spoken in this way, do not concern the nature of God the Word. How might the sentence, *[he who] comes after me* concern him? How could he say, *he was born before me, because he was before me,* if these words were spoken about the birth? In that case, it would have been necessary to say, "Because he was born before me, he was before me," not, *He was born before me because he was before me.* The things that are made are not made because they exist already, but on the contrary, they exist because they have been made.

What does the blessed John mean? [The Baptist] was already considered by all others to be more praiseworthy. Everyone came to him, while Jesus himself remained unknown. John testified; his testimony was, fittingly, about

---

[38]That is, the truth of the Jews which was based on the law rather than grace.

Jesus. In particular, while he baptized, Jesus actually received the baptism. Therefore he says appropriately, *This was he of whom I said, "He who comes after me was born before me: because he was before me."* In other words, "This is the one about whom I said, 'After me comes a man who will certainly be considered inferior to me because testimony about him came from me and he will be baptized by me. But in a short time it will become apparent that he is before me, and it is certainly more appropriate for him to be known as the one who is great, because he indeed is the greatest.'" He said *after me* and *before me* according to human opinion. If he said *was born* instead of "will be born," why should this be considered strange? As we have shown above, this is the usual way of writing in Scripture, and the Evangelist himself wrote "[it] did not grasp" instead of "[it] will not grasp."[39]

Let us examine the following words of John the Baptist, as the Evangelist relates them in an orderly way: [1:16] *From his fullness we have all received.* These are the words the Evangelist reports were pronounced by John the Baptist: *From his fullness*, he says, *we have all received*; that is, we have all received the grace of the Spirit which is given to us as a gift— this is what we received from his abundance. He says this about his human nature which has every grace in it, but at the same time demonstrates the dignity of the nature which is in him. Through his union with[40] God the Word, by means of the Spirit, he took part in a true sonship. We have received a portion of his spiritual grace, and through it we are made participants together with him in adoptive sonship, even though we are very far away from such dignity.[41]

And he appropriately added, *grace for grace*, indicating the law, as well, with the name "grace." He says, this grace is given instead of that grace [of the law]. In order that it might not be thought that identical words stood for identical things, he added, [1:17] *The law indeed was given through Moses; grace and truth came about through Christ.* At one time, he says, the law was given only for our instruction, and certainly was also conferred as grace even though those who received it were unworthy of it. But now true grace has been given. Therefore he did not say that through Jesus Christ it *was given*, but it *came about.* Certainly there a precept was given, here, on the other hand, the event of our regeneration is fulfilled which is first of all perfected in Jesus Christ, then is transmitted through him to believers, not only as a type but also in reality, so that we will be participants in his resurrection.

Since he had said above that he is full of grace and truth, and that he is the Only Begotten of the Father, [the Evangelist] wanted to confirm his words through the testimony of John in order to show that John had proclaimed this too. Therefore he added, [1:18] *No one has ever seen God: it is God the Only Begotten who is close to the Father's bosom who has made him known.* He also relates this as said by John. Therefore now we learn what true doctrine is all about. "Once," he says, "it was believed that God was seen. This occurred because of the way human speech is used. In fact, it is impossible to see God on earth. Now, however, the Only Begotten has become the master of truth for us. Anything he says is true because he is with the Father." And so from all this it appears that the Evangelist wanted to describe the dignity of the Messiah in comparison with the law.

He said, *[he] who is close to the Father's bosom*, because he is indissolubly connected with him. According to the custom of the

---

[39]Jn 1:5.　[40]Syriac: *bnqypwt' gyr dlwt 'lh' mlt'*. According to Robert Payne Smith, *Thesaurus Syriacus* (Oxford: Clarendon, 1879–1901), the word *nqypwt'* expresses the idea of *conjunction* or *connection* of the two natures in Christ without intermingling. This is how the word *union* should be understood here in order to remain consistent with Theodore's Christology.　[41]This passage introduces us to Theodore's typical "dualistic Christology" (see the translator's introduction, esp. the quotation from Norris, p. xxvi).

Holy Scriptures, our term *bosom* indicates what is united with us because what we keep in our bosom is intimately connected with us. So, for example, in the blessed David we read, "Return sevenfold into the bosom of our neighbors the taunts with which they taunted you, O Lord";[42] that is, cause their taunt not to withdraw from them, but to stick to their iniquities. And in the same sense we read, "The insults of many people that I bore in my bosom,"[43] meaning, [those insults] that never leave me. Therefore in our passage [the Evangelist] said, *[he] who is close to the Father's bosom,* to confirm the authority of him who taught these things. "Since," he says, "the one who is always with the Father and does not part from him related these things, he is true."

Through all this he confirmed the purpose of his words, intending to accuse the Jews and to show that the work of Christ was wonderful, and that believers found in him a great help while a grave punishment loomed over the unbelievers. And so he first demonstrated his case by portraying the dignity of Christ's nature, and then rehearsing the works performed by him. He further demonstrated his case through recording Christ's advent and the advent of John who testified about him. And then he included mention of his gifts, reporting the adoptive sonship which is to be bestowed by the one who exists with the Father as a coequal. He further recorded his advent as one who did not refuse to be in the flesh. This made it easy for those who wanted to receive him. And finally, after comparing his gifts with those that had been given to the Jews, he demonstrated that Christ's gifts far surpassed them. By adding John as a witness and using his words in his comparison, he described the superiority of Christ's gifts. All these aspects were a corroboration of the case of Christ and

a grave indictment of the unbelievers.

Therefore he continues, [1:19] *This is the testimony given by John when the Jews sent priests and Levites from Jerusalem to ask him, "Who are you?"* After he related that John had testified to him and had cried out by saying [. . .].[44] After reporting John's words, he now confirms what John said by observing that John testified about him when the leaders of the Jews were sent to him in order to inquire whether he was the Messiah. It was only right that [the Baptist] answered that he was not the Messiah, and added that he was not Elijah or the expected prophet. He was, according to the words of Isaiah, [1:23] *the voice of one crying out in the wilderness;*[45] that is, he was preaching in the wilderness in order that the listeners might be prepared for the one who would come. This is not the action of the king but of the messenger.

Then when he was asked again why he baptized if he was not Elijah or the prophet or the Messiah, he replied, "Even though I baptize, I do not baptize with the baptism of Christ, but only in water, and do not confer the Spirit. But the one whom you expect is already among you, although you ignore him; he who is now considered to be small, later will appear to be great. Compare him to me: his dignity is so great that I am not worthy to bend and untie the thong of his sandals."

After he had related the words said and testified by John, the Evangelist added, [1:28] *This took place in Bethany across the Jordan where John was baptizing.* Together with the events he described the place where they happened.

Since it is usually asked who that prophet was whom the Jews expected in addition to the Messiah, as they first asked John whether he was the Messiah—and when he said no,

---

[42]Ps 79:12. [43]Ps 89:50. [44]The editor J.-M. Vosté indicates a lacuna in the text here. This lacuna is present in the entire manuscript tradition, that is, in the archetypus A (N.-D. des Semences), as well as in all its recent copies: B (Borgianus Vaticanus); Berolinensis (not employed in Vosté's edition); P (Parisinus); Mingana (not employed in Vosté's edition). It evidently dates from a previous phase of the manuscript tradition of Theodore's commentary. See CSCO 4 3:i-iv and 40. [45]See Is 40:3.

whether he was Elijah, and finally whether he was *the prophet*—it must be known that there was a good reason why the Jews expected Elijah. In fact, he was supposed to come before the second advent of the Lord. But being ignorant they asked *whether he was the prophet*. Since the glory of the Messiah, before he came, was not fully known to humanity—just like now there are all these foolish and diverse opinions about the coming of that deceiver[46]— in the same way, at that time too, they held many incongruous opinions about the Messiah. Therefore, some people said that another was the Messiah, and another the prophet and were greatly in error because the prophecy said that a single prophet and Messiah was to be expected who would be rightly and appropriately called by both names.

[1:29] *The next day he saw Jesus coming toward him and declared, "Here is the Lamb of God who takes away the sin of the world."* As appears from the narrative of the Evangelist, John the Baptist spoke previously as if the Lord had come already and walked among crowds who still were ignoring him. Now, since he is coming to be baptized, he is described with the words: *This is the Lamb of God.*

Let us consider how Scripture usually places words in the appropriate context of facts. By saying here that *this is the one who takes away the sin of the world*, he did not call him "the Only Begotten Son" or the "Son of God" or "the one who is close to the Father's bosom," as it appears that he had said above, although now would have seemed the right time to express the majesty of his nature in order to confirm the promise of the things which he was about to give. But [the Baptist] did not say any of these things. Instead, he called him *lamb*, a name that signifies his passion. In fact, he was called a lamb and a sheep because of his

death, when he would wash away sin with his passion. Since sin reigned in our mortality, and death was strengthened in us because of sin, Jesus Christ, our Lord and Savior, came and relieved us of all of this. And after destroying death through his death, he also destroyed the sin rooted in our nature because of mortality. He has already made us immortal in promise; then he will render us so in actual fact when he defeats sin with the gift of immortality. For this reason, the blessed Paul writing to the Corinthians after recalling the resurrection said, "Then the saying that is written will be fulfilled: 'Where, O death, is your sting? Where, O death, is your victory?' "[47] And in order to teach us what the sting of death is that is to be destroyed with death, he added, "The sting of death is sin."[48]

Therefore he used the term *lamb* correctly here. [He refutes the opposing opinion and doctrine widespread among the Jews from ancient times by saying, "No one has ever seen God."[49] In fact, there was a firm belief among them that he had indeed appeared to them many times in different guises. And so, with good reason he added, "the Only Son who is close to the Father's bosom, has made him known,"[50] in order to confirm what he was saying through the trustworthiness of the teacher and to prove that this and nothing else should be believed.][51] While speaking about the grace that was given to us and about the destruction of sin, he uses the term *lamb* which conveys the nature of that grace he confers. Evidently, by saying, *Here is the Lamb of God*, he showed them that the one they expected had already come. He did this most appropriately according to the word of Isaiah, "Like a lamb that is led to the slaughter, and like a sheep that before its shearer is silent."[52] Since they already expected someone would come who, by dying for everyone, would wash away the

---

[46]That is, "the antichrist," according to 2 Jn 7, "many deceivers have gone out into the world, those who do not confess that Jesus Christ has come in the flesh; any such person is the deceiver and the antichrist!" [47]1 Cor 15:54-55. [48]1 Cor 15:56. [49]Jn 1:18. [50]Jn 1:18. [51]This portion of the text in brackets appears to be out of place and most likely was meant to be included with v. 18 above. [52]Is 53:7.

sin of everyone, John quite rightly said, *Here is the Lamb of God*. This was obviously the one about whom Isaiah prophesied. It is evident that this is what John the Baptist meant when the Lord came for baptism. This is also suggested by the order of the words that follow. In addition, it must be noticed that the Evangelist said that Jesus came to [John the Baptist], but does not add that he was baptized. It appears from all of this that the Evangelist accurately reports the details which had been omitted,[53] while he believed it was superfluous to repeat what had been said already.

[1:30] *This is he of whom I said, "After me came a man who was made*[54] *before me because he was before me"*; in other words, he is the one I talked about many times. Now it is necessary again to refute the cunningness of the heretics who take the words, *after me came* and *was made before me* as referring to the divine hypostasis, as has been already said above. We diligently demonstrated that *[he] was made* does not concern the hypostasis, or his eminent dignity, or even his divine nature. Rather, this was said about his human nature, as is revealed by the words, *after me came*, to which he adds *a man*. Evidently he means here no other but the one about whom he had spoken before. Therefore he says, *This is he of whom I said*. And then, since the speech is about the same one, if the term *man* follows, it is evident that here the speech concerns the man, and not at all the divine nature. And this is confirmed by all these elements. In fact, *I am not worthy to untie the thong of his sandals*, also hints at his human nature to which the sandals belong. In the same way also, *Here is the Lamb of God* indicates the nature that will suffer pain and a

violent death. The fact that even in his human nature he was much more powerful than John appears from his very great power and his joining himself to[55] God the Word by which he is elevated not only over every man, but over all creatures.[56]

[1:31] *I myself did not know him; but I came baptizing with water for this reason, that he might be revealed to Israel*. He revealed why he had lived in the wilderness. This certainly happened through a special arrangement by God in order that the Baptist might not have any relationship with the Messiah. In fact, an association would have certainly occurred between them if he had lived in the town since they were the same age and were related. The suspicion easily would have risen that he had spoken what he testified because of that previous relationship, and because they were friends and were related. In order to remove this suspicion, John was segregated from the time he was a young boy and grew up in the wilderness. Therefore, with good reason he said, *I myself did not know him*. "I had no familiarity or friendship with him. But I was sent to baptize him with water so that I might reveal him whom I did not know." He clearly showed that he baptized in order for all the Jews who came because of the baptism to have an occasion to hear his teaching and to see him about whom he testified. And above, when he was asked why he baptized if he was not the Messiah or Elijah or the prophet, he answered that he only baptized with water but that there was another to whom he testified, and that he had come to reveal him.

[1:32] *And John testified, saying, "I saw the Spirit descending from heaven like a dove, and*

---

[53]By the other Evangelists: Matthew, Mark and Luke.　[54]Most English translations treat this passage in terms of rank, but Theodore focuses on the word *gegonen* in Greek, or what we have in the Syriac: *whw' lh qdmy* = "and he began to (be)come into existence before me." Theodore's following comments on this phrase do not engage the Arian question of whether God the Word was created or generated since he sees the text as referring to the human nature of Christ, the man rather than the divine nature which has always existed, as Theodore held in arguments against the Arians.　[55]Syriac: *mṭl nqypwth* = from/because of his union, conjunction or connection.　[56]For Theodore's Christology and his concepts about Christ the Word and Christ the Man, see translator's introduction, esp. quotation from Norris, p. xxvi.

it remained on him." Here it is evident that the Spirit descending like a dove on the baptized Lord was not seen by all those present but only by John in a sort of spiritual vision, just as the prophets used to see things that were invisible to everyone else when they were among many people. It would have been superfluous to say that *John testified, saying, "I saw the Spirit,"* if all those present had been participants in the vision.

Therefore, what some say is extremely foolish, namely, that the Holy Spirit is inferior to the Lord Christ because the dove is inferior to man. In fact, what appeared was a vision, not its nature. Therefore no one present saw it. In a spiritual vision only the prophet received this kind of sight, as Peter praying on the roof saw a large sheet coming down full of every kind of animal.[57] What he saw was not its nature, but a spiritual vision of things to come. God himself appeared as fire,[58] and in such a vision he did not appear to be lower than if he had appeared in the guise of a man; rather, he adjusted the vision to his purpose.

[1:33] *And I myself did not know him, but the one who sent me to baptize with water said to me, "He on whom you see the Spirit descend and remain is the one who baptizes with the Holy Spirit."* He did not say, "I knew him when the Spirit descended on him." In fact, he had already testified about him before the baptism, and as the Evangelist said, he exclaimed at once, "Here is the Lamb of God who takes away the sin of the world." Matthew relates that the Baptist refrained from [baptizing Jesus] and said, "I need to be baptized by you, and do you come to me?"[59] But [here] he says, "I did not know him. He who sent me in order that I might reveal before everyone that he had come, and that he had given me the power to baptize with water, also predicted to me that the Spirit would descend on him." After these words were said to him in the wilderness, he

immediately came and set about to do these things. As the Lord came to him, he immediately received the vision so that he might recognize him, and then spoke publicly about his greatness.

When he saw in a spiritual vision the Spirit descending, while he was baptizing, as had been predicted to him, then he was sure that he was seeing the expected result of the prophecy. John the Baptist spoke these words—actually they were related by the Evangelist as spoken by John—[the same] John who, even before the event occurred, had heard in the wilderness that this would happen. It is as if he said, "What I was told about him I now see accomplished. Therefore I rightly and with good reason testify that I saw those things which I had learned would happen in the future fulfilled in him."

For this reason he adds, [1:34] *And I myself have seen and have testified that this is the Son of God*; that is, I have seen, and from that event I have acquired a greater certainty and therefore I testify about him.

He does not say, *this is the Son of God*, with reference to his divine nature which is revealed by his divine generation, but with regard to his human nature because of the conjunction of that [nature] with the Only Begotten. And so, after he said, "I saw the Spirit, and, it was said to me, 'He on whom you see the Spirit descend and remain is the one who baptizes with the Holy Spirit,'" he conveniently adds, *I myself have seen and have testified that this is the Son of God*. We too are regenerated by the power of the Spirit and are made children of God, and therefore it is called the "Spirit of adoption, in which we cry Abba! Father!"[60] And the beginning of all these things is what happened to the Christ-in-the-flesh who first was born in the Spirit, and through the Spirit was united to the Only Begotten so that he acquired the true dignity of sonship and communicates to

---

[57]See Acts 10:9-12. [58]See Ex 3:14. [59]Mt 3:14. [60]Rom 8:15.

us the gift of the Spirit by which we are also regenerated and received among his children according to the power of each one. He rightly connected the Spirit which he saw descending on him after the baptism to the words, *I myself have seen and have testified that this is the Son of God.*

[1:35] *The next day John again was standing with two of his disciples,* [1:36] *and as he watched Jesus walk by, he exclaimed: "Look, here is the Lamb of God."* It is evident that the blessed John baptized for many days and preached, announcing the advent of the Messiah. The apostles, therefore, did not care to relate these words accurately because they only intended to reveal the events. No other Evangelist was diligent in saying that these things happened on the first day, those on the second, those others on the third. Rather, each of them simply only recorded the events [themselves]. The blessed John,[61] intending to report also the omitted things which in his opinion had to be related completely, developed his story also according to a chronological order.

After the baptism of the Lord, John[62] persisted in that occupation and did not cease from baptizing. And after other things occurred, the Evangelist said that John was still baptizing in Aenon near Salim.[63] Therefore, when the Lord came back, he addressed him with the words [reported above].

[1:37] *The two disciples heard him say this, and they followed Jesus.* After hearing his words, his disciples who were with him left him at once and hurried to go to Jesus about whom he was testifying.

[1:38] *When Jesus turned and saw them following, he said to them: "What are you looking for?"* He does not say these things as if he was ignorant, but in order to give them an opportunity to have faith in him. They immediately called him "Rabbi" and showed their profound

intention, that is, that they had been led to Jesus by no other reason than the desire to obey him as teacher. At the same time they asked him where he lived, revealing the desire to visit him often.

He did not point out a house, but told them to come along with him and see, thereby providing them the space for greater familiarity and trust toward him. And since they followed him, and it was already the tenth hour,[64] they stayed with him for the rest of the day and all night. And then the Evangelist, by relating that they had passed the day with him, also shows that they left at daybreak, as the following context clearly reveals. He says that one of those who followed him was Andrew, brother of Simon, whereas he does not mention the other. Evidently this is the blessed John himself. He always appears to pass in silence over those things that personally concern him. Moreover, when he relates something concerning himself, he avoids subscribing his name. If those who received the Gospel had not indicated the writer in the prefixed title, we would not have known about whom the text is speaking. He then reports that Andrew found his brother Simon—he had not yet been called Peter—and announced to him that he had seen the expected Messiah.

Therefore the phrase, [1:41] *We have found the Messiah,* indicates that he was expecting him. He took him, the Evangelist goes on, and brought him to Jesus. And when Jesus saw him, in order to show that he needed no time to know the mind of each, and wanting to confirm for Simon the testimony of Andrew about him, Jesus said to him, [1:42] *You are Simon son of John. You are to be called Cephas.* Notice he first identifies who Simon is and whose son he is; then he designates how he should be called. Therefore, by hearing what would only happen later, they were able to believe. It was from clear signs like these that they learned

---

[61]John the Evangelist. [62]John the Baptist. [63]See Jn 3:23. [64]That is, four o'clock in the afternoon.

that he had no trouble knowing who each one was and whose son he was.

From this it appears that, after spending with him the day in which they had followed him, they left the next day. Then Andrew found his brother whom he instructed about Jesus, and took him and brought him to Jesus.

[1:43] *The next day Jesus decided to go to Galilee and found Philip and said to him, "Follow me." [1:44] Now Philip was from Bethsaida, the city of Andrew and Simon.* The Evangelist said that Philip was called by the Lord, but does not add that he followed him. Such a detail would seem to be necessary. However, he showed that this did, in fact, occur because he related that the other disciples such as Nathanael were brought by Philip. But he did not say this specifically. So it appears that the Evangelists endeavored to relate facts concisely, and described them simply. It is clear that the Lord did not tell Philip to come with him without a reason, because he was fully aware that he was well known to him as the Messiah. It is probable that many others, thanks to John's sound testimony, had his same opinion. And Philip would not have been persuaded by that simple invitation if he had not heard something similar about him already. I believe that this happens among people, that some, even though they desire it so much, are nonetheless ashamed to come to the one they like, while others, led by the trust of their burning love, do not fear to show with actions their intentions. As happens with others, so it happened with the apostles.

Some followed him immediately, thanks to the testimony of John about his love, even though they were reticent. When the Lord turned to them and began to speak to them he gave them confidence, because they revered him since the testimony of John made known how great he was. Philip wanted to do the same, but was prevented by his reticence which the Lord caused him to overcome by saying, *Follow me.* He shows that he allows him, and even wants him to come. And since he wanted him to have faith in him after overcoming his reticence, he offered him a sufficient opportunity to fulfill the will of the one who had told him to come along.

[1:45] *Philip found Nathanael and said to him, "We have found him about whom Moses in the Law and in the Prophets[65] wrote, Jesus son of Joseph from Nazareth."* Here it is clear that Nathanael followed Jesus. He would have not instructed others if in the first place he had not believed. He connected the words, *We have found Jesus, son of Joseph from Nazareth*, with, *about whom Moses in the Law and also the prophets wrote.* He does not mean that [Moses and the prophets] wrote that "Jesus, son of Joseph, is from Nazareth," but that, "we have found that the son of Joseph who is from Nazareth is the one about whom Moses in the Law and the prophets wrote, that is, the Christ."

[1:46] *Nathanael said to him, "Can anything good come out of Nazareth?"* But it was not meant to be taken in quite this way, but must be understood in a different and more dubious sense. In other words, "How is it possible that anything good comes out of Nazareth?" In fact, among the Jews the name of that village was much despised because its inhabitants were truly pagans,[66] and it seemed impossible that anything good might come from there. That is also why the Pharisees said to Nicodemus, "Search and you will see that no prophet is to arise from Galilee."[67] Therefore it is only right that Philip says to Nathanael, *Come and see.* "Since that previous opinion is now contradicted, I promise to show you the real facts."

---

[65]This is the reading of the Peshitta (the standard Syriac Bible employed by the Syriac translator of Theodore). In the Greek original: "in the Law and also the Prophets." [66]Theodore is probably referring to Is 9:1-2; or Mt 4:15, where Galilee is described as "Galilee of the Gentiles." [67]Jn 7:52.

But this would have been superfluous to say for one who had come to believe the truth.

[1:47] *When Jesus saw Nathanael coming toward him, he said of him, "Here is truly an Israelite in whom there is no guile."* [1:48] *Nathanael asked him, "Where did you get to know me?" Jesus answered, "I saw you under the fig tree before Philip called you."* In order to reassure those who were coming to him, our Lord began to speak more clearly to them so that he might reveal his secret omniscience. Thus also when Simon came to him, he told him the name by which he was called and whose son he was. When Philip wanted to follow him, but was prevented by reticence, Jesus said, "Follow me," in order to reveal the desire of his heart. And finally, when Nathanael was in doubt, Jesus praised him by saying, *Here is truly an Israelite in whom there is no guile*, and what he said was true. He did not praise him for anything that he was not. With these words, *in whom there is no guile*, he means that Nathaniel did not engage in subtlety but rightly said what he thought. Therefore, Nathanael was in doubt about what Philip had said, and naively and frankly revealed his thoughts. But even though he was praised, he did not yield to that praise but immediately asked where Jesus had found out about him. The Lord, even though he was not present, clearly pointed out the place and the tree under which he was before he had been called by Philip, so that he might show the excellence of his power in this way.

Therefore Nathanael, convinced by those deeds, said to him, [1:49] *Rabbi, you are the Son of God. You are the king of Israel;* that is, "You are the Messiah who has already been announced." The Messiah was certainly expected by them as someone more intimate with God than anyone else—like a king of Israel—even though they conceived of him in a fairly obscure and carnal way. It was impossible then for the Jews to know how he was the Son of God, or the king of Israel. Evidently Nathanael himself did not say he was the *Son of God* because he knew about his divine birth, but because it was a familiar way of saying things, since those who by their own moral virtue drew near to God were called sons of God. It was impossible for Nathanael to know immediately what we see that the apostles themselves came to know later after a long time. Those things that were said to him by the Lord could not be sufficient to demonstrate his other nature.[68] Such things are related about the prophets. For instance, Elisha blamed his disciple because he had taken gold from Naaman.[69] Even though he was far away, he revealed how he had committed the act. This was how the prophets acted who knew these things through the revelation of the Spirit. And this will appear more clearly in the following passages.

What did the Lord answer him? [1:50] *Do you believe because I told you that I saw you under the fig tree? You will see greater things than these.* Therefore he shows that nothing he had said was great or sufficient to demonstrate fully who he was. And then he declares what the greater things are that he would have seen, [1:51] *Very truly, I tell you, you will see heaven opened and the angels of God ascending and descending upon the Son of Man.* Now, if Nathanael had called him "son" according to divine birth, what greater thing would he have seen? And how could seeing angels ascending and descending upon him be greater than that? Certainly that is the greatest and most wonderful thing!—not only because it is consistent with his confessed divine nature which is the beginning of everything, so that Nathanael would know that angels ascend and descend upon him (which always happens for the benefit of all humankind)—but also in order that Nathanael might understand that he is the creator of the angels. Now, after that confession,

---

[68]That is, his divinity. [69]2 Kings 5:26.

he says that something greater than what had appeared from the title "Son of God" (used in the sense of which we spoke) was expressed by Nathanael.

The Lord spoke of angels ascending and descending upon him because they assist him with his creation. The Evangelist Matthew, after the temptations, said, "Angels came and waited on him."[70] Clearly they were with him to serve him in all the things God was doing to him so that he might be the winner in the fight with the devil. But we learn from the Gospel that the angels assisted him also throughout his passion.[71] And after he rose again, angels were seen near the stone.[72] And similarly, when he ascended to heaven, they stayed close to the apostles.[73] Through all these things the dignity of Christ was revealed because the angels assisted him constantly by serving him in everything that happened around him. Therefore he says rightly that they would see greater things than these, namely, that the angels would always be with him, ascending and descending, or assisting him in all that happened around him in the most dedicated manner. This is certainly greater than what was said before, but as far as his divine nature was concerned, it was of little consequence. It was enough that he was known as the creator of the angels. On the other hand, those things that happened thanks to the divine nature inhabiting him were of no small importance for his human nature, especially since grace was given to all humanity through those things that happened in him.

[2:1] *On the third day there was a wedding in Cana of Galilee, and the mother of Jesus was there.* It is evident that this third day must be calculated as the third day after the baptism. The Evangelist relates that the first day was that in which Andrew and his companion followed him and then passed the night with him. The second is that in which the events related concerning Philip and Nathanael oc-

curred. The third day, finally, is that in which the events of this wedding party happened. Clearly all these events took place in Galilee. He had left immediately after his baptism and was living there. Those things which happened in the fight with the devil, and which Matthew reports,[74] evidently took place later. Matthew, in fact, did not care about the order of events, but only reported the events themselves.

[2:2] *Jesus and his disciples*, he continues, *had also been invited to the wedding.* He calls *disciples* those whom he had mentioned above and who were already with him. The Twelve did not yet believe nor had they yet been gathered. Therefore the Lord did not yet make them undergo difficult training. Instead he went to the celebration of a wedding.

[2:3] *When the wine gave out, the mother of Jesus said to him: "They have no wine."* His mother, according to the habit of mothers, incited him to perform a miracle, wanting the greatness of her son to be revealed and thinking that the lack of wine offered the perfect occasion for the miracle.

[2:4] *And the Lord said to her: "Woman, what concern is that to you and to me? My hour has not come yet."* This must be read in a different sense: *Has my hour not come yet?* That is, why do you press me and annoy me? Do not think that for me there are two distinct moments: one for knowing, the other for doing, like what happened with Moses, who at one time was able to give manna, at another to give meat and then caused the water to spring out from a stone—each action occurring according to the necessity of those receiving the benefit. It was obvious that Moses granted them these gifts thanks to the power he received [from God]. However, he says, it is not the same with me. I always possess the power to act at any time and in any way I want. And I am not incapable of revealing my power unless urged to do so by the necessity of the guests. Therefore

---

[70]Mt 4:11. [71]See Lk 22:43. [72]See Mt 28:2. [73]Acts 1:10-11. [74]See Mt 4:1-11.

the pretext of the lack of wine which you put forward is an offense to me—as if I only acquired my ability to act because of the need of others, and not, on the contrary, because I am powerful, so that this need occurred [according to my will].

Having understood what he said, therefore, [2:5] *his mother said to the servants: "Do whatever he tells you."* Understanding that he needed no predetermined hour or moment to show signs, nor was he motivated by the guests' needs to confer his gifts, which also might anticipate a predetermined time—he could, in fact, act whenever he wanted—she all the more confidently ordered the servants to obey him.

If, on the other hand, the words, *My hour has not come yet*, had been spoken in a definite or imperative sense, as some have thought, as if he refused to perform the deed, his mother would have given up and would not have ordered the servants to obey him.

[2:6] *Now standing there*, as the Evangelist says, *were six stone water jars for the Jewish rites of purification*. It is probable that everyone had such water jars in his house, because according to the law there often was need for purification.

[2:7] *He ordered to fill them with water; and they filled them up to the brim*. He did not add *up to the brim* without a reason, but in order to allay any suspicion that might arise that, if there had only been a little water, the wine could have been mixed [with it]. Then Jesus, by deceiving their taste, could have just simulated the change of the water into wine. Indeed, those who drew the wine [from the jars] also distributed it. The water, according to the will of the one who had ordered, was changed into wine. On top of this, the thirst of the drinkers was not only satisfied but he also provided the couple with wine more abundantly for the next day. The Lord intended with this action to demonstrate what he had said, that is, that

there was no predetermined time for him to perform miracles, nor was he motivated by the need of others in this activity. Rather, thanks to the abundant riches of his power, he was able to show his work whenever he wanted.

Then the Evangelist says that the chief steward tasted the water that had become wine. He calls "chief steward" the one who oversaw the service at the table and the preparation of the wedding. After he had tasted the wine (the text continues) and did not know where it came from—whereas the servants knew because they had filled the jars with water—he called the bridegroom and began to scold him because the usual human custom is to offer the good wine first, but he had kept it to the end when the guests had already drunk a lot.[75]

To this the Evangelist added nothing else. It is probable that [the chief steward], after hearing that the wine had given out, would have wondered because he knew that the bridegroom had no other wine. And, after inquiring where the wine had come from, he learned that a miracle had been performed. And yet, John did not add any of this, except that the chief steward called the bridegroom and scolded him because he had kept the *good wine* to the end. He preserved this detail in order to show that the water was not only changed into wine but also changed into an admirable quality of wine. He omitted all the other details as superfluous and extraneous to his narrative.

After narrating this, he concludes, [2:11] *Jesus did this, the first of his signs, in Cana of Galilee, and revealed his glory; and his disciples believed in him*. If the bridegroom had not answered the chief steward, and those words in which the performed miracle appeared had not been said, it would now be maintained that he revealed his glory superfluously. It is evident that these words refer to the moment in which the miracle and the performer of it appeared. And for this reason, as the Evangelist says, *his*

[75]See Jn 2:10.

disciples believed in him, even though they had already believed earlier. Obviously he is indicating that they were more confirmed in their faith since he often uses *faith* for "confirmation." On the other hand, he avoided relating those details which he considered to be useless to his purpose.

It is evident that this is the first sign. The Evangelist asserts this clearly, also indicating the place where the miracle happened. It is certainly foolish to believe that any of those events reported about our Lord during his childhood ever happened.[76] This is not only demonstrated by this text but also by the fact that John the Baptist indicated that he was unknown. If those things that are commonly said about him had really happened, he would have been well known because of them more than because of the simple word of John.[77]

But if he had previously performed no[78] miracle, and this was the first he accomplished, we must wonder how his mother—as if she was aware of his power—came to him when the wine gave out and said, "They have no wine!" How did she know he could do this? His mother certainly already held a great opinion about him when he was a child. In fact, when according to the rite of the law she brought him while still a child to the temple in order to offer a sacrifice for her firstborn, she came to know how great her son was from the words of Simeon prophesying about him, as well as from the words of Anna.[79] And she learned the same thing from the angel who announced his conception by saying, "Without a man, from the Spirit, you will conceive. He will be great and will be called the Son of the Most High."[80] Then, when he was born and placed in the manger, the shepherds were instructed by the

angels, and they came to see him and spread the news about him.[81] To this the Evangelist added, "But Mary treasured all these words and pondered them in her heart."[82] And the words of Elizabeth were not of small importance either. But the most wonderful thing of all was the visit of the wise men.[83] From all this evidence [his mother] could see his greatness. And if we also add the testimony of John, it was only right and with good reason that she held him in great admiration.

After this miracle [the Evangelist] says, [2:12] *After this he went down to Capernaum with his mother, his brothers, and his disciples; and they remained there a few days.* Then he passes to another episode and omits many events which occurred in the meantime since they had already been related by others. He did not twist the chronological order of the events but said that they occurred "later," that is, they happened after the events that he had related first.

Then he says, [2:13] *The Passover of the Jews was near, and Jesus went up to Jerusalem,* as everyone used to go up; [2:14] *and he found people selling cattle and dealing with money*—he called them *moneychangers*—[2:15] *and made a whip of cords*, not because he wanted to hurt anyone, but to provide an occasion for his entry when he drove all of them out by saying, "These things are not suitable to this place."

[2:17] *His disciples remembered that it was written, "Zeal for your house will consume me."*[84] This was not said about *him* in the prophecy,[85] but he took the opportunity to do what was appropriate for the temple. It is appropriate for the righteous to have zeal for the house of God and then to remove what is not suitable to it.

---

[76]Theodore alludes to the apocryphal Infancy Gospels, which must be rejected as pure fables. [77]John the Baptist. [78]The negative adjective is missing from the manuscript of Theodore's commentary (see CSCO 4 3:59), and is added on the basis of the quotation in Isho'dad (see *The Commentaries of Isho'dad in Syriac: Luke and John*, Syriac text edited by M. Dunlop Gibson, HSem 7 [Cambridge: Cambridge University Press, 1911], p. 220). [79]See Lk 2:22-38. [80]Lk 1:31-32 (the quotation is not literal, but slightly adapted). [81]See Lk 2:7-18. [82]Lk 2:19. [83]See Mt 2:1-12; Lk 1:42-45. [84]The disciples quote Ps 69:9. [85]An example of Theodore's limited view of Old Testament prophecy referring to Christ.

The Jews, however, asked for a sign that would reveal why he did this, even though a sign for this was not necessary. The very thing he did was itself serious enough, and if a sign was required, it had already been given.

As I said above, the Evangelist seems to relate these events not according to an order, but by omitting many facts that happened in the meantime. The Lord, in fact, would not have taken on such an extreme measure if he had not already revealed himself through his miracles; nor would the merchants there have allowed themselves to be expelled if someone who was unknown had forced them to do so.

However, he says to them, [2:19] *Destroy this temple, and in three days I will raise it up.* In fact, since he seems to have stopped not only the commerce, but also the custom of the sacrifices—the people selling cattle and doves had their market there in order that the pilgrims coming from faraway places might be able to buy victims for the sacrifice—he logically moved on to talking about the resurrection as if he were saying, "If you want to know why I do these things, just wait a little bit. When you have killed me, after my resurrection, I will show everyone who I am. And those ancient and obsolete rites will be replaced with a new rite, a new order, and a new age that will be proclaimed after my resurrection."

But our Lord said these things in an obscure and mysterious way. He had a symbolic purpose in mind that only foreshadowed his intention with allusions. He did not do anything openly. He believed that his hearers could not yet understand what he was saying. The disciples themselves did not understand either, as the Evangelist observes. They believed that by driving away the sellers of cattle and sheep, he abolished the market, but in truth it meant that the sacrifices of brute animals were to be abolished.

Because the Jews did not understand the power of those things that he said and did, they believed that he spoke about the material temple. And so they said, [2:20] *This temple has been under construction for forty-six years, and you will raise it up in three days?* They say that the construction of the temple lasted for forty-six years. Obviously they meant since the return from Babylon. In fact, it was built throughout that stretch of time. This is not because such a long time was necessary for the construction but because there were different reasons to hinder it so that its construction was protracted for a long time, as can be seen in the historical books.[86]

Truly, the Evangelist says, [2:21] *But he was speaking of the temple of his body*, because he believed it was appropriate to explain the meaning of these more obscure words of Christ.

But how is it possible that the heretics do not consider that he, after the words, "destroy this temple, added, "I will raise it up in three days?" In this way he clearly shows that he did not refer the destruction to himself, but to the temple [of his body] that was going to be destroyed. He did not need anything else to restore the temple. He could do it himself.[87]

"In three days," he says, "I will raise it up," that is, I will resurrect it. Therefore, even though it is said that the Father raises Christ, there is no doubt what this expression means. The agreement that is between them both in all operations causes them to be attributed with equal right to both the Father and the Son.

Then, explaining the word of our Lord, the Evangelist says, [2:22] *After he was raised from the dead, his disciples remembered that he had said this; and they believed the Scripture and the word that Jesus had spoken.* The Evangelist says this in order to show that the disciples had not

---

[86]Theodore is referring not to the temple constructed by Herod but to the temple reconstructed by Zerubbabel and Jeshua after their return from the Babylonian exile. See Ezek 3:1–6:14; Hag 1:1–2:9. [87]Again Theodore clearly shows his concept of the two sharply separated natures of Christ: the temple, that is, the body, only belongs to Christ the man. See also see translator's introduction, esp. quotation from Norris, p. xxvi.

understood the Lord either when he said those things. But the fulfillment of the events will make them understand what was said and will render them more certain about the full sense of his words and works.

The other Evangelists also relate that he drove the sellers of cattle and sheep away from the temple.[88] [John] actually recorded this event—even though he only speaks of those things they had omitted to write—as if Christ had done the same thing twice. And this does not happen without a reason, as we can see in many cases. He did not repeat what had been said by the others, except because of the power of the doctrine that was connected with the miraculous event. The others only said that Jesus had expelled them from the temple. He actually added the words with which the Pharisees opposed him and the reply given to them by Jesus. And he not only alluded to the event of the resurrection but also to the time when it would happen, hinting that there was thought to be a great difference between the one who suffered the passion and the one through whom he was raised.[89] In addition we hear that the disciples themselves did not understand many words that were said at that time. Because of all those things that he desired to say, he recorded the event that appears to have been already related by the other [Evangelists].

End of the First Book.

Book Two (John 2:23–5:47)

[2:23] *When he was in Jerusalem during the Passover festival, many believed in him*[1] *because they saw the signs that he was doing.* With these words the Evangelist shows that Jesus did many signs through which many came to faith. However, John omitted them because he did not intend to describe all of his works but only those which included an exhortation or a doctrine of faith, or those which needed to be related since they had not been mentioned by the others.

[2:24] *But Jesus did not entrust himself to them, because he knew all people and needed no one to testify about anyone; for he himself knew what was in everyone.* If they believed, why did he not entrust himself to them on his part? Clearly the words, *many believed in him*, are not said about a firm and true faith, such as the faith of those who, after believing once that his words were true, considered him as a teacher of truth without doubting what he said. This is what is typical of true believers. John refers here, however, to people who were astonished when confronted by the events that occurred and praised him as a great and admirable man. However, not all of them approved his words by showing their respect for him to others—which is what true believers do. And so, John added, *But Jesus did not entrust himself to them.*

In these words, however, there is also a forceful exposition of true faith. Indeed, they reveal the power of Christ's knowledge that enabled him to avoid being deceived by the outward appearance of those who came to him. Instead, he recognized precisely who each of them was, already knowing who his true disciples were and who were in doubt and coming to him under false pretenses.

And in order to confirm these words the Evangelist relates the story of Nicodemus. After the miracles were done, he too admired our Lord but still did not firmly cling to what our Lord said without any doubt so that he might believe by considering him as a master of truth. Through the words of Nicodemus to our Lord and his reply, John clearly shows what he had said above, that is, *Jesus did not entrust himself*

---

[88]See Mt 21:12-13; Mk 11:15-19; Lk 19:45-48. [89]Theodore's dualistic Christology is furthered even more as he speaks of the difference between the assumed man, who would suffer, and God the Word, who raised the assumed man from the dead. **Book Two** [1]The Syriac text of the Gospel of John (Peshitta) reads "him" instead of "his name."

to them, because he knew all people.

[3:1] *There was a Pharisee named Nicodemus.* The Pharisees were those who gloried in the doctrine of the law. Many Jews respected them, and their sect was renowned among the people. He came to him *by night* because nighttime best reflected his own state of mind. Since he was distrustful of the Jews, he chose that time so that he might cautiously hide from them.

As soon as he came, he said, [3:2] *Rabbi, we know that you are a teacher who was sent[2] from God; for no one can do these signs that you do apart from the presence of God.* His speech begins with praise. People usually begin with these kinds of words especially when they address an illustrious person. Therefore Nicodemus says, "We know that you are a true teacher, and that you were sent by God because the miracles which you have accomplished demonstrate this to us." But our Lord did not pay attention to his flattery. Since Jesus knew, according to the testimony of the Evangelist, that his own deepest thoughts did not correspond with his own words, he began to speak to Nicodemus words prepared for a person who desired to teach, and all the more directed to one like Nicodemus, who had at one time confessed he was sure the Lord had been sent as a teacher from God. But the situation only served to further accuse the already doubtful mind of the one who approached Jesus, so that Nicodemus[3] did not accept any of his words.

Therefore Jesus said, [3:3] *Very truly, I tell you, no one can see the kingdom of God without being born again:*[4] "If you believe that I was sent as a teacher from God, and the miracles I did convince you of this, as you say, then our teaching requires another way of life and expects the beginning of a new birth." In this way, we hope indeed to see the kingdom of God because, while we are mortal, we cannot go there unless we are resurrected to an incorruptible state after our death. We believe that this happens through the type of baptism. We are born again in a type of the resurrection since we enter into a new state of being.

[3:4] *Nicodemus said to him, "How can anyone be born after having grown old? Can one enter a second time into the mother's womb and be born?"* This was the question of an unbeliever. He inquired about the nature and manner of birth as if he did not believe that it could really happen. This clearly appears from the fact that he did not accept the truth of these words without doubting, even after he had learned that a spiritual birth was under discussion. In order that he might not take his words in a material sense and thus be prevented from reaching their true meaning, our Lord clearly replied to his question by explaining how this birth happened: [3:5] *Very truly I tell you, no one can enter the kingdom of God without being born of water and spirit.* Since Nicodemus had asked, "Can one enter again into the mother's womb and be born?" our Lord explained how this could happen through water and Spirit. He mentioned water because it is in water that the work is accomplished. He mentioned Spirit because the Spirit exercises its power through the water. This is why the Spirit is mentioned, and not the water, in the phrase "Spirit of adoption,"[5] because we are regenerated through the Spirit's power. For this reason in baptism we name the Spirit together with the Father and the Son, but we do not mention the water, so that it may be clear that water is employed as a symbol and for a [visible] use. But we invoke the Spirit as the agent together with the Father and the Son, because when Nicodemus asked, "Can one enter again into the mother's womb and be born?" our Lord answered his question saying, through both *water and Spirit.*

[2]The Syriac text of the Gospel of John (Peshitta) reads "who was sent" instead of "who has come." [3]Nicodemus. [4]Other testimonies of the Greek manuscript tradition read "from above" instead of "again." [5]Rom 8:15; Gal 4:5-6; Eph 1:5.

Just as in the case of natural birth the womb is the place in which the child is formed, and then it is perfected by the divine power that forms it from the beginning, so also in this place the water represents the womb, while the Spirit of the Lord is the real agent. Baptism is said to be a symbol of death and resurrection, and so it is called regeneration. Just as the one who is resurrected after his death is considered to be created again, so also one who is begotten in baptism is said to be born again, because first he dies in water, then in a similar way, he is resurrected from it through divine power. The immersion represents the burial, and the lifting of the head at each invocation and the ascent from the water symbolize the resurrection that takes place through the power of the Spirit.

Then, in order to lead him further away from comprehending [these words] as referring to corporeal birth, the Lord says, [3:6] *What is born of the flesh is flesh, and what is born of the Spirit is spirit.* He means that what results from the birthing process is necessarily similar to the nature of the one giving birth. When flesh gives birth to flesh, the birth is necessarily a bodily one; when the spirit is the one giving birth, it is necessary that we understand the birth as incorporeal and spiritual. Through this he also demonstrates that the water which he united to the Spirit does not operate with him, but is mentioned as a symbol and for a [visible] use. Therefore he did not add, "what is born of water," but only says, *what is born of the Spirit*, thus clearly attributing the birth to the Spirit.

And since Nicodemus was still in doubt about those words, he added again, [3:7] *Do not be astonished that I said to you, "You must be born again,"* that is, "Do not have doubts about what has been said." "And how should I have no doubts," [Nicodemus asks], "when these words surpass my nature?" [3:8] *The Spirit,*[6]

the Lord says, *blows where it chooses, and you hear the sound of it, but you do not know where it comes from, or where it goes.* "Do not consider your nature, but understand the power of the one giving birth. The Holy Spirit, because it is omnipotent, performs everything as it wants, and nothing can resist its operations. You hear its voice, that is, you perceive the sound of its coming. You cannot ascertain in which place its person is contained so that you may understand its way of operating. As its nature is immense and therefore it is everywhere it chooses to be, so also its action is ineffable because it does everything according to its will." He said rightly: *you hear the sound of it*, because by descending first on the apostles it came with a noise. They heard the sound of a strong wind, and spoke different languages through the power of the Spirit that was over them.[7]

So after he had elevated everything to the higher level of the one giving birth, he concluded perfectly, *So it is with everyone who is born of the Spirit*; that is, such is the birth from the Spirit. It cannot be comprehended by human thought. And since it is beyond their grasp, it can only be perceived through a noise for the benefit of those who receive it.

It is amazing that some think this is said about the spirit of the air.[8] How could the words, *it blows where it chooses*, be rightfully applied to this spirit, or wind, that has no will since it is moved by inanimate puffs of air? And how can it be said, *but you do not know where it comes from, or where it goes*? On the contrary, everyone knows where the wind comes from, and those who want can protect themselves from its billowing. Many immediately give a name to the wind when it blows, and so indicate the places through which it rages. The expression, *so it is*, is not said in a comparative but in a demonstrative sense, and means, "in this way, as has been said." And in the same manner, in the sentence, "God so

---

[6]The Greek word *pneuma* means both "wind" and "spirit."   [7]See Acts 2:1-4.   [8]That is, the wind.

loved the world that he gave his only Son,"[9] the particle *so* is said in a demonstrative sense,[10] and not at all in a comparative sense.

[3:9] *Nicodemus said to him, "How can these things be?"* He clearly reveals that he has doubts about what was said to him. And for this reason the Lord ironically said to him by way of accusation, [3:10] *Are you a teacher of Israel, and yet you do not understand these things?* Since [the Pharisees] always professed to teach by narrating the exploits of Moses, Elijah, and any of the prophets, and since they expected their audience to have faith in their words, even though the exploits [of the prophets] were wonderful and went beyond the grasp of human minds, [Christ] rightly blamed Nicodemus's disbelief by considering his duty as a teacher.

And he, explaining this even more clearly, added, [3:11] *Very truly, I tell you, we speak of what we know and testify to what we have seen; and yet you do not receive our testimony.* Now, he says, "I teach things I certainly know and have witnessed and authored, because I perform them by the Spirit. And you, even though you teach things that you ignore, expect that your audience believes you." To be sure, the words, *we speak of what we know, and testify to what we have seen*, indicate the divine nature. But he indicated this in a subtly obscure way, because the one who heard this was not capable yet of understanding. On the other hand, anyone who considers this attentively will find the same in any of his words.

Then he added, [3:12] *If I have told you about earthly things and you do not believe, how can you believe if I tell you about heavenly things?* He calls baptism earthly because it is performed on earth. He calls his divine birth heavenly because it is quite superior to the spiritual birth that happens among human beings. "If you do not accept these words, how will you be able to believe me when I touch on sublime topics and discuss my own nature?" These things, however, are not said openly but are insinuated circumspectly.

And he explains more clearly his insinuation by saying, [3:13] *No one has ascended into heaven except the one who descended from heaven, the Son of Man who is in heaven.* This appears to be said more clearly than what he had said previously. But up to this point, even this can only be considered an allusion. If one asserted that *ascended* and *descended* are referred to the Godhead, that would be a sign of great foolishness. What ascent and descent can there ever be for the one who is always in heaven and on earth? He certainly refers to himself when he said, *[he] who is in heaven*, in order to prevent us from understanding his descent as a movement from a certain place. In fact, if he is in heaven, he does not descend by moving from heaven. If he descended by moving from heaven, he would not be in heaven anymore. But the Evangelist also demonstrated this clearly at the beginning of his book by saying, "He was in the world."[11] He who once was already on earth and at the same time in heaven clearly is always in heaven and on earth. Therefore *ascended* and *descended* are used in a physical sense. But there is another meaning according to a true interpretation.

If this was said about his human nature which did indeed "ascend from earth into heaven,"[12] the term *descended* does not appear to be consistent because [his human nature] was born of the seed of David and did not in fact descend from heaven. Rather, he joined these two things together when speaking about what concerned his human nature. And since the meaning of his words overwhelmed the mind of Nicodemus, by linking them with divinity he established what he intended to say. In the same way, if one calls a human being rational, he calls him so for his wisdom and therefore establishes what he meant. Never-

---

[9]Jn 3:16. [10]That is, "in this way," God loved the world. [11]Jn 1:10. [12]Acts 1:9.

theless, since heavenly things should not have been given to [Nicodemus] because he did not believe in his words, he added, *No one has ascended into heaven*, and so forth. And by this, he meant, "Even though you do not believe his words, there will be very clear events that will overcome your disbelief. The Son of Man will ascend into heaven, and this is something that has never happened to anyone until now. Therefore, when he ascends, he will clearly demonstrate the nature dwelling in him that naturally descended without moving from any place. He is also now in heaven, without being far away. Since [God] lived in him both here and there, and united him to himself, and wanted him to become the participant with him in his honor, he therefore assumed him into heaven as the one who must be exalted over everything.

After talking about his ascension, since this would have appeared incredible because he [still] had to be given over to suffering, he added, [3:14] *And just as Moses lifted up the serpent in the wilderness, so must the Son of Man be lifted up,* [3:15] *that whoever believes in him may not perish, but have eternal life.* It is as if he said, "Let no cross frighten you in any way or make you doubt my words." For, just as Moses in the wilderness lifted up the serpent[13] which is bronze in its nature, and the power of him who ordered it to be lifted up saved those who looked at it, so now Christ bears his human destiny and suffers the pain of the cross. But thanks to the power dwelling in him, he has made those who believe worthy of eternal life. And as at that time [the bronze serpent] which did not possess life, through the power of another, delivered from death those who perished because of the bites of the serpents—as long as they turned to look at it—in a similar way, even though he appears to be mortal and suffers, [Christ] through the power dwelling in him gives life to those who believe in him.

[3:16] *For God,* he continues, *so loved the world that he gave his Only Begotten Son, so that everyone who believes in him may not perish but have eternal life.* "This is," he says, "a sign of the love of God who gave his Only Begotten Son for the salvation of the world." And notice how he took up, just a few lines above, the example of the serpent, which indicates the human who was taken up, in order to demonstrate, as in the case of the serpent, that he gave believers something that he does not possess through his own power but through the power that lives in him. How then did he say, *he gave his Only Begotten Son?* For it is obvious that the Godhead cannot suffer; nevertheless, they[14] are one through their conjunction. Therefore even though the other suffers,[15] the whole is attributed to the divinity.

Usually whenever the Holy Scripture describes the greatness of the passion, it mentions the divinity in order to confirm what is being said. The blessed Paul does something similar when he, intending to signify the greatness of the passion, says, "If they had understood this, they would not have crucified the Lord of glory."[16] Just as the greatness of the passion is indicated here in this very title,[17] so also our Lord, in an effort to demonstrate the abundance of his love that caused him to undergo suffering, says appropriately, *[he] gave his only Son.*

And since he said that the Son of Man would be raised up and that God gave his only Son [for the redemption of humankind], and since there would be those who would not believe who thus would be condemned, he therefore added, [3:17] *Indeed, God did not send his Son into the world to condemn the world, but in order that the world might be saved through him.* And so he comes back to the purpose of what happened to him. "The purpose established by God is not that someone may by damned, but that all may be saved." And then what? [3:18]

---

[13]See Num 21:8-9. [14]That is, divinity and humanity. [15]That is, the humanity. [16]1 Cor 2:8. [17]That is, "Lord of glory."

Those who believe in me are not condemned; but those who do not believe are condemned already, because they have not believed in the name of the only Son of God. "The intention of God is this," he says, "that all may believe and be saved, and this is why I came to be among humanity. Those who do not believe are the cause of their own damnation. But believers have the right to salvation. If some do not believe, they are the authors of their own condemnation: indeed, his grace is offered to all who want it."

[3:19] *And this is the judgment, that the light has come into the world, and people loved darkness rather than light because their deeds were evil.* "This is why," he says, "they deserve to be accused even more, because the light did come to them. If they had wanted to, they could have enjoyed happiness. But they closed the eyes of their soul and turned to evil." He declares why this is so: *Because their deeds were evil*; that is, they did not devote themselves to virtue. He makes it clear that a sick mind has no regard for the doctrine of truth. And in order to confirm this he says, [3:20] *All who do evil hate the light and do not come to the light, so that their deeds may not be exposed.* [3:21] *But those who do what is true come to the light, so that it might be clearly seen that their deeds have been done in God.* Those who enjoy evil do not turn their attention to the good. In fact, they hate it because they know that it condemns their evil. Those who do what is true pursue virtue.[18] They know virtue is praiseworthy and a good testimony of their conscience.

Notice then that he said, *all who do evil* and *those who do what is true*, and not "whoever did" or "committed." Certainly it happens that those who have done evil sometimes abandon their inclination to evil and tend toward goodness, while those who appear to do what is true sometimes fall into evil. Therefore he said, *All who do* and *those who do*, because one who is devoted to wickedness is never brought to virtue, and anyone who is a lover of truth is always a follower of virtue as well.

After reporting these words the Evangelist added, [3:22] *After this Jesus and his disciples went into the Judean countryside, and he spent some time there with them and baptized.* He described the events he related above as happening in Jerusalem.[19] Then he added those things that Jesus did after he had left the city when he was traveling through the places and the region of Judea, teaching and baptizing.

He then said, [3:23] *John also was baptizing at Aenon near Salim because water was abundant there; and people kept coming and were being baptized.* And he added, [3:24] *John, of course, had not yet been thrown into prison*, in order that it might be known that all these events happened before the imprisonment of the Baptist, although all the other Evangelists [record his imprisonment] immediately after the baptism of the Lord and the temptations of the devil.[20] Matthew said, "Now when Jesus saw that John had been arrested, he withdrew [from Judea][21] to Galilee;"[22] Mark: "Now after John was arrested, Jesus came to Galilee";[23] and it is well known that Luke followed the same order.[24] If by relating these events he also reconnects his narrative to those events that happened in the temple, when our Lord drove away the cattle and sheep—while, on the contrary, all the other Evangelists report this fact at the end, especially Matthew, who joined this event to the entry of the Lord riding a donkey[25]—we conclude that this event either happened twice, or, if it happened only once, John endeavored to relate it according to proper order. All the others only reported the bare fact, and we have seen that they do this often, since they had no care for the order of the events but were only interested in narrating the facts.

---

[18]Or, beauty. [19]See Jn 2:23. [20]See Mt 4:12; Mk 1:14; Lk 3:20. [21]"From Judea" is added by Theodore. [22]Mt 4:12. [23]Mk 1:14. [24]See Lk 3:19-20. [25]See Mt 21:12-13.

[3:25] *Now a discussion about purification arose between John's disciples and a Jew.* [3:26] *They came to John and said to him, "Rabbi, the one who was with you across the Jordan, to whom you testified, here he is, baptizing, and all are going to him."* He mentions *a discussion*, not "an argument"; in other words, an inquiry had been made about purification, namely, about baptism. If there had been a difference of opinion among themselves, they would not have come to John with a unanimous agreement. It is evident that they discussed and examined among themselves the difference of the baptisms: the Jews naturally praised the purifications of the law; John's disciples exalted the baptism of their master. This discussion led them to bring up the baptism by which the Lord baptized.

Since this baptism seemed useless to both parties, they came to John to provoke his jealousy. Indeed, the one who had needed *his* baptism and had been revealed publicly by *him* was now gathering a great number of disciples. Therefore in order to correct their misguided opinion and to show them that not only did he not envy the good fortune of the Lord but that he also enjoyed the splendor of his glory and the fact that a wonderful event was connected with it—because the Lord, in fact, was great and, as such, it was only fitting that he should be known by everyone—the blessed John said to them, [3:27] *No one can receive anything except what has been given from heaven.* "No one can possess a spiritual gift unless God has given it to him." And so the words, "no one can receive anything without the permission of God," must have been intended to refer to spiritual gifts. On the other hand, many take any number of earthly things outside the will of God.

Why did I say this [the Baptist asks]? [3:28] *You yourselves are my witnesses that I said, "I am not the Messiah, but I have been sent ahead*

of him.'" "Remember my words," the Baptist says, "and remember that when I was questioned, as you know, I answered that I was not the Christ, but a messenger sent before him. Therefore I came to reveal the Messiah. The one whom I indicated is the Messiah. Everything belongs to him and is due him. He needs no one to teach him; he is entirely sufficient unto himself because the greatness of the nature dwelling in him causes him to need nothing else. I, because I am a man, cannot receive anything spiritual on my own, nor would I be able to testify or to impart baptism if this right was not given to me by God. I am not the Christ, but he is, and every good thing resides in him."

And, insisting and explaining the same concept more clearly, he says, [3:29] *He who has the bride is the bridegroom. The friend of the bridegroom who stands and hears him rejoices greatly at the bridegroom's voice.* Even though human beings seem to be different in this life because each person is distinct, we are nonetheless all a single human being[26] because of the affinity of [our] nature. This is apparent from the fact that all of us are of one and the same body: each of us is a member of a whole. We are all this mortal and corruptible man,[27] and all of us are included in the decree of death. But our Lord in his generous grace wanted to recreate and bring this man to a naturally better state in the future life after death in which we will all be resurrected. And we will not only receive being again and life, but we will remain always incorruptible. Therefore, after this change has been accomplished, our body will remain in an incorruptible state.

Adam was, for us, the beginning of the condition of our present life; Christ our Lord will be the condition of the real life yet to come. As Adam was the first mortal man, and because of him all other human beings came into exis-

---

[26] Latin *homo.* [27] The man referred to here is Adam, who stands for universal humanity. See Rom 5:12.

tence, so Christ was the first after death [to be raised], and gave the beginning of resurrection to those coming after him. We came to this visible life through corporeal birth, and therefore we are all corruptible. But we will be transformed toward the life to come through the power of the Spirit and so will be resurrected incorruptible. This is what is going to happen then, but our Lord Christ desired that we would already be transferred to that [new life] symbolically by granting us baptism and the regeneration that comes with it. And since the present [spiritual] birth is a figure of the resurrection and the regeneration that will be fulfilled in us when we migrate to that life, he also called baptism *regeneration.*

Most appropriately, the apostle said, "Do you not know that all of us who have been baptized into Christ Jesus were baptized into his death? Therefore we have been buried with him by baptism into death, so that, just as Christ was raised from the dead by the glory of the Father, so we too might walk in newness of life. For if we have been united with him in a death like his, we will certainly be united with him in a resurrection like his."[28] With these words he clearly shows that the birth through baptism is a figure of the resurrection after death. Indeed we will also receive this resurrection through the power of the Spirit, as was written, "What is sown is perishable, what is raised is imperishable. It is sown in weakness, it is raised in power. It is sown in dishonor, it is raised in glory; and then: It is sown a physical body, it is raised a spiritual body."[29] This means, "As this body of ours enjoys visible life here when the soul is present, even so there [in heaven] it will receive eternal life through the incorruptible power of the Spirit."

Also, in a similar way, we receive grace through the same Spirit in the birth that is conferred to us here through baptism, namely, through a figure of the resurrection. But we only receive a small amount as a pledge.[30] We will receive all of it when we are truly resurrected, and incorruptibility is actually conferred upon us. Therefore also the apostle, discussing the nature of our future life and desiring to strengthen his audience with his words, said, "And not only the [creation], but we ourselves who have the first fruits of the Spirit, groan inwardly while we wait for adoption, the redemption of our bodies."[31] Because we receive the present grace as first fruits, we also expect to attain perfection when the delights of the resurrection[32] will be given to us as a gift.

In the same way also Christ-in-the-flesh, who is our beginning in everything, received the resurrection. For the descent of the Spirit was not useless even for him with regard to the conferring of grace. Therefore, since we as creatures hope to take part in the same things as he did, the apostle said, "If the Spirit of him who raised Jesus from the dead dwells in you, he who raised Christ from the dead will give life to your mortal bodies also through his Spirit that dwells in you."[33] He clearly demonstrated here, since the power of the Spirit in the resurrection [of Christ] had not been revealed completely yet, that we who have received the same Spirit expect to receive the same resurrection. In a similar way, since it had to fulfill perfectly in himself the figure of resurrection, the Spirit descended upon him. "And John testified, 'I saw the Spirit descending, and it remained on him.'"[34]

Adam was created the first of all human beings. Then God took a part from him and formed the woman,[35] whom he also united to Adam through marriage, as was said, "and they both shall be in one flesh."[36] The constitution of the entire human race had its beginning from there. In a similar way Christ-in-the-flesh was the first to be born by spiritual birth—both in reality, because he was the first

---

[28]Rom 6:3-5. [29]1 Cor 15:42-44. [30]See Eph 1:14. [31]Rom 8:23. [32]See 1 Jn 3:2. [33]Rom 8:11. [34]Jn 1:32. [35]See Gen 2:21-22. [36]Gen 2:24.

of all to be resurrected, and in a type, because he was the first to receive birth in baptism through the grace of the Spirit which fulfilled both the fact and the type. God took a portion of this grace and gave it to all so that they might participate in that same [grace]. He made everyone participants in the Spirit in order that they might be born again in a spiritual way. And since, through similarity of birth, we possess a natural affinity with him, so through him we receive a familiarity with God the Word. Therefore, it is not the union of marriage but faith and perfect charity that unite all the faithful with our Lord Christ. For this reason, the church has also been taken by our Lord as a bride, either because it has retained, to a small extent, the similarity of affinity with him or because it is connected to him by the love that it spreads in its faith around him. And so the apostle, inviting the husbands to love their wives, used the example of Christ in his admonition to them. And after he had said that the two were one flesh, he added, "This is a great mystery, and I am applying it to Christ and the church,"[37] in order to note that previously it had happened in a corporeal manner.

Since the church of the faithful has through regeneration been made the bride of Christ-in-the-flesh, and through him it has received a relationship with God the Word, [the Baptist] says in our present passage, [3:29] *He who has the bride is the bridegroom*, that is, "This role [of bridegroom] is not mine but his." For there is a divine nature in him in whom we first believed, and then, through regeneration, it is as if a natural relationship has now been established toward the man who was assumed. And thus we too receive an ineffable union with God the Word.

"I," the Baptist says, "as the friend of the bridegroom, do not rashly desire to gain the love of the bride for myself. Rather, because of my friendship with the bridegroom, I enjoy the love the bride has for him. *For this reason my joy has been fulfilled.* My joy is that I see his incorruptible bride keeping her love for him. That all would love him and believe in him— this is the kind of love that is fitting and due him—and most certainly due to him as Lord! If I, instead, wanted to attract the bride to myself, I would be committing an act of spiritual corruption because I would deceitfully pursue a union for which I have no right, and would be committing adultery." It was very appropriate that he called the church *the bride* and Christ *the bridegroom* to show that love and the faithfulness of the church are due to Christ and that it is evil for the church to turn aside from him to anyone else.

[3:30] *He must increase, but I must decrease.* "This certainly will not happen in a short time," he says, "but it is necessary that the things that are his increase while those that are mine decrease." Why? [3:31] *The one who comes from above is above all; the one who is of the earth belongs to the earth and speaks about earthly things.* "Since he came from above," he says, "he is consequently above everything. I, because I am of the earth, am necessarily like one who is of the earth."

Again, he repeats the same thing: *The one who comes from heaven is above all;* [3:32] *and he testifies to what he has seen and heard, yet no one accepts his testimony.* The words *from above* and *from heaven* are not referred to places but to the eminence of his nature. "He is superior to all," he says, "and does not speak according to tradition but rather teaches those things about which he himself has gained an accurate knowledge. But still you refuse to believe." Our Lord spoke in the same way to Nicodemus, "We speak of what we know and testify to what we have seen,"[38] that is, "I teach those things I know for certain."

[3:33] *Whoever has accepted his testimony has set his seal to this, that God is true.* [3:34]

---

[37]Eph 5:32. [38]Jn 3:11.

He whom God has sent speaks the words of God.
"Whoever believes in his words," he says, "confesses openly and embraces the truth of God.
He who was sent by God speaks his words.
Therefore whoever believes his words as true
openly confesses him and testifies to God that
the words said by him are true. But whoever
does not believe appears to despise those words
as false since such a person would not have
refused to believe in him if he had considered
them to be true."

And after he had talked about the divine
nature, [the Baptist] turned his attention to
the human nature, saying, *He whom God has
sent speaks the words of God.* This one does
not possess such dignity by nature, however,
which is why [the Baptist] added, *God gives the
spirit without measure.* [3:35] *The Father loves
the Son and has placed all things in his hands.*
"God did not only give him," he says, "a small
part of the grace of the Spirit, as all human
beings have received. Instead, he gave him
its entire fullness because he loved him and
entrusted him with dominion over everything."
And this is logically consistent with his human
nature which, in its union with God the Word,
received dominion over everything. Therefore
he rightly mentioned the Spirit first, through
which he received the union, regeneration and
dominion over everything. Then, he rightfully
said, *[God] has placed all things in his hands,*
because he thought nothing other than that
he had perceived the truth about the human
nature of our Lord, in other words, that it had
received universal dominion only through the
power of the Spirit. And he would, without
any doubt, establish the faithfulness of this
word.

After he had said all this in order to prove
the power of Christ our Lord, he rightly concluded by adding, [3:36] *Whoever believes in
the Son has eternal life; whoever disobeys the Son
will not see life, but must endure God's wrath.*

"Since these things are so ," [the Baptist] says,
"whoever believes in him will participate in
eternal life; whoever does not believe will
face eternal damnation. Therefore, because
of this, it is all the more fitting that everyone
should become diligent so that through faith
in him they might be worthy of the promise
of future blessedness and escape the threats of
judgment." These are the words of John [the
Baptist].

After the Evangelist inserted this story and
related the words that the disciples of John
said to the Jew when they came to John, and
related John's words in reply where he clearly
taught the greatness of Christ, he returned to
the order of his narration by saying:

[4:1] *Now when Jesus learned that the Pharisees had heard, "Jesus is making and baptizing more disciples than John"—*[4:2] *although
it was not Jesus himself but his disciples who
baptized—*[4:3] *he left Judea and started back to
Galilee.* Actually, this should have been noted
when he had reported [earlier], "After this
Jesus and his disciples went into the Judean
countryside, and he spent some time there
with them and baptized,"[39] which can be read
above. According to the sequence of the events,
what is said now followed later, that is, as soon
as Jesus learned that the Pharisees had heard
about this and were angry with him, he left
Judea and returned to Galilee. But the Evangelist related first that John was baptizing at that
time and reported his answer to those who
questioned him about the Messiah. These facts
then were related and occurred while our Lord
walked in Judea and baptized. And finally
[the Evangelist] added the reason why [Christ]
left Judea and stopped baptizing. After first
reporting this account and then returning now
to the sequence of the story, he corrected what
he had omitted by saying, *It was not Jesus himself but his disciples who baptized.* He thought
that what he had omitted before should be

[39]Jn 3:22.

said now in order to show that it was not Jesus himself who imparted baptism but his disciples. It is evident nevertheless that also those who were baptized were brought to faith. Then, after saying that he had left Judea to go to Galilee—since in the course of the journey the incident of the Samaritan woman occurred which the other Evangelists omit—he took the opportunity to report this occurrence as well, in order to relate what the others omitted and to keep the historical order of his different speeches.

Therefore he says, [4:4] *But he had to go through Samaria.* This necessity to go [through Samaria] gave [the Evangelist] the opportunity and the starting point for his narrative. He did not report this fact in vain. He does not say "on the way to Judea" or "on his return to Galilee from Judea he also came to the Samaritans." Because of the Samaritans' separation from the Jews Jesus certainly avoided, giving an occasion for their[40] just complaint. And so he did all this as though he were passing through so that those who were worthy among the Jews might not be deprived of his benefit. He acted for their benefit so that it might be thought that he did what he did there by happenstance. In this way also he appeared to extend goodwill to the Samaritans for whom a mere passing through [of the Lord] was sufficient to recognize the truth, while for the Jews not even his long stay among them brought about any result.

After beginning his narration of the encounter with the Samaritan woman and the Samaritans, he continues, [4:5] *So he came to a Samaritan city called Sychar, near the plot of ground called Shechem.*[41] This is the name of the plot of ground *that Jacob had given to his son Joseph.*[42] [4:6] *There was a spring there that was called Jacob's*, because he himself had dug that well. With the name of *spring* he indicates the source from which the water originated,

calling it a spring. This is clarified from what the Samaritan woman said to him, *You have no bucket and the well is deep.*

And Jesus, tired out by his journey, was sitting by the well. It was about noon. [4:7] *A Samaritan woman came from the town to draw water.* Even though our Lord knew she was able to receive true doctrine, he did not immediately begin to teach her. It did not seem appropriate to him to begin in such a way with strangers. Rather, it was better to begin conversation with something readily available taken from the order of visible things. Therefore he said to her, *Give me water to drink.* What this man said, tired out by the journey and the heat of the day, caught the attention of the woman who was about to draw water. [The Evangelist] also added that his disciples had entered the town to buy food, demonstrating that Jesus did not talk to strange women by chance or without purpose, but with due modesty so that anyone who came to him might respect him for his words.

The Samaritan woman said to him, [4:9] *How is it that you, a Jew, ask a drink of me, a woman of Samaria? Jews do not share things in common with Samaritans.* It is evident that the blessed John wanted to reveal the virtue of the woman through this story. She did not take the matter of offering water to him lightly. First she reminded him of the rules of the law. She demonstrated great integrity, not tolerating this infringement of the commandment even with strangers, even if it was easy to do and appeared almost even as a necessity.

Therefore, in order that it might not appear that the woman did not want to give water out of meanness or hostility to foreigners, the Evangelist added these words, *Jews do not share things in common with Samaritans*, so that we might know that she refused to give him water not as someone who was a stranger to her religion, but because she wanted to warn him

---

[40]That is, "of the Jews." [41]Variant: Sichem. [42]See Gen 48:22; Josh 24:32.

not to transgress the rules of the law because his thirst led him to do so. At this stage our Lord took this answer of the woman as a ripe opportunity for teaching. Since she reminded him of the precept of the law, as if he wanted to proceed along this subject line, he took the start for his preaching by revealing who he was, [4:10] *If you knew the gift of God*, he says, *and who it is that is saying to you, "Give me a drink," you would have asked him, and he would have given you living water.* He says, in effect, "I approve of you wanting to remind me of the commandments of the law, but it seems that you ignore the dignity of the one who is speaking to you. I am not the kind of person who needs instruction from you to attain virtue; on the contrary, I can provide those who ask with virtues superior to human nature."

However, since the [Samaritan] woman did not yet understand these words, and did not know what *living water* was, she said to him, [4:11] *Sir, you have no bucket, and the well is deep: where do you get that living water?* The tone of her conversation has changed. Above she had dared to say, *How is it that you, a Jew?* Now, she appropriately uses the title *Sir* before her words. Before, she talked to him, suspecting that he would transgress the law because of his strong thirst. Now, after understanding from his answer and his peaceful words that he had not asked for water because he was oppressed by thirst, she treated his words with appropriate dignity. She says, "From where will you give me that living water? You have no bucket, and the well is deep."

But since she wanted to know more, she said to him, [4:12] *Are you greater than our ancestor Jacob who gave us the well, and with his sons and his flocks drank from it?* "Do you possess a greater power than he who dug this well? He used it for his and his children's benefit, and left it for us so that we might enjoy the fruit of his labor. Therefore we necessarily expect from you something wonderful, because you are able to give water to drink without human work or activity, and without even having a bucket."

Our Lord, explaining that his words did not concern this water, said, [4:13] *Everyone who drinks of this water will be thirsty again,* [4:14] *but those who drink of the water that I will give them will never be thirsty. The water that I will give will become in them a spring of water gushing up to eternal life.* "There is a great difference," he says, "between that water and the water I promise to give. That [water], after they have drunk it, extinguishes their thirst for a short time. But then, when it has been consumed, because of the kind of water it is, it again leaves the one thirsty who shortly before had drunk it. The water that I give, by its very nature, is the kind that not only does not disappear once it is consumed, nor does it leave the one who drinks it oppressed by thirst. Quite the contrary, it becomes in him like a spring gushing up forever. Just like the water from a spring does not run out or need to be brought from another place or to be poured into the [spring] but constantly offers a perpetual refreshment fruition to those who want it—in a similar way the power of this water also provides the one who receives it with perpetual help and will always preserve him and will not allow him to perish. Therefore the one who receives this grace will never die." And it was right that he said this, and with good reason, because this is how it is with the power of the Spirit. And so we also receive from him the first fruits of the Spirit with the hope of a future resurrection. Indeed, now this operation is performed as in a type, but in the future we hope to receive perfect grace when through participation in him we will remain imperishable.

The woman, however, understood these words in a bodily sense. And so she said to him, [4:15] *Sir, give me this water, so that I may never be thirsty or have to keep coming here to draw water.* What did the Lord say? By showing his inner nature and confirming his promise, and by explaining what had up to this point remained hidden from her, he began with a suitable pretext and said, [4:16] *Go, call*

your husband. After she had replied that she
had no husband, Jesus said to her, [4:17] *You
are right in saying, "I have no husband"*; [4:18]
*for you have had five husbands, and the one you
have now is not your husband. What you have
said is true.* By revealing all her hidden secrets,
he precisely revealed his own inner nature,
proving that his promise to her was not false,
and demonstrating that he does not promise
little things.

From what he says here, it appears that
this woman did not lead a chaste life. It turns
out that the husband she had was not married to her according to the law. Therefore she
answers, *I have no husband*, since our Lord
had also demonstrated that this was not her
husband. The five men who had been with her
do not seem to have married her in public or in
successive order. This is also demonstrated by
the wonder of the woman—that stranger had
revealed what was hidden to her fellow citizens
both accurately and openly. So she said to him,
[4:19] *Sir, I see that you are a prophet.* Indeed
only a prophet can reveal what is hidden to everyone else. What then? "I must certainly ask
important questions of a prophet. Come then
and solve for me this question about which
I am uncertain, and which has become even
greater because of the antiquity of those who
discussed it without ever being able to find an
agreement. Our fathers always worshiped God
on this mountain, and considered it a crime for
worship to be performed anywhere else. But
you maintain from the most ancient times that
the mount of Jerusalem is the place of God."[43]
After hearing this, the Lord thought that she
had to be instructed accurately because she
had asked this question as one addressing a
prophet.

Therefore he said to her, [4:21] *Woman,
believe me*—it was appropriate for him now
to say, *believe me*, once he had clearly demonstrated the truth of the words that he had spoken to her above—*the hour is coming when you
will worship the Father neither on this mountain
nor in Jerusalem.* "This," he says, "is what you
want to learn about. Know then that there will
be a time when both these places will end."

However, in order that it might not appear
that Jews and Samaritans should be considered
equal because he had predicted the end of both
their sanctuaries, he says, [4:22] *You worship
what you do not know*, that is, you Samaritans.
We worship what we know, that is, we Jews.
And then he adds, *for salvation is from the
Jews.* He did not say "in the Jews" but *from the
Jews.* In fact, salvation was not in them, but
from them, because Christ-in-the-flesh came
from them. "Therefore," he says, "the truth
is with the Jews, but both sanctuaries will be
emptied out. He then declares how this will
happen. [4:23] *But the hour is coming*, he says,
*and is now here, when the true worshipers will
worship the Father in spirit and truth, for the
Father seeks such as these to worship him.* [4:24]
*God is spirit, and those who worship him must
worship in spirit and truth.* "There will be a
time—indeed it has already begun—when
God is worshiped as he should be and in the
way appropriate to his nature. God, in fact, is
incorporeal in nature and cannot be circum-
scribed into any place. He is everywhere, and
it is necessary that he be worshiped according
to this understanding. The true worshiper
is one who honors him with the right intention and believes with a pure conscience that
he can speak with the Infinite one anywhere.
There should be no discussion as to whether
God is only here or there, so that he should
be worshiped in only one place. Such a question gives more offense than honor to God and
runs counter to the right understanding that
worshipers have.

And so this woman, understanding that a
new doctrine higher than the traditional one
and superior to Jewish weakness was being

---

[43]See Jn 4:20.

taught, says to him rightly, [4:25] *I know that Messiah is coming. When he comes, he will proclaim all things to us.* "We expect a Messiah." she says, "And since he will teach us truths much superior to what we have traditionally been taught, could it be that you are the Messiah?" He answered her, [4:26] *I am he, the one who is speaking to you,* that is, "I am the one whom you expect." His disciples came to him while he was speaking and were amazed to see him speak to a woman. Nobody, however, asked what the conversation was about. Indeed, the words, [4:27] *What do you want?* mean, "What are you talking about?" It is evident that they were not astonished because he talked to a woman—he frequently spoke with different women—but because he had not personally avoided speaking with a stranger. And [the Evangelist] had suggested the same thing above when he said, "His disciples had gone to the city,"[44] because he did not speak with strangers or the daughters of other people in a familiar way, or in any other way that might affect their modesty in their conversations with him. But he not only spoke with those who were his companions in love and faith but also instilled great confidence in them. This appears in different events, especially in those that happened in the house of Martha and Mary. One of them sat at the feet of our Lord, who was instructing her, and the other asked if he might make her sister get up so that she might not become weary serving all by herself.[45]

Therefore, after these words, the woman abandoned her jar and forgot about her family and the duty she had come to fulfill and went to the city to invite everyone to see the Messiah. But she related the miracle in a very cautious way by saying, "He told me exactly all that I had done in secret." Actually she did not assert that he was the Messiah, but—as if she were in doubt—said, [4:29] *He cannot*

be the Messiah, can he? This was because she thought that the suitable opportunity to judge from these facts about her words should be left to them. The more they knew that she spoke without being certain, and that even after an evident proof she still investigated, the firmer they believed her words. So all of them came out eagerly in order to learn the truth about what she had said to them.

At this point the Evangelist related what was said in the meantime by the disciples to the Lord and by him to the disciples. Since those who had been invited by this woman had not yet come from the city, the disciples asked him to eat something. But he answered that he had a food unknown to them. This was at the same time the solution to their doubt. They were astonished to see that he spoke to a woman, ignoring the reason why he had deigned to speak to her. He declares, therefore, that his attention toward humanity is holier than any other activity, and that it was more pressing upon him than any need for food. This is why he spoke with the woman.

The disciples understood these words concerning food in a material sense and so they discussed among themselves whether anyone should have brought him something to eat. But Jesus was about to reveal the entire sense of the words, saying, [4:34] *My food is to do the will of him who sent me, and to complete his work.* What is this work? The conversion of human beings. And, quite appropriately, speaking like a human being himself, he said that this work was more important than any bodily food and that he did the will of him who sent him because he had been entrusted with that work. The conversion of humankind, which continued to live in the flesh, had been put under his care because he had faith in divine help more than any one else who had been asked to accomplish this task.

So, he says, [4:35] *Do you not say, "Four*

---

[44]Jn 4:8. [45]Lk 10:38-42.

months more, then comes the harvest?" But I tell
you, look around you, and see how the fields are
ripe for harvesting. He indicates here the time
to which he was referring. After four months
the harvest would come. Therefore our Lord
also said, "Do you not say that there are four
months up to the time of the harvest? But I
will show you a better and more immediate
harvest," alluding to the coming of the Samaritans and their conversion.

[4:36] The reaper is already receiving wages
and is gathering fruit for eternal life, so that
sower and reaper may rejoice together. [4:37]
For here the saying holds true, "One sows and
another reaps." He calls himself the sower
because he has begun to teach and preach.
He calls the apostles reapers because they
have taken their initiative from him, offering
human beings as fruits to God. Therefore he
adds, and the reaper is already receiving wages,
that is, "Your labor will not go unrewarded
simply because the purpose and the initiative of your work came from me; rather, you
too will receive wages for the work you do.
Therefore we both benefit: I because I sowed;
but also you because you reap. You rejoice in
gathering the fruits while I rejoice in seeing the seed grow. The truth of grace is more
clearly revealed here as well, because such
great power has been given to you through the
seed sown by me that you will be able to lead
many to faith through the help derived from
me. And the fact that you are able to do these
things through the power proceeding from me
confirms the excellence of my power."

[4:38] I sent you to reap that for which you
did not labor. Others have labored, and you have
entered into their labor. Even though he called
himself the sower of divine adoration, the teaching concerning the worship of God had clearly
been initiated before his coming in the flesh
through the prophets and the righteous who followed. He clearly shows that this initiative, too,
had been given by him. "I sent you," he says, "to
reap and enjoy the labor of others. Their hard

labor ensured that the seed of adoration would
remain among humanity. And then you came,
and from this crop that was sown you will then
gather people and lead them to the adoration of
God. I would not have invited you to reap and
enjoy the work of others if that cultivation was
not mine from the beginning. I entrusted some
with sowing, others with reaping, according to
the season. I portioned out the different phases
of cultivation."

After inserting here these words about the
doctrine of our Lord, the Evangelist proceeds
by saying, [4:39] Many Samaritans from that
city believed in him because of the woman's
testimony. And immediately they asked him to
stay with them. Therefore, since he remained
there for two days, many believed in him. They
told the woman her testimony was no longer
the reason why they believed in him. Indeed,
after they had experienced evidence stronger
than the testimony of her words, they firmly
believed that he was the Messiah on the basis
of the facts themselves.

After he had spent two days there, he
continued his journey to Galilee just as he
had planned. He looked on this not only as
an opportunity but also [4:44] testified that
a prophet has no honor in the prophet's own
country, referring to Judea as his own country,
which he had left for this very reason, that is,
because the Jews clearly sought any number
of ways to persecute him because they envied
him so much. Everything that the Evangelist
had included about the Samaritans was clearly
inserted in the plot of his narrative. Among
other things, Samaria was not the homeland
of the Messiah. And the phrase has no honor
could not refer to the Samaritans because they
believed in him and received him with great
honor. However, the Galileans, the Evangelist
says, also received him with honor since they
knew and had seen what he did in Jerusalem.
Therefore what we have said above is now
clear. In other words, the Lord did not come
and drive out of the temple those selling cattle

and sheep without due consideration but only did so after he had worked miracles there and revealed his power with various signs.

[4:46] *Then [Jesus] came again to Cana in Galilee where he had changed the water into wine. Now there was a royal official whose son lay ill in Capernaum.* [4:47] *When he heard that Jesus had come from Judea to Galilee, he went and begged him to come down and heal his son, for he was on the point of death.* [4:48] *Then Jesus said to him, "Unless you see signs and wonders you will not believe."* Jesus said this as a rebuke, certainly meaning to single out the royal official who asked him to come down and heal his son, but who had approached him with less than perfect faith. After hearing those words,[46] the official asked him to hurry before his child died. But our Lord, in order to rebuke him because he had come without a mature faith, said to him, [4:50] *Go; your son will live,* that is, "It is not necessary that I come down. All I need to do is merely speak." *The man believed the word that Jesus spoke to him and started on his way.* By writing here *the man believed*, the Evangelist does not intend to say that he believed completely and perfectly. Rather, he means that he accepted the word without hesitation and hoped for something excellent from him. This is similar to what we said at the beginning of this book about the words, "many believed in him."[47] Indeed, the Evangelist adds there, "but Jesus on his part would not entrust himself to them."[48] He certainly would not have written this if they had believed with certainty.

The events that follow clearly demonstrate that the royal official left his encounter with Christ with an imperfect faith. Upon reaching his house, his slaves met him and reported to him his son's recovery. He did not, however, come back to give thanks for the miracle but instead asked at what time the child had recovered. When he had ascertained that it was

the same hour in which the Lord had promised him the healing of the child, [4:53] *Then he himself believed, along with his whole household.* For this reason [the Evangelist] also said, *The father realized that this was the hour when Jesus had said to him, "Your son will live." Then he himself believed, along with his whole household.* If he had perfectly believed after Jesus' words, it would have been superfluous to now add, "His father realized . . . and believed." But it is evident in the previous instance[49] that "he believed" indicated that "he received his word." But here it is used to indicate that "he himself was confirmed [in his faith]," and his whole household, because of the evidence received from the event itself. And our Lord, who knew this would be the case from the beginning, had said, *unless you see signs you will not believe.*[50]

After relating this fact, the Evangelist underlines, [4:54] *Now this was the second sign that [Jesus] did in Galilee.* The first was the miracle of the wine. Then he moves on to report another event not narrated by the others:

[5:1] *There was a festival of the Jews, and Jesus went up to Jerusalem.* It is clear from John's mention of this that Jesus wanted to help as many people as possible, and so he chose to attend the festival. Just as it was previously said, "The Passover of the Jews was near, and Jesus went up to Jerusalem,"[51] so also at this point there was another festival. He chose a time when everyone would be gathered so he could help everyone. Therefore he went to Jerusalem at that time too. He did not think it was necessary to travel around and go to every place where sick people were. Otherwise it might appear that he was looking for fame. Instead, he healed a single person and revealed himself to many through that person.

It was for this reason that he came to the pool [5:2] *called in Hebrew Beth-zatha which had five porticoes.* Besides the four that surrounded it, there was one in the middle. Here

---

[46]See Jn 4:49. [47]Jn 2:23. [48]Jn 2:24. [49]Jn 2:24. [50]Jn 4:48. [51]Jn 2:13.

a great crowd of people who were sick with different infirmities had gathered, hoping to be healed, as if those waters might accomplish something because the entrails of sheep offered as victims to God were washed in them.[52] And God also supported this belief by causing the waters to stir sometimes. Since people believed that these waters were stirred by divine power, when they went down into the water they obtained the grace of healing. Not many people were healed on the same occasion, but the one who came down first did obtain this gracious help. This happened in order that the ease of the healing might not diminish the effect of the miracle. Therefore, because their attention and desire were so focused on the stirring of the waters, once they recovered their health, they would better remember their healing. Even though many lay ill there, he did not heal all of them. Instead, in order to show his power, he chose one person who was affected with a very serious infirmity and who was already beyond hope about his recovery. There was a paralyzed man among them who had already been ill for thirty-eight years. When the Lord passed by him he did not at once say to him, [5:8] *Stand up, take your mat and walk.* Instead, he first started talking to talk to him, as we have shown he did with the Samaritan woman.

But why did he question him first by saying, [5:6] *Do you want to be made well?* There was no need for this question. It is obvious that anyone who is sick desires to be healed from his illness. He had already been lying in that place for a long time with only this one desire. However, as we said previously, [the Lord] approached the miracle according to a certain order of events: first by questioning him, and then, after getting the proper answer, conceding the benefit of healing to him. The one who

was paralyzed did not understand the reason for this line of questioning. He suspected that Jesus had asked him, *Do you want to be made well?* as a way of suggesting that he had not received the grace of healing because of his own negligence and that this was why he was ill for such a long time. And so the one who was paralyzed answered him, [5:7] *Sir, I have no one to put me into the pool when the water is stirred up; and while I am making my way, someone else steps down ahead of me*, that is, "I certainly want to be healed. I have not been lying here in my infirmity for all this time because of my own negligence. It is the seriousness of my illness that constantly deprives me of grace. Indeed, I cannot move ahead of anyone else because those who are stronger always get there ahead of me. I have no friend who otherwise might put me into the waters when they are stirred up. This is the reason why I have not obtained any grace up to this point."

After he said these things, the Lord took the opportunity to answer, [5:8] *Stand up, take your mat and walk.* "Since," he says, "you have no hope that you can be healed—your infirmity has, in fact, bound you and not even allowed you to crawl—you have been deprived of the benefit of healing which is available here for all. Therefore, I will now give it to you. You are released from your infirmity and are completely healed. Therefore, *Stand up, take your mat and walk.* And as he had said this, at once the miracle followed the word.

Now it was on the sabbath when this incident occurred.[53] He commanded him to take his mat and walk on the sabbath and therefore on a holy day. As a consequence, since according to the law of Moses it was necessary to rest on that day, everyone began to murmur and reprove the paralytic as a transgressor of the law because of what took place. Therefore he

---

[52]Theodore seems to ignore the section of text following 5:3, which is inserted here by a part of the manuscript tradition of the Gospel of John, and is usually indicated as 5:3b-4: "waiting for the stirring of the water; for an angel of the Lord went down at certain seasons into the pool, and stirred up the water; whoever stepped in first after the stirring of the water was made well from whatever disease that person had." [53]See Jn 5:9.

was compelled to defend himself by making known both the miracle and its author.

Therefore all the Jews rebuked him and told him to lay down his mat. But in his own defense he answered, [5:11] *The man who made me well told me to do this.* After receiving such great benefit, it was only right that he would necessarily obey Jesus' commands. Therefore they questioned him, "Who ordered you to do so?" But the healed man did not know who he was because Jesus went into hiding as soon as he had healed him. It would have been typical of someone looking for glory if Jesus had remained with the one whom he had healed. It would have been typical of someone who desired public exposure. But we see that our Lord carefully avoids this. In fact, even though it would have been appropriate for him to be acknowledged as God, because he appeared as a man and many had this opinion about him, he nonetheless protected himself from the judgment of those who saw him.

When our Lord later saw the paralytic in the temple, believing the man had no conscience worthy of the healing he had received—indeed Jesus thought that the paralytic might even point him out to the Jews since they were enraged and threatened to execute him—he said to him, [5:14] *See, you have been made well! Do not sin anymore, so that nothing worse happens to you,* as if he wanted to signify implicitly to him that he should not incline toward wickedness. On the contrary, as one who had received such kindness, he ought rather to repay the one who had bestowed this kindness to him with love. Even though it was only fitting that the Lord should be known as the author of the miracle, he nonetheless could read the mind of this man and aptly alluded to his [evil] intention. But this man did not benefit from his words. Instead, he went and revealed to all who the author of his healing was.

Some have actually composed words of praise for the paralytic's actions, concluding

he is worthy of such praise because he pointed out to the Jews who it was who had healed him. He indicated who his helper was, they say, out of joy and out of a desire to make him known to everyone. If a sophist, looking for the applause of the audience and having no care for the truth, wanted to write this, perhaps we could say this would be the logical conclusion for such a person. But if someone loves and pursues the truth and honors it above everything else—and it is appropriate for an interpreter of the Holy Scriptures to act in this way in order that he might not offer his own private interpretation but rather expose that interpretation to every place where the testimonies of the Scriptures speak to it—how could he not see that such an interpretation is highly censurable and inept? How could the paralytic be worthy of praise when he revealed our Lord to the Jews who had even openly threatened him because he had taken his mat on a sabbath and had therefore rebuked him as a transgressor of the law?

After the paralytic defended himself before the Jews, saying that another had ordered him to take up his mat on the sabbath, the Jews turned their rage against the one who had said this to him. And so they questioned him, "Who told you to do this?" implicitly accusing him and, with this accusation, in effect censuring him for his violation of the law. And they did this even when they had already ascertained who it was who had given him this order. When he pointed Jesus out to such an enraged and furious people, he did not act as a friend. Rather, in order to comply with the rules of the Jews, he betrayed his own benefactor. Nor can one excuse his actions as being done out of necessity because he felt pressured by the violence of the questioners. Therefore, our Lord spoke words such as these to him when he approached him in the temple, thus disclosing to the paralytic his inclination to sin. But he gained nothing from these words. Instead, following his own evil will and giving in to the threats which the Jews were threatening to carry out, he spontaneously betrayed his benefactor and brought on him all kinds of trouble. As soon as the Jews came to know who healed him, they persecuted Jesus as one who was impious, a breaker and destroyer of the ancient laws decreed by God and given through Moses, which had been established among them for a long time. When our Lord was accused of violating the sabbath, he escaped their accusation by relating accurately who he was. He did not recall anything about all the others who had done something during the sabbath, even though he might have said much about the invisible natures[54] fulfilling the divine precepts on the sabbath, and also about the things that were moved on the sabbath by these invisible natures according to the command of God.

What did he say then? [5:17] *My Father is still working, and I also am working.* He did not want to describe those [invisible natures mentioned above], because each of them moved according to the command of God. Instead, he recalled his Father, who always acts according to his own will and power. Even on the sabbath he does not abstain from those works which are for our good, knowing that any time is suitable for our salvation. [Christ refers to the Father] in order to show us that this same authority is also in him. Just as [the Father] has the authority to work at all times without being subject to the law—even though he is the one who decreed the law of rest on the sabbath—so Jesus has the same privilege, and there is no commandment or law that would prevent him from doing whatever he wants.

Therefore, when they objected to the disciples harvesting ears of corn and preparing them with their hands and eating them on the sabbath, he replied with the example of David and the priests, and also with the word written in the Law.[55] In this way he showed them

that they were allowed, when appropriate, to do what appeared to be forbidden by the law. But now, since he only was accused for his own action, he did not recall any of those who were under the law—in fact, the reason for their action seemed to have another purpose. Instead, he mentions the Father who is working by saying, *My Father is still working, and I also am working.* It is as though he were saying, "My Father never ceases from working, and neither do I. Just as it is his work to provide for people, and there is no law averting him from that and forbidding him to do that, so I too work whenever I want, and there is no fixed time for my work in promoting the salvation of the human race. And just as he always has the authority to do work, so do I. If you rebuke me because I work on a sabbath, you must also rebuke my Father, because he is working too. If no one accuses him because his dominion gives him this authority, neither should anyone accuse me because I, indeed, have the same authority to work whenever I want."

The Jews could not stand such a reply. They considered it to be a great profanity, even worse than the previous one. More to the point, they believed that his words were an iniquity even greater than the violation of the sabbath itself. Such an impious expression would be taken quite seriously, if it was judged according to a human way of thinking. The violation of the sabbath was, in fact, a transgression of the commandment, but [Christ's] words implied equality with God himself! And there was no greater iniquity than that if his words were considered to be spoken by a man.

Therefore the Evangelist took the opportunity to add, [5:18] *For this reason the Jews were seeking all the more to kill him, because he was not only breaking the sabbath, but was also calling God his own Father, therefore making himself equal with God.* It is appropriate that John included the words, *for this reason . . . all the*

---

[54]Perhaps the angels are meant here. [55]See Mt 12:1-8.

more and *not only*, in order to show that this second censure against him arose from his own words which they used to increase the accusation against him for the things he had said. First, he had said that they were persecuting him because he had violated the sabbath. Then John reported what the Lord answered them when he had been accused of violating the sabbath. Therefore John now aptly adds, *For this reason the Jews were seeking all the more to kill him*, signifying that the accusation had become more serious because of what he had said. *Not only for this reason*, he says. And he was quite right in noting that this was not the only reason they had threatened him. There were other reasons besides this one. And so, he adds, *But [he] was also calling God his own Father, therefore making himself equal with God*. If he had simply called God his father, they would not have grumbled. Instead, he called him his *own* Father, as if he proceeded directly from him and was equal with him in strength and power. He openly asserted this when he was being accused of violating the sabbath in his reply, "My Father is still working, and I also am working." However, some, for whom it is quite easy to twist everything, without considering the whole context, assert that Jesus indeed did not make himself equal with God, but that the Jews only thought he did.[56]

Therefore, such people say, the Lord himself, desiring to remove this opinion they held, answered them, [5:19] *Very truly, I tell you, the Son can do nothing on his own*. Later, with the help of God, we will show in what sense this was said. Now let us inquire how, if the Lord did not teach this through his words, the Jews were led to such an opinion. By considering every aspect of the question, it seems impossible to me that the Jews conceived this opinion about Christ by themselves. According to the narrative of the Evangelist, they persecuted him

because he had violated the sabbath. But they had not yet censured him because he had made himself equal with God. They were only charging him then with the crime of violating the sabbath. Only after he had answered them, "My Father is still working, and I also am working," does the Evangelist mention that they persecuted him not only for this,[57] but also because *he was calling God his own Father, therefore making himself equal with God*. It is only logical for us to assume that they obviously concluded that he made himself equal with God because he had called God his Father.

Who would be foolish enough to believe that these words might have suggested to Jewish hearers an opinion concerning equality with God when, at that time, people everywhere were called sons of God and God was called the father of human beings not only collectively, but also with reference to a single person. The blessed David, for instance, says, "He will call on me, 'You are my Father' . . . and I will make him the firstborn and will exalt him over the kings of the earth."[58] This refers to those who are going to receive the kingdom, since anyone who preserves the law of God is appropriately called by this name as one who must be considered a son and the firstborn. However, it is clear that the Jews were accustomed to using this name to such an extent that they called God their Father out of mere familiarity. And so, when they spoke to Christ, as this Evangelist reports, they did not hesitate to tell him, "We have one father, God himself."[59] They called God their Father without in any way thinking they were equal with God. So how was it—on the basis of this way of speaking to which they were accustomed and which was in use among them since antiquity—that they intentionally and spontaneously concluded that [Christ] had said he was equal with God?

---

[56]Theodore alludes again to the Arians who tried to find in the Holy Scriptures proofs of the Son's inferiority to the Father. [57]That is, the violation of the sabbath. [58]Ps 89:27-28 (88:27-28 LXX). [59]Jn 8:41.

We again ask how the Jews suspected this about him when this way of speaking was quite common and was used by many. And evidently they understood both these points from his words because they found both in them. In other words, they understood that he had called God his Father as well as that he made himself equal with God. They found both assertions in his words when he told those who were accusing him of violating the sabbath, "My Father is still working, and I also am working," proving that he had the power to work just like the Father and that he was, like the Father, immune from any rule and law. He also maintained and demonstrated his equality with God when he said that God was his Father, not in the usual way, but in a higher and more sublime way because he was born of him and was of the same nature as his Father. Like a son toward his father, and yet distinct from any of us, he rightfully shares with him in his works and authority and is beyond reproach in everything he does according to his will. Human beings, on the other hand, cannot share in this because he is their Father not by nature but by adoption.

Therefore, since in his words they found that he called God his Father, indicating a natural birth and that he made himself equal with God, they thought they had a good reason to grumble against him. They determined this not on the basis of mere suspicion but from his own words concluded that he had to be accused of great arrogance. For there were two things that both they and our Lord were saying: first was that he had violated the sabbath, and second, that he had called God his Father. The first of these, as we have just demonstrated, could not have suggested an opinion of equality to the Jews because profaning the sabbath was considered a sin and transgression of the commandment. They pronounced a sentence against those who were guilty in

this respect just as they would against anyone who transgressed against a commandment, like those for instance who gathered wood on a sabbath in the desert.[60] But they did not punish them at all as though they were people who wanted to usurp equality with God. Similarly, since calling God his Father was the usual and customary usage among them, this did not arouse any such suspicion among them either.

Therefore there is nothing else to say except that they understood from his words that God was called Father by him in the literal sense, not as a title of adoption. And it was only right that he declared himself to have equal authority as a Son who is coequal in everything with the Father.[61] We have explained these things in their context, with the help of God.

What the Arians say in addition is quite surprising, that is, that our Lord, in order to refute this idea, added, [5:19] *Very truly, I tell you, the Son can do nothing on his own.* This sentence disproves even more their evil intent. From the words that follow it appears that not only does the Lord not want to remove this idea but wants to confirm it even more.

What did he say? *Very truly, I tell you, the Son can do nothing on his own.* Will they also deny his power to do what human nature can do? We ask them: Can human beings do anything on their own or not? If they cannot, those who are evil are not evil on their own. The same can be said about the righteous. Judas is not a betrayer on his own, and the same may be said about Peter. If this is how things really worked, the first should not be condemned for his sin nor should the second be praised for his goodwill. Neither of them acted on their own, then. However, if instead we deem such an opinion ungodly—for Judas, in fact, is punished with good reason for his evil will and Peter is praised above everyone, receiving honor suitable to his good intention—how is it possible that human beings are

---

[60]See Num 15:32-36. [61]Here Theodore refers to Christ the Word only, according to his Christology.

what they are on their own, but the Lord cannot do anything on his own? Any one of them does what he wants on his own; our Lord, on the contrary, did not break the rule of the sabbath on his own. This is the kind of argument he could have offered against their accusations. Therefore even Satan is not what he is by his own will. So our Lord did not possess goodwill toward his Father on his own, as they say. Rather, he obeyed because he was forced to do so by a command. These arguments are, however, full of impiety.[62]

The meaning of his reply, rather, is this: We use the word *cannot* in two ways, as do the Holy Scriptures. When the text says "the blood of bulls and goats cannot take away sins,"[63] it clearly means that the blood of goats has no power to take away sins. When, on the other hand, the text says, "There are two unchangeable things in which God cannot lie,"[64] it is not assumed that there is any inability on the part of God; rather, it is asserting that it cannot be the case that God would lie. And this is a great sign of his power. "It is impossible, or, it cannot be the case that God would lie" is said about God because of his great inclination to virtue. Since he is firm and faithful in his truth, he would never indulge in a lie because of weakness.

It is evident from what has been said that the words, *the Son can do nothing on his own*, must not be understood as referring to inability, then, because people do all kinds of things on their own. It is necessary, therefore, that we turn to another meaning. Why is it impossible that the Son would do anything on his own? Because of his undivided equality with the Father—because this natural union creates a great unanimity of will, thanks to which it is impossible for the Son to want what the Father does not want. Divine nature does not learn events in time and successively. Rather, from the beginning, his foreknowledge is fully aware of all future events and what must happen because of these events. The Son, too, equally possesses this knowledge. He has everything in common with the Father, including the will. Therefore, neither his intention nor his thought differs from that of the Father because both will to do everything equally. This is what the Evangelist reveals by means of the Lord's own words.

For, after he has said, *the Son can do nothing on his own*, he also added the reason for this by saying, *but only what he sees the Father doing*. Now, if he had wanted to signify that he was lacking in strength or power, he should have said, "except for what the Father orders, or, what [the Father] gives him the power to do." But now he has added, *but only what he sees the Father doing*, which indicates similarity. Actually, if the Son only does what he sees the Father doing, it is clear that he possesses a perfect similarity with the Father in his actions. But this would be impossible if he did not also have the same power. How could he be similar to him and do the same works unless he possessed strength equal to his Father's? And this is by no means different from what he had said above, "My Father is still working, and I am also working," except for the fact that above he spoke clearly but here he speaks with a certain obscurity in order to moderate the strength of his assertion because of the weakness of the hearers.

Therefore, after saying, *but only what he sees the Father doing*, in order to clearly teach that his actions were the same as the Father's— he also said this so that we might not believe some things were made by the Father and others were made by the Son, which might cause a distinction concerning creation to arise in our minds, as if a part of creation should be attributed to the Father and another part to the Son—he added, *whatever the Father does, the Son does likewise*. He did not say, "The Son

---

[62]Again Theodore alludes to the Arians, who always tried to demonstrate Christ's subordination to the Father. [63]Heb 10:4. [64]Heb 6:18.

also does similar things to those the Father does." The Father does not do some things and the Son then does similar things to those done by the Father. Rather, he says, "Whatever the Father does, I do it too." "The operation is common as he and I accomplish the same thing." And he underlines his argument by not simply saying, "The Son also does these things," so that we might believe that he acted in obedience to [to the Father], but adding *likewise* in order to indicate not only that the operations are common but that the way of operating is common as well. Everything that is made is made by him and the Father in the same way because of the sameness of power and will. With good reason he has said, *the Son can do nothing on his own.* Since the works are common and the will is one from which they come, how can the will and the decision for what is done be divided? These things confirm the sentence, "My Father is still working, and I am also working," and show that the offence against the Son also includes the Father. In a similar way, they demonstrate his equality with the Father and do not separate the one from the other in any way, as [these heretics] maintain.[65]

But after he said these things and clearly demonstrated that he did the same things as the Father, and that he did them in the same way, he turned his speech to his human nature by saying, [5:20] *The Father loves the Son and shows him all that he himself is doing; and he will show him greater works than these, so that you will be astonished.* It is evident from the previous context that these words, if they are taken in a literal sense, are not appropriate nor should they be referred to the Godhead. For what are the works to be shown to him by the Father which God the Word will see—he who is the Creator of things visible and invisible, he whose nature is more excellent than anything, he who does likewise whatever the Father does, as he said above?

But since our Lord and Savior Jesus Christ is both God and man—and since the deity according to nature possesses everything, whereas the man came to posses everything through his union with God the Word—when he was rightly accused as a man of violating the sabbath, he demonstrated from the greatness of God that he had not violated the sabbath since he was allowed to do whatever he wanted to do. Therefore he talks about the dignity of this nature,[66] taking the accusation of the Jews as an occasion to reveal this nature, what it was, as far as it was possible. Then in good order he turned the discussion to his human nature because his words would be considered quite incongruous in relation to what they were seeing. Therefore he said, *The Father loves the Son and shows him all that he himself is doing.* And certainly it would be superfluous to show, out of friendship, something to him who naturally can do everything like [the Father]. But he shifted to this subject, as we have said, because the development of the narrative led there. When he was rebuked as a man by them, but could not accept the accusation leveled against him as undeserved since he was considered to be simply a man, he accomplished two things by passing on to a discussion of his divinity: he revealed himself, as far as it was possible, and he strongly rejected the insult leveled against him. But since these words did not seem suitable to him in his visible state, he fittingly added, *The Father loves the Son and shows him all that he himself is doing.* The implication is that he possesses dominion also when he is visible. He possesses many things too which overcome nature because of his union with God, so that he figuratively uses the word *shows* for "gave." Since he was speaking about all these things with the Jews, he accommodated his speech to their weakness, indicating the distinct natures with distinct words. By mentioning those two things as though speak-

---

[65]Here Theodore refers again to the Arians. [66]That is, the divine nature.

ing about one, he signified the unity of the person. And even though the Jews could not understand these topics at the time, he nonetheless spoke about them, so that later they might consult this book. The disciples, at the time, did not understand many of the things he said either. But later, when they preserved his words, they understood their meaning, as the Evangelist observes. Therefore after our Lord says, "Destroy this temple, and in three days I will raise it up," the Evangelist adds, "After he was raised from the dead, his disciples remembered that he had said this; and they believed."[67] He shows this and more with the words that follow.

He said that *greater works than these*—evidently greater than the healing of the paralytic—would be shown by him that would astonish them. Here he alludes to the general resurrection and to those things that he will appear to do when he stands and judges everything and they themselves will see his dignity in this action. With good reason, they will be astonished at that time, learning who he is and what role has been given to him. And undoubtedly, after seeing this, they will agree to believe in the nature dwelling in him. He relates this in various places in the passages that follow.

After saying these things, knowing that such words pertain to a nature higher than can be seen, he confirms again his speech with an allusion to the excellence of that divine nature by saying, [5:21] *Indeed, just as the Father raises the dead and gives them life, so also the Son gives life to whomever he wishes.* And this also agrees perfectly with what he had said above. Indeed, there is no difference between the phrase, "whatever he sees the Father doing, he does likewise," and the phrase, *indeed, just as the Father raises the dead and gives them life, so also the Son gives life to whomever he wishes,* except for this: while in the first phrase he extended his speech to include everything,

in the second phrase he speaks about a precise issue,[68] just as the development of the argument demanded.

After he had confirmed his words on the basis of the greatness of the [divine] nature, he added, [5:22] *The Father judges no one, but has given all judgment to the Son.* He links the [general] resurrection with the judgment because, since they will occur at the same time, they will demonstrate the dignity of our Lord. All will be resurrected by him and judged by him. Usually when the Scripture relates things that concern the human nature of the Lord, if the subject matter is more elevated than the nature under discussion, it immediately makes mention of the greatness of the Godhead, therefore rendering the discussion beyond doubt for the hearers. For instance, when Paul says, "He has spoken to us by a Son whom he appointed heir of all things,"[69] he intends us to understand the assumed man, and signifies that he has spoken in a human way. And this assumed man, even though he is not the lord of [all] things, has received dominion over them through his union with God the Word because the Word, being the author of all things, has dominion over them as well. But since he understood that his statement was more elevated than the nature about which it was concerned, Paul added, "through whom he also created the worlds,"[70] so that by attributing this to the divine nature he might demonstrate that universal dominion is due to this visible [Christ] too. In a similar way, when Christ revealed these things that belong to the divine nature, he defended himself from the accusation mentioned above and intentionally turned the discussion toward his human nature in order to demonstrate that it had received supernatural qualities from the divine nature.

Because he wanted to make known which qualities he had received—since they were more elevated than his human nature—he first

---

[67]Jn 2:19, 22. [68]That is, resurrection. [69]Heb 1:2. [70]Heb 1:2.

confirmed what he had said by referring to the greatness of his divinity, and then adds an extensive narration about the qualities that were given to him. He says, *The Father judges no one, but has given all judgment to the Son.* It is evident that this does not pertain to the divine nature because God the Word, as he himself has said, does everything like the Father. It is not possible that he who does everything like the Father judges anything other than what the Father judges. Therefore, the Son is said to have received the judgment, while the Father is said to have given it. This actually fits with his human nature. Indeed, since the divine nature is invisible to all creatures, and yet it is necessary for the judge to be seen by those who are judged, God the Word has assumed the man, investing in him everything that pertains to our salvation. And he has given him the role of judge, judging through him in order that he who judges and gives orders might be visible. It is evident that [the assumed man] does not have this honor and power by nature but has been granted through his union with the glorious nature dwelling in him that power which belongs to it.[71]

Therefore *The Father judges no one* cannot be said to refer to the Father's power or strength. In fact, the Father never loses his power to judge. Since he is the creator and Lord of everything, it is only right that he judges everyone. If it is a question of being seen and of appearing to those to be judged, we would have to say that the Son too judges no one, because he can never be seen. But the man who has been assumed will come down from heaven,[72] as it says, "This Jesus who has been taken from you into heaven, will come in the same way as you saw him go into heaven."[73] He will judge everyone by repaying each person according to his merit and pronouncing his sentence upon everyone he pleases. And since

he cannot do this by his own nature, he has said rightly, *[The Father] has given him judgment.* What he did not have, he received from his union with God the Word so that, since he is by his nature the judge of all, he has the right to judge his servants. And since he does everything like the Father, he likewise judges all as well. Some are quite foolish in saying that the judgment has been given to God the Word. But how can it be the case that those things which equally belong both to the Father and the Son are outside of [God the Word's] power of judgment? If what he said is true, he does everything like the Father.

He then expresses the consequence of this judgment by saying, [5:23] *so that all may honor the Son just as they honor the Father.* But the honor of all is not due to God the Word because he judges, but because he is the beginning of all the things that were made through him. Therefore the honor of all is necessarily due to him. Creating things that did not exist is highly superior to rendering judgment. Consequently, this honor is also aptly attributed to the man because, through what he received, he was made a participant of this honor together with the Father. Therefore, there is no incongruity in honoring him just like the Father. Indeed, since he did not receive by nature the honor of all, but only after being united in the adoration of God the Word, he is necessarily honored with the same honor with which the Father is honored together with God the Word. Therefore he added, [5:23] *Anyone who does not honor the Son does not honor the Father who sent him.* "The dishonor inflicted upon me," he is saying, "overflows to the Father as well."

He goes on to note what benefit those who honor him or believe in him receive, [5:24] *Very truly, I tell you, anyone who hears my word and believes him who sent me has eternal*

---

[71]That is, that belongs to the divine nature. [72]Another typical instance of Theodore's Christology: see also translator's introduction, esp. quotation from Norris, p. xxvi. [73]Acts 1:11.

life, and does not come under judgment, but has passed from death to life. "Whoever obeys my words and believes," he says, "is made a participant in eternal life and will not only avoid the judgment, that is, the tribulations of judgment, but will even receive honor. And honor will certainly be attributed to him by the judge himself." Thus, from this point on, he talks about the honor of his human nature with increasing intensity and focuses on this as the subject of his narrative. The greater the things that were said about it, the more they revealed the nature that was in him.

He then immediately confirms his words by saying, [5:25] *Very truly, I tell you, the hour is coming, and is now here, when the dead will hear the voice of the Son of God, and those who hear will live.* Since it was hard to believe that the dead would pass from death to life, he added correctly, "This hour is coming. Indeed, even now many who are dead already hear my voice and are rising up," so that as they saw what he was doing now, they would not have doubts about what he was saying. This happened with the son of the widow,[74] with the daughter of the leader of the synagogue,[75] and was fulfilled gloriously in Lazarus,[76] and similarly on many other occasions. Not all these events were even recorded.

He then tells them where his power to perform these miracles comes from. [5:26] *For just as the Father has life in himself, so he has granted the Son also to have life in himself;* [5:27] *and he has given him authority to execute judgment.* "The Father," he says, "gave him his same power to raise the dead and conferred upon him the same power to judge." And rightly he said these things about the man, because in his union with God the Word he received omnipotence like the Father had. God the Word who was in him can do everything just like the Father.

Therefore it is evident that all these things

are said about the assumed man since, from the words, *the Father judges no one,* it is obvious that all the discussion has become focused on the [assumed man], just as it is obvious from the phrase, *The Father loves the Son.* And the sentence, *Indeed, just as the Father raises the dead and gives them life, so also the Son gives life to whomever he wishes,* is introduced into the narrative to offer further support for what has just been said.

But when he realized that such a speech was too elevated for his visible nature, he added, [5:28] *Do not be astonished at this; for the hour is coming when all who are in their graves will hear his voice* [5:29] *and will come out—those who have done good, to the resurrection of life, and those who have done evil, to the resurrection of condemnation.* "Although you are considering only this visible nature," he says, "do not doubt what I have said about the hour that is coming when all who are in their graves will hear his voice and will come out and be divided into groups with each having his reward according to his merit." *The hour is coming* follows *do not be astonished.* However, *the hour is coming* is not the reason why they should *not be astonished.* Since he had previously said above, *the hour is coming, and is now here, when the dead will hear the voice of the Son of God, and those who hear will live,* and again, *and he has given him authority to execute judgment*—since these events, if referred to his visible nature, were not really credible, he consistently repeats the thought, "When considering this nature, do not be astonished about what you hear, and do not think these events I am talking about are beyond belief."

And then he says why they must not be astonished: [5:30] *I can do nothing on my own. As I hear, I judge.* When he says this, he means, "The power and the strength I have to judge come from someone else." A mere mortal does not have the power to be able to judge

---

[74]Lk 7:11-17. [75]See Mt 9:18-26. [76]See Jn 11.

everything according to justice. And who is the one from whom he received the power and the strength to judge? It is clearly God the Word who, in his union with him, granted him the strength and the power to judge, whereas his [human] nature would have never been able to do so.

Therefore, he says, [5:30] *and my judgment is just because I seek to do not my own will but the will of him who sent me.* "So," he says, "my sentence against unbelievers is just, because I do not speak to you as one who wants to take you away from the worship of God in order to lead you to me; rather, I am leading you to God and preaching what he wants you to know. This leaves no pretext or excuse for those who refuse to believe in me."

It is evident that he did not mean the same thing when he said, *I can do nothing on my own,* as when he had said earlier, *the Son can do nothing on his own.*[77] Here in our present context he is talking about the resurrection and the judgment. And since these words are higher than would be appropriate for the visible human nature, he rightly said, *I can do nothing on my own,* in order to show that he is a participant in this power and strength through his union with God the Word. He then added, *As I hear, I judge,* meaning, because of what the Word teaches me, I have the excellence of God the Word who dwells in me." Above, since he was accused of violating the sabbath, he said, *the Son can do nothing on his own.* But it was possible for anyone to break the sabbath who wanted to. Therefore, in this case, it was not a question of possibility but of the impossibility of wanting to do anything against the will of the Father. That is why above he added, *but only what he sees the Father doing*; but here says, *as I hear, I judge,* which indicates knowledge. Above he indicates similarity. The entire context in both passages

reveals their difference. Indeed, above, after saying, *but only what he sees the Father doing,* he lingered on the similarity and equality by adding, *whatever the Father does, the Son does likewise.* Here, after the phrase, *as I hear, I judge,* he added, *my judgment is just,* in other words, "because I do not want to convert you to me, but intend to lead you to the divine nature." So the context and the purpose for why this is said demonstrate that this is referred to his human nature because it can do nothing on its own if it is removed from its union with God the Word. The other sentence, however, has a different meaning. Because of his communication in nature and in will with the Father, we cannot conceive that the works of God the Word might be in opposition or contrary to the will of the Father. Above, since he was rebuked for violating the law, he had the right to declare this. Here, lest he be considered arrogant—and rightly not believed because what he was saying was incredible—he rendered the elevated nature of his speech credible by referring it to God the Word.

For an accurate interpretation of the text, we also note here that the words, *the Son can do nothing on his own,*[78] are not appropriate at all if they are attributed to the divine nature. They imply weakness. But whatever the divinity performs, it performs through its innate power—unless one wants to interpret these words in the sense that [God the Word] cannot operate separately from [God the Father], as we have shown above. However, if they are referred to his human nature, they make perfect sense because all the things that are elevated above this nature—and there are many in which he now participates through his union with God the Word—do not proceed at all from that nature, but from no other nature than the divine nature which is united to him.[79]

---

[77]This and other italicized references in this paragraph are to Jn 5:19. [78]Jn 5:19. [79]See translator's introduction, esp. quotation from Norris, p. xxvi.

[5:31] *If I bear witness to myself, my testimony is not true;* [5:32] *there is another who bears witness to me, and I know that his testimony about me is true.* But how could one possibly say that our Lord's testimony about himself is not true? If this is how things had remained, the Jews had good reason not to believe his words. But he evidently adjusted many things he said toward the audience with whom he was speaking. Therefore since they were about to object to the words pronounced by our Lord about himself, "Your words are not true, nor worthy to be accepted because you bear testimony about yourself" —since in their argument with him, I say, they were about to put forward this objection—our Lord forestalled them by saying, "You must not accept me as true because I bear testimony to myself: this is what you undoubtedly mean. But you only have the right to say that if I am the only one testifying about myself. But now someone else said something similar to what I said about myself, and he was a very sound witness."

Who was that someone else? [5:33] *You sent to John, and he has borne witness to the truth.* "Besides," he says, "what I had to say against your objections, you also received a testimony from John when you sent envoys to him." Then, exercising caution in order not to appear to destroy the certainty of what he had previously said with these words, he added, [5:34] *Not that the testimony that I receive is from man; but I say this that you may be saved.* "I say this," he says, "not because I need his testimony. Human testimony does not add anything to the words I have spoken about who I am. Rather, I chose to say this with your salvation in mind and therefore wanted you to recall the words of John so that, perhaps, after being convinced by the testimony of John, you might agree to believe my words without further hesitation.

"Why don't I need his testimony?" [5:35]

He was a burning and shining lamp, and you were willing to rejoice for a while in his light. "He acted as a lamp which, in the absence of the sun, was useful to those who were in darkness. But after the sun had risen, the lamp was superfluous since it was of no use for those whom it illuminates. In a similar way [John] too, before I came, was certainly useful for your instruction. But after I came—I, the true light to which everyone must turn and look—the use of that temporary [lamp] must cease. This is how great the difference is between him and me. It was appropriate for me to recall his testimony because he came to you so that you might be saved. When he was far away from you, you seemed to obey him. But that was not true obedience. For a short time you rejoiced in him, and for a short time you appeared to believe in him, but then you demonstrated your disobedience by your own actions when you did not want to accept his testimony about me or obey my words. If it is necessary to resort to truthful testimony, I have an even higher testimony against those who resist." Therefore, he says, [5:36] *But the testimony which I have is greater than that of John.* And so he adds, *For the works that the Father has granted me to accomplish, these very works that I am doing bear witness to me that the Father has sent me.* The testimony of the works is the greater: the oral testimony may fail sometimes, but in the works the truth is undisputed. "The works that are done by me certainly demonstrate my union with God. I would not be able to do such works if I were lacking in that nature."

[5:37] *And the Father who sent me,* he continues, *has himself borne witness to me.* "Besides the works, I have also received a testimony about me from the voice [of the Father]." He talks here about the voice that was heard spoken over him in the course of his baptism that said, "This is my beloved Son with whom I am well pleased."[80] That voice spoke con-

[80]Mt 3:17.

57

cerning Christ-in-the-flesh in order that the Jews might be instructed. Great crowds were present who learned the identity of the one for whom that voice spoke. But since *sons* was a common designation among them—for example, "Sons have I reared and brought up,"[81] and, "I say, 'You are gods, sons of the Most High, all of you,'"[82]—he declared that the dignity of this son was different. Therefore he says, "This is my beloved Son, with whom I am well pleased."[83] He was not similar to them, nor was there only a verbal familiarity in the name. Rather, he was worthy of the highest love because, in his union with the true son, he was made a participant in the honor of sonship.

And again he added, *You have never heard his voice or seen his form,* [5:38] *and you do not have his word abiding in you because you do not believe him whom he has sent.* He justly directed his reproach against them. "Now," he says, "even though you have never seen him or heard the word of him who spoke, you were considered to be worthy of hearing his voice coming from heaven. But this did not bring about humility in you so that you would believe his words. On the contrary, you forgot his word and did not believe in me, the one who was sent by him and for whom testimony was given."

And then, as if this was not sufficient, our Lord confirms what was said about him by discussing those things that were considered to be important among what was said. [5:39] *You search the scriptures because you think that in them you have eternal life; and it is they that testify on my behalf.* [5:40] *Yet you refuse to come to me to have life.* "If you do not want to believe in my works," he says, "you should at least have respect for the scriptures to which you entrust your faith and which you accepted as suitable to prepare you for eternal life. Indeed, you will find abundant testimony in them about me. But you do not even want to obey them

so that, through what is written in them, you might believe my words and have the true life you hope to have through the Holy Scriptures."

After using all that he had said here to reproach those who refused to believe in him and to confirm with many other [arguments] what was said about him, he took the opportunity to reject the foolish conclusion that some might draw from his words by saying, [5:41] *I do not accept glory from human beings.* [5:42] *But I know that you do not have the love of God in you.* "I have used these words not because I want glory from you or because I expect that your faith will be for my advantage but so that I might reprove you for not having the love of God. In fact, you even use what you call your love for God as a pretext for tenaciously persecuting me as if I were vainly or even impiously boasting of equality with him. I can only hope that after being rebuked, you might turn to virtue." He then said aptly: οὐ λαμβάνω, that is, "*I do not accept* glory given to me. My nature is not increased in dignity by the glory that comes from human beings."

With many and varied valid arguments he prevailed against the unbelief of the Jews and confirmed and established beyond doubt what his words meant through the logical arrangement of his argument. When it seemed that they justly accused him of violating the sabbath—if he was only a man like all other men who are subject to the law, then he transgressed the rules—he took the occasion in his reply to their accusation to respond with a logically ordered argument that immediately rehearsed what belonged to the divine nature so that he might demonstrate that he was not subject to the law, like all other men. For the one who is perfectly equal with the Father dwells in him and fully cooperates with him in what he does. "My Father is still working, and I also am working";[84] and again, "whatever the Father does, the Son does likewise."[85]

---

[81]Is 1:2. [82]Ps 82:6. [83]Mt 3:17. [84]Jn 5:17. [85]Jn 5:19.

Then he turned to a discussion of the human nature in order to demonstrate that he had authority and strength from there as well, saying, "The Father loves the Son and shows him all that he himself is doing."[86] Since he wanted to demonstrate the dignity that he had assumed, he again brings up his divinity in order to confirm what had been said. And after he had expanded his subject a bit further with the words that followed, he introduced in an orderly way the question of his honor.

These words were meant to accomplish two things: in the first place, to reply to the accusation alleged against him by the Jews concerning his violation of the sabbath; second, to demonstrate that his dignity was above his visible nature. He accomplished both by confirming by what he said that these had both been done by his divine nature.

Therefore, immediately after alluding to such dignity, he returned to his discussion of the human nature in order to demonstrate that here too he was allowed to do whatever he wanted. And since he needed to speak in the same order about the dignity and honor of the assumed [man], again, after confirming his words with the mention of his divinity, he came back to the order of his narrative by utilizing all these things in his teaching and by noting that he would be the one who would resurrect everyone as well as the one who would be their judge.

He then refuted the opinion of those who thought this was incredible by saying, "You should not be astonished that a man can do these things, because he does them not on his own but through another nature." And in order to fulfill in every aspect the truth of his words, he says that even *now* he does things that amply demonstrate the future resurrection. He not only mentioned John, who testified to those things, but bolstered what he said

even further by noting that the Father himself had testified to them. The accomplished miracles too were sufficient testimony to his words, along with the Scriptures that pronounced many prophecies about these events.

Through all this he demonstrated that the Jews were arrogant because they did not believe the miracles that happened right before their eyes, nor did they believe the prophetic books or even the very prophet who came to them. If they would have believed him it would have been to their definite advantage. And, worst of all, they did not even believe the voice of the Father himself! They only had one reply to all of this: they believed they were fighting in defense of the Father and could not believe someone who said that he had the same power as the Father and asserted that whatever the Father did, he, the Son, could do likewise as he willed. Therefore Christ finally forcefully responded to all of this by saying, [5:43] *I have come in my Father's name and you do not accept me; if another comes in his own name, you will accept him.* He alludes here to what must occur with the antichrist.[87] "At that time," he says, "your arrogance will be shown for what it is when you take refuge in him and receive him. I, on the other hand, refer what I say and accomplish to the Father because my glory is the glory of my Father. Therefore I lead you to the Father and do not offer a pretext for your unbelief. But when the antichrist comes, he will not mention the Father at all but will do everything for his own glory. He will refer to himself as god, making himself appear magnificent and admirable before everyone. Then you will take refuge in him instead of offering supplications to the Father, even invoking a sense of duty toward God as a pretext for what you've done, so that you will at least have the appearance of being steadfast. Therefore, from all that you are doing now, and will do

[86]Jn 5:20. [87]This allusion to the antichrist is rather forced and does not appear in the Gospel text. Theodore is probably influenced by the fact that John is considered to be the author of Revelation as well.

then, it is evident that you are acting according to your inclination to evil."

He then declares why they will believe in [the antichrist]: [5:44] *How can you believe when you accept the glory of a man and do not seek the glory that comes from God?* "Since I," he says, "lead you to God without making any magnificent promises for this life, you run away from me because what I say is too difficult. On the other hand, since the antichrist puts all his glory on display in this life by promising great security and dignity to those who believe in him, because you are enticed by the greed of this life, you will take refuge in him."

After clearly demonstrating by what he has said that they did not persecute him because of their love for the Father, he also proves that they did not even do the will of Moses, who was the minister of the law. Indeed, they even persecuted him as if they were defenders of both![88] This made it clear that they did not honor the giver of the law, nor did they love his minister. Therefore he says, [5:45] *Do not think that I will accuse you before the Father; your accuser is Moses, on whom you have set your hope.* [5:46] *If you believed Moses, you would believe me, for he wrote about me.* [5:47] *But if you do not believe what he wrote, how will you believe what I say?* "You must know this," he says, "that I do not need to accuse you before the Father. The accusation against you is already in the Scriptures. Certainly already once, many centuries ago, Moses wrote about my advent. But now you despise him like me with your disobedience. Therefore, he will act as your severe but also just accuser. You did not want to obey his prophetic words. If you had believed Moses, you would have undoubtedly received me as believers. But since you paid no attention to his words, it is no surprise that you do not believe my words either."

End of the Second Book.

Book Three (John 6:1–8:59)

From here the Evangelist moves on to the account of the miracle of the bread, which all the other Evangelists related as well.[1] However, John reported this episode because of the doctrine that was drawn by our Lord from it and that had been omitted by the others. He believed that this doctrine was essential to his narrative.

[6:1] *After these* words and deeds, he says, *Jesus went to the other side of the sea of Tiberias.* [6:2] *A large crowd kept following him, because they saw the signs that he was doing for the sick.* [6:3] *Jesus went up to the mountain and sat down there with his disciples.* In acting this way he ensured, and appropriately so, that no one would have the false impression that he was always running after the crowd. It was the crowd, rather, that eagerly ran after him. The Evangelist also indicates the time when these events happened, [6:4] *Now the Passover was near,* in order to show that the facts which he was about to relate happened just before this festival.

[6:5] *When he looked up and saw a large crowd coming toward him, Jesus said to Philip, "Where are we to buy bread for these people to eat?"* Through his question to Philip, he intended to expose his disciples to doubt so that they might observe more clearly the miracle he was about to perform. Even though he appears to speak to one disciple only, his words concerned all of them and were offered for their common benefit. The Evangelist explains why he asked this question, adding, [6:6] *He said this to test him, for he himself knew what he was going to do.* To test him, he says, but he means, "to provide him with proof." Indeed, he first kept him in doubt and difficulty with regard to the shortage [of food], but then, when [Philip] saw the miracle accomplished, he learned that everything must always be committed to God and that no one should ever feel embarrassed

---

[88]That is, of both the Father and Moses.   **Book Three** [1]See Mt 14:13-21; Mk 6:31-44; Lk 9:10-17.

because of any shortage.

But Philip answered the question from a human point of view, [6:7] *Two hundred denarii of bread would not be enough for each of them to get a little.* That is, "We cannot spend two hundred denarii, because we do not have them. Such an amount of money is well beyond our means, and even if we had it, it would not be enough for each of them to receive even a small morsel of bread. This means: even if we bought bread for such an amount of money, [the quantity] would be barely enough for each of them to have even a small taste."

After Philip had said this, Andrew, the brother of Simon, added, [6:9] *There is a boy here who has five barley loaves and two fish. But what are they among so many people?* Andrew said this so that they might not think he was hiding the food for his own use. Indeed, Andrew was right in observing that those five loaves were nearly nothing for that great crowd. And he had no other food.

After Philip's expression of profound anxiety and Andrew's acknowledgment of the shortage of food, the Lord himself prepared to accomplish the miracle. First he ordered them to make the crowd sit down. Then the disciples, who did not know what was about to happen, fearfully told the crowd to sit down, fearful of the possibility that there might be some troublemakers among the crowd. [6:10] *So they sat down,* he says. *Now there was a great deal of grass in the place.* Therefore the place where they sat down was pleasing, and the weather was good. It was Nisan,[2] when the earth is usually adorned with growing grass, especially in a region warmer than others. He also indicated the season when he said before, *Now the Passover was near.*

[6:10] *So they sat down, about five thousand in all.* [6:11] *Then Jesus took the five loaves, and when he had given thanks, he distributed them to those who were seated; so also the fish.* The Evangelist also adds, *as much as they wanted,* in order to show that Jesus multiplied the loaves and the fish as much as they wanted and could eat. This is a sign of great power, because he not only solved the shortage of food for those who were hungry but also bestowed his grace so generously that after all were satisfied, the people still found food to carry along with them on the journey or to offer at home according to human custom. This is what the words, *as much as they wanted,* mean.

Thus he continues, *when he had given thanks, he distributed the bread.* He did not do this without a reason. According to common opinion he was considered to be a man, and so he had to begin by giving thanks in order to teach those who saw him that food cannot be received if due thanks to its provider is not given first. After the people had eaten as much as they wanted, he ordered his disciples to gather the fragments left over. [6:13] *So they gathered them up, and filled twelve baskets.* Our Lord ordered them to gather the fragments in order that the experience of the miracle might linger longer in their memory. At the same time, they could still enjoy the food left over too. And after giving this order, he added, *so that nothing may be lost.*

Obviously he didn't care whether anything might get lost. What damage would have derived from that? There was another and more proper pretext for ordering them to gather the fragments left over. He foreknew what would happen later. Indeed, by enjoying that bread a little longer, they would better remember the miracle Jesus had done and would report what happened to other people. Indeed those who saw all that food in the hands of the disciples were bound to ask where it came from, and therefore would learn that a miracle had been done. In his actions the Lord, according to his foreknowledge, usually seems to say one thing while he is doing another so that no suspicion

---

[2]A month of the Jewish calendar that corresponds more or less to April.

of pride might be raised against him because of the greatness of the signs that he did. This is how he acted, for example, with the woman suffering from hemorrhages. Indeed when he asked, "Who touched me?"[3] this enabled the woman to reveal the miracle. In a similar way, through this leftover bread, he shows that he did not perform his miracles according to the necessity of those receiving them, like the prophets, but according to the excellence of his power. When Moses gave the manna to the Jews in the desert, he gave them a certain amount each day. If anyone took more, the usefulness of the food they had gathered for that day was lost. But on the coming of the sabbath, since they had to abstain from work on that day, only then were they allowed to gather a double portion.[4] However, when they reached the region where the fruits of the earth could nourish them, then the bestowing of the manna was suppressed.[5] We see the same thing happening with Elijah. For when he promised the widow that she would lack neither flour nor oil, he placed a limit to his miracle: "Until," he says, "the day that the Lord sends rain on the earth."[6] In a similar way Elisha gave oil to the woman who had debts as far as she had vessels to fill. When they were all full, the oil stopped flowing.[7]

Our Lord, however, did not act in this way. Instead, first he gave them as much as they wanted. Then, after those for whom the miracle had happened were satisfied, he caused all these fragments to remain for those for whom the miracle had been accomplished so that they carried away twelve full baskets. And in order that it might be known everywhere that these fragments had remained according to his will, he arranged things so that the number of the baskets might be equal to the number of the disciples. Therefore this miracle demonstrates the abundance of his grace through the abundance of the food left over and also shows

that he can do anything as he pleases, since he arranged his gifts so that the number of the bearers might be sufficient for the baskets to be carried.

After the miracle was performed, the crowd said, [6:14] *This is indeed the prophet who is to come into the world.* But our Lord knew that they wanted to make him king because they were amazed at this miracle, and so he ran away alone to the mountain. And he did not do this without a purpose either, but in order that they might not believe he had gained authority for his kingdom by election of the people. The disciples, on the other hand, remained where they were while the Lord ascended the mountain.

Since it was getting late, they got into a boat and started to sail toward the shore of Capernaum. The darkness oppressed them in the middle of the sea. Our Lord had not yet come to them, and the sea was highly agitated from the blowing winds. But our Lord was merely setting the conditions for a truly miraculous manifestation [of his power]. When the disciples had already sailed for twenty-five or thirty stadii,[8] the Lord appeared to them while walking on the water. When he came near the boat, a great fear overtook those who were watching this great and wonderful spectacle, especially because it was in deep sea that the Lord easily walked upon the water, when for them it was a fearful thing to merely sit in the boat. But the Lord, in order to calm their fear, said, [6:20] *It is I; do not be afraid.* There was good reason that they were terrified, especially when they thought they were seeing some apparition of the devil. In order to increase the miracle before their eyes, he walked upon the water and did not get into the boat. But the Evangelist says, [6:21] *Then they wanted to take him into the boat, and immediately the boat reached the land toward which they were going.* He records this in order to demonstrate that

---

[3]Lk 8:45. [4]See Ex 16:4-5, 19-22. [5]See Ex 16:35. [6]1 Kings 17:14. [7]See 2 Kings 4:1-7 [8]That is, about 3-4 miles.

not only did they not take him into the boat, but while they were trying to bring him in, both the boat and the Lord reached land at an awesome speed. There was no way they could doubt what the Lord had done or consider him a ghost when they saw that the boat at such speed had reached the land toward which they were going, coupled with the fact that the Lord was with them.

[6:22] *The next day the crowd that had stayed on the other side of the sea saw that there had been no other boat there beside the one the disciples had boarded, and that our Lord had not gone aboard with the disciples, but only the disciples themselves had boarded.* [6:23] *Then some boats from Tiberias came near the place where they had eaten the bread after the Lord had given thanks, and when they saw that neither the Lord nor his disciples were there, they too* [6:24] *got into the boats and went to Capernaum,* where they knew that the disciples had gone, so that they might question them about the Lord. [6:25] *When they found him,* they asked him when he had arrived. Since the disciples could not explain the miraculous nature of his arrival, the crowds, according to a human way of thinking, thought he had perhaps come by boat. Therefore they only questioned him about the time, since they wondered how he had been able to arrive so quickly. They knew well that he had not gotten into the boat with the disciples. And, on the next day, they had not found him among themselves. Therefore they eagerly questioned him about the time only because this aspect was so wonderful for a human mind—when actually it was how he had arrived that was more spectacular than the time element. But it still escaped their comprehension.

Our Lord paid no attention to their inquiry, or to the manner in which they looked for him, which seems to be full of affection. He foresaw their intention, that is, how and why they looked for him. And so he said to them, [6:26] *Very truly, I tell you, you are looking for me, not because you saw signs, but because you ate your fill of the loaves.* "I know," he says, "the reason why you look for me. It is not my power after performing the miracle that you admire, nor is it that your love for me is properly intentioned. On the contrary, you run after the abundance of bread as dedicated followers of gluttony and pleasure, as if you believe that happiness consists in being filled with food while living in sloth. This is also why you tried to make me king. Through sheer force of royal authority I would be bound to take care of you, and by necessity would be compelled to provide you always with food in this way."

After he had reproached them on both these counts, namely gluttony and sloth, he continued by saying, [6:27] *Do not work for the food that perishes, but for the food that endures for eternal life which the Son of Man will give you. For it is on him that the Father has set his seal.* "I," he says, "ask you not to revel in sloth but in a willingness to cultivate and perform works that are good and excellent—not those by which the belly is satisfied for a short time but then is hungry again because the food previously received perishes, but those works whose nourishment makes you a participant in eternal life where you can remain incorruptible without needing any more food. This concept is similar to that expressed to the Samaritan woman.[9] Indeed he also said there, "Everyone who drinks of this water will be thirsty again, but those who drink of the water that I will give them will never be thirsty. The water that I will give will become in them a spring of water gushing up to eternal life."[10] He demonstrates the uselessness of natural water that satisfies thirst for only a short time, whereas he displays the power of that which he will give for eternal life in which whoever receives the Holy Spirit becomes participant. He says the

---

[9] See Jn 4:4-42, where Jesus speaks of the living water, that is, the eternal life in Christ.   [10] Jn 4:13-14.

same thing in this passage, "This is the effect of material food: it satisfies our hunger for a short time, but soon leaves us hungry again. But the food which I give confers eternal life," since the purpose of his coming is to give [the gift of] resurrection to every person, and after resurrection, incorruptibility. This is what he appears to be expounding in everything he says. His actions in the episode of the paralyzed man are also similar to this. There,[11] when replying to the accusations put forward by the Jews, he only mentioned his dignity and divinity. Had he done otherwise, they would never have believed what he had said about his human nature because of its apparent weakness. So here too he uses the question of the Jews as an opportunity to talk about himself and to demonstrate what he was able to give and would give to those who believed in him. He alludes to his divinity in order to confirm what he had said—that is, that this gift can occur by means of food.

After making this great and wonderful statement that this food would give eternal life and make the body incorruptible instead of nourishing it for only a short time, he went on to say, which the Son of Man will give you. "You will taste this food," he said, "through what I do. I will suffer for you, and with my suffering I will forgive your sins. The food that you must eat is a symbol of my death." And in order to clarify what he had said, he most appropriately added the words, It is on him that God the Father has set his seal; that is, [the Father] made him the origin of this spiritual food—the very one who himself was healed, according to the inscrutable decision of God, when he was raised after he died. Through his union with God the Word, he rightly and deservedly invites to this kind of life those who come to the sacrament[12] according to his will.

[The Evangelist] always uses the expression set the seal for the word confirmed. This expression does not at all refer, as some have thought, to the similarity of his divine generation. John [the Baptist] too had said, "Whoever has accepted his testimony has set his seal to this, that God is true";[13] that is, he has confirmed and established the truth of God as much as that is possible, just as a "blessing" is spoken by us to God, and by God to us. A blessing is spoken by us, certainly, when it is said, "Bless the Lord, O my soul,"[14] and by God to us when it is said, "The Lord bless you from Zion."[15] But the same power is not present in both. A blessing is pronounced on our part when we speak of the greatness of God in what we say; on the part of God when he grants us his help. In the same way, when among ourselves we say, "Set the seal," we for our part demonstrate the truth about God through our faith and, as much as we can, show that his words are true. It is said with reference to God when he causes the assumed man through his works to grant eternal life to others as well.

The Jews, either because they did not understand the power of his words or wanted to hear them more clearly, said, [6:28] What must we do to perform the works of God? Our Lord answers them, [6:29] This is the work of God, that you believe in him whom he has sent. Knowing that what he had said about the mysteries was beyond their comprehension, he did not rush immediately into a discourse about it. Instead he found a way suitable for such teaching, saying, "This is the work of God, that you believe in me. This is, indeed, the way through which you may come to be instructed about all the other [mysteries]. It is impossible to have doubts about the things that have been said if you believe in me. And you cannot accept them unless you believe because they are well beyond your comprehension."

[6:30] So they said to him, "What sign are you going to give us then, so that we may see it and believe you? What work are you going

---

[11]Jn 5:9-47.　[12]The sacrament of the Eucharist.　[13]Jn 3:33.　[14]Ps 103:1.　[15]Ps 128:5.

to perform?" Great is the arrogance of the Jews! When that magnificent miracle was still before their eyes, and while the crumbs of the food which they had enjoyed were still between their teeth, they asked him for a sign to confirm his power. But maybe, since they understood the magnitude of the miracle he had done and that it was useless to ask for another—maybe they wanted to lessen this sign through a comparison with another. Therefore in order for their question not to appear too rash—hoping people would believe that they rightly wanted to see a greater sign—they say, [6:31] *Our ancestors ate the manna in the wilderness; as it is written, "He gave them bread from heaven to eat."*[16] Through the comparison with the manna they intended to diminish the gift of the bread so that they might demonstrate that they rightly considered Moses superior to Jesus. But the Scriptures show us that the opposite is true. Indeed, when the manna was given to them in the wilderness, this did not stop them from saying about God, "Even though he struck the rock so that water gushed out and torrents overflowed, can he also give us bread?"[17] Back then, they asked for bread as if there were something better, and offended God by insinuating that he could not give it to them. Now, these people prefer the gift of the manna more, even when they are receiving something that appears to be far greater, because they considered the bread given to their ancestors as something extraordinary. It was only right that they would follow in the tracks of those whom they called *fathers* who, after receiving what had appeared to them to be so uncommon, should have been able to recognize the greatness of the one who was to come. But the ingratitude of those who came before[18] and those who now come later is one and the same: both dared to criticize the gift they had before them by comparing it with what they were missing.

[6:32] *Then Jesus said to them, "Very truly, I tell you, it was not Moses who gave you the bread from heaven, but it is my Father who gives you the true bread from heaven. [6:33] For the bread of God is that which comes down from heaven and gives life to the world."* Even though the Lord could have used the words proffered by their ancestors in the wilderness to show that his gift of bread was greater than the manna, he abstained from doing so because even when the gift of the manna was attributed to God, they still grumbled as if he would have not been able to give bread to them. He appropriately avoided trying to prove that [his miracle] was greater than the other by way of comparison. Indeed, by comparing himself to the Father and not to Moses, he might have suggested that he considered himself to be greater than the Father. That would have rightly given the Jews a reason to rebuke him. But he gave them an enigmatic reply, bringing together under one concept many different strains of thought. Since he did not express all of these concepts, but compressed them into one, he made his doctrine appear enigmatic. The words: *it was not Moses who gave you; but it is my Father who gives you,* seem to be united with regard to sense, and apparently their meaning is one. But they are also distinct from each other, and each of them possesses its own meaning. Certainly the words, *it was not Moses who gave you the bread from heaven,* have a meaning complete in themselves. But they are still also said enigmatically. He means, in fact, "If those ancient [gifts] seem to you to be extraordinary, it still was not Moses who gave them to you, but I." But this is only suggested by his silence, because it would have been quite difficult for his hearers to understand if he had said that he himself had given them bread in the wilderness. After all, he was a man and looked like a man. When he later said, "Before Abraham was, I am,"[19] they did not want to lis-

---

[16]See Ps 78:24. [17]Ps 78:20. [18]Those who ate manna in the wilderness under Moses. [19]Jn 8:58.

ten to him, but threw stones at him. Therefore, with good reason he enigmatically hinted by his silence that he was the giver of the manna. But he added, *it is my Father who gives you the true bread from heaven*, meaning, "you also received this from me. However, if you want to obey me, leave the gift of the bread and the manna; both of these are worthless and weak. Desire the true bread, which the Father gives you from above and which comes down from heaven and gives everyone eternal life."

Evidently he speaks here about his own body, which must be eaten symbolically as part of the institution of the mysteries.[20] The bread that was given by our Lord to his disciples is the symbol of the nourishment of his body, which up to this day we place on the altar and take with our hands as the body of the Lord. He expounds this clearly through the following words: "And the bread that I will give is my flesh."[21] Therefore we must not be amazed if he says that his body *comes down from heaven and gives life to the world*. It is from heaven, indeed, that the Son of Man who was assumed comes on the last day for the resurrection and life of all, as was said by the apostle, "The first man was from the earth, a man of dust; the second, the Lord, is from heaven."[22] When our Lord descends from heaven, it is most certainly not with the earthly body of Adam, for it is clearly evident that body[23] was formed in the womb of Mary. Rather, the apostle intends to indicate the future general resurrection [when he writes] of our Lord's advent from heaven. If our Lord now says here that his body has descended from heaven, realize that this was his custom so that he might attribute to his human nature those qualities that concerned his divinity, but not because it[24] possesses these by its own nature, according to what we have explained above. If, therefore, he said this about his future descent when he will give life to the world and raise everyone, everywhere

from the dead—and if he also said this about his present advent, meaning that the divinity that exists in him while it is in heaven was always in him and now is in him—he said this with good reason.

[6:34] *They said to him, "Sir, give us this bread always."* Since they were still consumed by their gluttony, when they heard of the true bread, they thought that the Lord was promising to give them material food forever. Therefore they asked for this bread because they hoped that they would be fed without having to do any work from then on if they tasted this bread. What does the Lord answer them? [6:35] *I am the bread of life. Whoever comes to me will never be hungry, and whoever believes in me will never be thirsty.* "If you really desire to taste this bread," he says, "I am this bread. Whoever, indeed, obeys and believes in me will receive such blessings that he will never suffer from thirst or hunger again." He did not immediately say, "whoever eats me," but *whoever comes to me and believes in me*, avoiding for the moment what he first said because of its difficulty and holding it for a more appropriate time. Moreover, since they did not believe when he said these things, he showed himself by no means ignorant of their unbelief, admonishing them by what he said so that they might believe, which was the only suitable way to teach people like this. And so he said, [6:36] *But I said to you that you have seen me and yet you do not believe.* "I said this," he says, "because I certainly knew that, even after seeing the miracle, you would remain in your unbelief. I knew this well and predicted it to you."

And so, since he intended to teach them— as he had done in his previous conversations with them[25]—that even though they thought they believed in the Father and that it was their love for him that incited their hostility toward Jesus,[26] they were entirely wrong. Therefore he said, [6:37] *Everything that the*

---

[20]The Eucharist. [21]Jn 6:51. [22]1 Cor 15:47. [23]That is, his body. [24]That is, his human nature. [25]See Jn 5:19-47. [26]See Jn 5:18.

Father gives me will come to me, and anyone who comes to me I will never drive away. "Do not think that you believe in the Father if you do not believe in me," he says. "Such thinking is so far from the truth that it actually opposes the truth. For the Father receives those who believe in me, and he brings to me those who truly belong to him. Whoever obeys the will of the Father has no doubts about me. I do not drive away those who behave in this way. Just as those near to the Father come to me, so I love those near to me whom he gave me." And he corroborates what he said by saying, [6:38] *for I have come down from heaven, not to do my own will, but the will of him who sent me.* How could he not also do his [Father's] will? If indeed he wants the same things as the Father, he not only did the will [of the Father], but also his own. But the meaning of his words is, "I came not in order to gather a following only for myself in opposition to the Father, but to bring everyone to my Father through their faith in me. Nobody can believe in me and be alienated from the Father." He said this in order to reprove the Jews, demonstrating that there was no logic in their unbelief.

[6:39] *And this is the will of him who sent me, that I should lose nothing at all that he has given me, but raise it up on the last day.* [6:40] *This is indeed the will of my Father, that all who see the Son and believe in him may have eternal life; and I will raise them up on the last day.* He said two things: that all must believe in him and that eternal life must be granted to all those who believe. Appropriately, he connected both to the will of the Father by saying, "This is the will of the Father, that all should believe in me," and, "those who believe in me should receive this gift from me." In this way, they are reproved by these two arguments as if they were opposing the will of the Father himself. Therefore, if the Father equally desires both of these things, which they first did not accept and then did not believe, in both they were caught as resisting the will of the Father.

[6:41] *Then the Jews began to complain about him because he said, "I am the bread that came down from heaven."* [6:42] *They were saying, "Is not this Jesus, the Son of Joseph, whose father and mother we know? How can he now say, 'I have come down from heaven?'"* The cause for their complaining was not in his words but in the obstinacy of their minds. There could only be two reasons, in fact, why those who heard him did not accept what they heard: either what he said did not convince them, or what he said was full of wickedness. Our Lord was safe from either accusation. He fully removed any suspicion of iniquity by referring everything to the Father and attributing to his [Father's] will everything that happened. He also threw out any possibility that his words might prove unconvincing because he performed the miracle of the multiplication of the bread. He then proceeded to talk to them about spiritual nourishment in order to convince them through an accomplished sign about something that seemed unbelievable. But the Jews understood none of this, challenging him instead with a question about his father and mother, saying that someone who had a human birth could not have come from heaven, because they did not understand the Lord's symbolic way of speaking.

[6:43] *Jesus answered them and said, "Do not complain among yourselves.* [6:44] *No one can come to me unless drawn by the Father who sent me; and I will raise that person up on the last day."* It is clear that Jesus always spoke cautiously with the Jews lest it seem that he was averting their attention from the Father. He also did not want to provide them with any justification in their argument with him. Here too, he reproves their foolishness by saying, "Your complaint is not leveled against me but against the Father. If you really were close to the Father, you would not refuse to believe me. Indeed, it would be impossible for someone to be mine if the Father had not accepted him out of the goodness of his own heart and brought him to me. These are the kinds of people I receive, and I have due concern for this deposit entrusted to me by the Father. I will crown them and give them the reward of being raised again." All these words confirm what he had said above: *And this is the will of him who sent me, that I should lose nothing at all that he has given me, but raise it up on the last day.*

And he further corroborates what he has said with the following words, [6:45] *It is written in the Prophets, "And they shall all be taught by God."*[27] *Everyone who heard and learned from the Father comes to me.* "Recognize," he says, "that it is written in the Prophets that everyone must be taught by the Father at one time or another. This has now, in fact, occurred. Indeed, through his invisible grace the Father is bringing to me those whose goodwill has made them worthy, since what he has done is just as valuable as a sermon or teaching would be for them." And since, when he said, *everyone who heard*, they could have taken this literally as though the *father* to whom he was referring might be construed as his father Joseph, he added, [6:46] *Not that anyone has seen the Father except him who is from God; he has seen the Father.* "I do not say this," he says, "as if you were able to see the Father. Only the one who is from the Father knows the Father, and he is the only one who always enjoys looking upon him."

After saying this and referring everything to the person of the Father, he added, [6:47] *Truly, truly, I say to you, he who believes has eternal life.* "Therefore," he says, "do not doubt what I am saying. I will give eternal life to those who are mine." [6:48] *I am the bread of life.* He was right in concluding that his words, "I give eternal life," did not convince his hearers. In fact, bread that can be eaten hardly seems to possess in its nature the power to give eternal life. How could they possibly believe that it might give others what it did not have

in its own nature? He now solves the difficulty concerning what he had said by calling himself *bread* as an example of using the word symbolically. Bread, indeed, even though it does not have life in its own nature, can improve and support human life because, according to the design of God, it was destined for this purpose from the beginning. "Therefore," he says, "not even now, when you consider the nature [of bread] should you doubt what I am saying." Indeed, he had said earlier, "The Father set his seal on him,"[28] in order to reveal that he confers these gifts because God entrusted him with this task.

Then, since he wanted to indicate his dignity by a comparison, he said, [6:49] *Your fathers ate the manna in the wilderness and they died.* [6:50] *This is the bread that comes down from heaven, that a man may eat of it and not die.* "Your fathers who ate manna," he says, "were not only *not* delivered from the sentence of death, but every last one of them in fact died in the wilderness, and not one of them was found worthy of entering the promised land. But whoever eats this food is freed from death." It is worth noting that he says, *may not die*, not "may not taste death." Indeed there is no real death when one dies and believes that death has been defeated. This is what the blessed Paul said, "But we would not have you ignorant, brothers, concerning those who are asleep, that you may not grieve as others do who have no hope,"[29] by referring to "those who are asleep" as all those who hope in the resurrection. In another passage he says, "What do people mean by being baptized on behalf of the dead?"[30] referring to "the dead" as those who have no hope of resurrection, as if those who do have the hope of resurrection were not mortal. Our Lord did the same thing when he said, "He is not the God of the dead but of the living."[31] He had no desire to call those who expect the resurrection "dead."

---

[27]Is 54:13.   [28]Jn 6:27.   [29]1 Thess 4:13.   [30]1 Cor 15:29.   [31]Mk 12:27.

[6:51] *I am the living bread that came down from heaven; if anyone eats of this bread, he will live forever; and the bread that I shall give for the life of the world is my flesh.* Here he clearly appears to call his body *bread.* He calls it by this name figuratively either because bread is eaten or as handing over a type of the mysteries. He mentioned that this bread came from heaven, as we have explained above. He does not mean that his body came down from there but is rather highlighting the sublime nature of his gift, and by alluding to the greatness of the Godhead, confirms what he is saying. Therefore his use of allegory was not difficult for the Jews either. And afterward this teaching would become clear and certain to those for whom these words were said and written.

After our Lord had said these things, clearly indicating that the word *bread* referred to his body because it was to be eaten, the Jews argued again with each other, saying, [6:52] *How can this man give us his flesh to eat?* when nature itself does not allow this. And they opposed what he was saying as something difficult and sinful as though he were asking them to really eat human flesh.

[6:53] *So Jesus said to them, "Very truly, I tell you, unless you eat the flesh of the Son of Man and drink his blood, you have no life in you."* He does not say, "You do not live," but "you have no life in you." In other words, you will not be immortal. Certainly it is possible to live because the cause of this mortal life comes from somewhere else. But no one can be immortal if he does not receive this life in him. Therefore he repeats the same idea, [6:54] *Those who eat my flesh and drink my blood have eternal life, and I will raise them up on the last day;* [6:55] *for my flesh is true food and my blood is true drink.* "This is," he says, "true food and true drink for those who eat it." [6:56] *Those who eat my flesh and drink my blood abide in me, and I in them.* Here he refers to the fact that

our food and drink are usually transformed into the nature of our body, which is nourished in this way. And what constantly perishes is renewed through the assimilation of those elements that appear to have an affinity with our body. Using the example of what happens in our body, he therefore repeated his argument and said, "Those who eat my flesh and drink my blood," will be joined to me through the effectual working of the Holy Spirit. They will possess, as it were, a natural union with me, enjoying eternal life." This is also what the apostle Paul said, "He will transform the body of our humiliation that it may be conformed to the body of his glory."[32]

It is clear that everything he said here does not touch in any real sense on the Godhead. And to illustrate this even further, he adds, [6:57] *Just as the living Father sent me, and I live because of the Father, so whoever eats me will live because of me.* Against the heretics who assert that these words diminish the divinity of the Only Begotten,[33] the order itself of the words is sufficient for us because it shows the purpose of his argument. The addition that he immediately makes is also sufficient. *And I live because of the Father* is connected to the sentence, *so whoever eats me will live because of me.* Who is so foolish as to say that the Godhead is eaten? We will now show in our commentary, with the help of God, the meaning of this section.

Since it is impossible for a body to give eternal life, he offers the following concise explanation: "The Father," he says, "who always lives, gave me eternal life—something that does not belong to my [created] nature. And through me, he gives life to those who eat me." After referring to the Father all that is elevated above the nature of the body, and after confirming this accurately so that the Jews might not object to it—they could not object that a body had no power to give if it has received

---

[32]Phil 3:21.   [33]This verse was usually quoted by the Arians to prove the alleged inferiority of the Son.

that power from the Father—as if further corroborating his argument and definitively setting his seal on it, he says, [6:58] *Not like your ancestors who ate manna and died: the one who eats this bread will live forever.* "This is the bread," he says, "that I mentioned to you at the beginning, and that came down from heaven and gives eternal life. This bread is highly superior to the sustenance the manna provided because those who ate the manna died like all other mortals. This bread received from the Father what it did not have in its nature, and therefore gives others the possibility of actually participating in him." He adds here as well *that came down from heaven* in order to suggest—by saying "it was given to them by the Father"—that he is also alluding to something else, that is, to the nature that is in him.

After this the Evangelist said, [6:59] *He said these things while he was teaching in the synagogue at Capernaum.* It is evident that the crowd, after moving immediately to Capernaum and seeing the Lord in the synagogue, addressed these words to him and listened to the entire discussion as well as the preaching. When they heard these things, as the Evangelist reported, many among the disciples said, [6:60] *This teaching is difficult; who can accept it?* Since they had understood in a human sense that flesh had to be eaten, they thought that it was sacrilegious and certainly too difficult. The Evangelist probably means that the disciples said those words among themselves, because he adds, [6:61] *But Jesus, being aware that his disciples were complaining about it, said to them, "Does this offend you?"* It would have been superfluous to say "being aware," if the disciples had said what they did openly. Rather, standing in awe of him because of his dignity—as is appropriate for disciples—they kept these things among themselves. But Jesus knew what they were thinking because of his

divine power. And so he said to them, *Does this offend you?* [6:62] *Then what if you were to see the Son of Man ascending to where he was before?* "I know that you were offended by these words that seem to you to be completely incredible because you only look at the nature that is visible. But when you see him[34] ascending to heaven and returning to his higher dignity, will you not even then believe his words? Will you not rather blush at such a vision?" He proves here as well, when he talks of the great things that his human nature does, that these things do not happen because of that nature but because of his divine nature. The phrase, *ascending to where he was before*, is not suitable to his human nature. In fact, he did not come down from heaven and then ascend to it again. But [this is said] in order to assert allegorically that "he will ascend to heaven," that is, to the place where the one who is in him resides and who, according to the majesty of his nature, gave to him of himself and brought him up above. Therefore that nature through which he was able to ascend conferred upon him the power of giving eternal life.

[6:63] *It is the spirit that gives life; the flesh is useless.* Above, after a long discussion, he ended that discussion by saying he was the Son of Man and telling them, "Do not be amazed, I can do nothing on my own."[35] In the same way, here too, after telling them what his body would give to those who eat it, he aptly resolved their doubt about his words by saying, "It is not the flesh that through its nature grants this benefit, but it is the divine nature which is not immersed in matter that bestows this life through the body."[36] Here he is clearly speaking about the [divine] nature of the Only Begotten. Indeed after the phrase, *ascending to where he was before*, he added, *It is the spirit that gives life; the flesh is useless.* In other words, through his union with this

---

[34]That is, the Son of Man. [35]See Jn 5:27-28. [36]This is clearly Theodore's paraphrase. See translator's introduction, esp. quotation from Norris, p. xxvi.

[spiritual/divine] nature he gives [eternal life] to those who eat him. Indeed, in the eucharistic mystery—a mystery accomplished among us by means of a symbol of the body of the Lord through the descent of the Holy Spirit—we believe that this same thing happens. This should make it clear that his nature is equal to the Spirit. And [the Spirit] was also in the body of our Lord in the form of anointing[37] and is always with him. It prepared for him his union and participation with God the Word. [6:63] *The words that I have spoken to you are spirit and life.* "Therefore," he says, "the things I am saying to you must also be understood in a spiritual way, and then you will be able to believe that they are eternal life."

[6:64] *But among you there are some who do not believe.* Through these words he demonstrates that even though his preaching is addressed to the entire crowd, he knows the thoughts of all and does not teach only for the sake of appearances. Therefore the Evangelist adds, *For Jesus knew from the first who were the ones that did not believe, and who was the one who would betray him.* [6:65] *And he said, "For this reason I have told you that no one can come to me unless it is granted by the Father."* "I," he says, "knowing your inner thoughts, said that no one who was not chosen by the Father could come to me. Indeed whoever is far removed from knowledge of the Father cannot have any association with me either."

[6:66] *Because of this many of his disciples turned back and no longer went about with him.* Evidently here he refers to disciples other than the Twelve. Indeed, he immediately adds, [6:67] *Jesus asked the Twelve, "Do you also wish to go away?"* He shows that it was not the number but the thought that counted. Simon answered for them all by saying, [6:68] *Lord, to whom shall we go? You have the words of eternal life.* [6:69] *We have come to believe and know that you are the Christ, the Son of the liv-*

ing God. "Their opinion is not ours. We know, indeed, and are certain that you are the Messiah, the Son of God whom we expected. And your words prepare eternal life for believers and grant what they promise."

What did the Lord say after this? [6:70] *"Did I not choose you, the Twelve? Yet one of you is a devil."* [6:71] *He was speaking of Judas son of Simon Iscariot, for he, though one of the Twelve, was going to betray him.* Since Simon answered in the name of all, Jesus clearly showed that he knew who in his inner thoughts intended to follow him and who would go in the opposite direction.

[7:1] *After this Jesus went about in Galilee,* since up to this point he had avoided going to Judea because of the hatred of the Jews. Because the Festival of Booths was near—and everyone had to go up quickly to Jerusalem for the festival—his brothers said to him, [7:3] *Leave here and go to Judea so that your disciples also may see the works you are doing;* [7:4] *for no one who wants to be widely known acts in secret. If you do these things, show yourself to the world.* Their human thoughts led his brothers to say these words to him. They wanted him to reveal himself before everyone through his signs so that they might also be glorified through him. They did not possess a mature faith in him if they believed that he needed to reveal himself completely before everyone concerning the nature hidden in him and that he had to be exalted over everyone. The Evangelist alludes to this by saying, [7:5] *For not even his brothers believed in Jesus,* meaning that their opinion about him was extremely weak and vile.

[7:6] *Jesus said to them, My time has not yet come, but your time is always here.* He says, "Any time is good for you to go up[38] and reveal yourselves. Indeed, time makes no difference where you are concerned. I, on the other hand, keep this wonderful and excellent nature hid-

---

[37]That is, "the chrism."   [38]To Jerusalem.

den within because this is necessary for the plan of salvation. My time will come when I will clearly make known who I am before everyone." Here he refers to his crucifixion and to the events that happened afterward, as he also said in another passage, "The hour has come for the Son of Man to be glorified."[39] Therefore, in order to show why he avoided going up to Jerusalem, he said, [7:7] *The world cannot hate you, but it hates me because I testify against it that its works are evil. [7:8] Go to the festival yourselves. I am not going to this festival, for my time has not yet fully come.* "You go up, as is convenient, because nothing prevents you. But they hate me because I reprove their iniquity. Therefore I will abate their anger through silence and delay. And so it is prudent for me not to go up now. I will go up at the right time." Cautiously, but appropriately, he said, *I am not going now,* meaning that he would go up, but just not right at the beginning of the festival.

The Evangelist added, [7:9] *After saying this, he remained in Galilee. [7:10] But after his brothers had gone to the festival, then he also went, not publicly but as it were in secret.* Some people were angry with him, but others wanted to see him, being led by their love for him after the miracles he had performed. And so this delay was advantageous for both parties—for his adversaries because their anger was abated, for the others because their love was increased.

Then the Evangelist says, [7:11] *The Jews were looking for him at the festival.* It was as if the miracles he had performed and the words he had spoken still resounded in their ears. *And they were saying, "Where is he?"* Evidently these were the words of those who were angry at him, and so he adds, [7:12] *And there was considerable complaining about him among the crowds. While some were saying, "He is a good man,"* others were saying, "No, he is deceiving

the crowd." [7:13] *Yet no one would speak openly about him for fear of the Jews.* His delay came about because of his extraordinary prudence. In this way, the anger and fury of those who did not see him was immediately abated, while the love of those who wished to see him was inflamed even more. Therefore the Evangelist says, [7:14] *About the middle of the festival Jesus went up into the temple and began to teach. [7:15] The Jews were astonished at this, saying, "How does this man have such learning when he has never been taught?"* And how does he employ such great doctrine? Our Lord, intimating the reason for their disbelief, according to his custom, said to them, [7:16] *My teaching is not mine but his who sent me. [7:17] Anyone who resolves to do the will of God will know whether my teaching is from God or whether I am speaking on my own.* "Do not make the reason for your disbelief a reason to avenge God," he says. "Indeed, I am making it clear to you that these words are his,[40] and I am leading you to him through my words." If you want to do the will of God, you will understand that my teaching is his, and is not at all foreign to him." He makes it clear here that the phrase, *I am not speaking on my own,* refers to his counterpart,[41] certainly not to his own weakness. Through the words, *You will know whether my teaching is from God or whether I am speaking on my own,* he means, "You will understand whether my teaching is from him or against him." In a similar way it was said, "The Son can do nothing on his own,"[42] as we have already explained above. This merely indicates perfect harmony.

And then he further clarified his words even more. [7:18] *Those who speak on their own seek their own glory; but the one who seeks the glory of him who sent him is true, and there is nothing false in him.* "If," he says, "I had wanted to turn you away from God and draw you to me, it would have been evident that I was

---

[39]Jn 12:23. [40]That is, God's. [41]Theodore is probably using the term *counterpart* to describe the equality of will and action in the Father-Son relationship. [42]Jn 5:19.

teaching you a doctrine contrary to God. But since I lead you to him through my words, it is clearly evident that these words that are said to you are just, and that those who want to reprove them as sinful have no reason to do so." But since in the previous festival he had been accused of violating the law when he healed the paralyzed man,[43] he again directed his words toward this topic by saying, [7:19] *Did not Moses give you the law? Yet none of you keeps the law. Why are you looking for an opportunity to kill me?* "If," he says, "you really defend the law of Moses, prove to me that you actually keep it and tell me why you want to kill me. What you are doing is contrary to the law more than any other violation."[44]

[7:21] *Jesus answered them, "I performed one work, and all of you are astonished."* The expression, *you are astonished*, must not be interpreted here as praise. It means, "You were amazed at something you thought was extraordinary and admirable and at the same time were angry at something you thought was a violation of a command that God gave us through Moses." Then he added, [7:22] *Moses gave you circumcision (it is, of course, not from Moses, but from the Patriarchs), and you circumcise a man on the sabbath. [7:23] If a man receives circumcision on the sabbath in order that the law of Moses may not be broken, are you angry with me because I healed a man's whole body on the sabbath?* He employed a very convincing argument. "Moses," he says, "established circumcision and the sabbath, and ordered that men be circumcised on the sabbath. It was appropriate for him to have established the sabbath—indeed nobody had observed it until then. On the other hand, when he established circumcision, it was superfluous to do so because it had already been established by the patriarchs. But he established circumcision too in order to teach us that observance [of the sabbath] is not compulsory in case of necessity, and that there are occasions when it can be broken. If the sabbath can be broken for circumcision because Moses so ordered—and we don't consider such instances to be a violation of the law—why do you think the fact that a man was healed on the sabbath is a violation of the law?"

And he further shamed them by saying, [7:24] *Do not judge by appearances, but judge with right judgment.* "If a transgressor of the law," he says, "is someone who performs something on the sabbath, the first to be blamed is Moses. But if he is not considered to be a transgressor of the law, then how much more should my action remove me from blame." After he had said these words, they remained silent because they had been struck by an evident rebuke.

[7:25] *Now some of the people of Jerusalem were saying, "Is not this the man whom they are trying to kill? [7:26] And here he is, speaking openly, but they say nothing to him! Can it be that the authorities really know that this is the Messiah? [7:27] Yet we know where this man is from; but when the Messiah comes, no one will know where he is from."* Since what they said was clearly false—they knew from the word of the prophets that the Messiah would arise from Bethlehem and from the house of David; this much is clear from those who were questioned by Herod and answered him[45]—for this reason the Lord said to them, [7:28] *You know me and you know where I am from. I have not come on my own. But the one who sent me is true, and you do not know him. [7:29] I know him, because I am from him, and he sent me.* "Now," he says, "you know where the Messiah

---

[43]See Jn 5:1-47. [44]According to J.-M. Vosté, editor of the Syriac text, the comment on 7:20 which must have followed this passage, was expunged because of the verse's content, which might appear to be disrespectful to the divine dignity of Christ: *The crowd answered, "You have a demon! Who is trying to kill you?"* In the Greek fragments published by Migne (see PG 66:749B-C) the comment on 7:20 is actually included, but it appears to be a mere interpolation of a passage taken from John Chrysostom *Homilies on the Gospel of John* 49. See CSCO 4 3:158; Latin translation, p. 112. [45]See Mt 2:4-5

would come from and certainly know where I am from. From this you can ascertain that the prophecy about me is true. I indeed did not come to do my will against the Father [. . .].[46] If you really consider the fact that you do not know where he comes from as a sign of the coming of the Messiah, realize that you do not know me perfectly. Even though you know me by external appearance, you do not know what abides inside of me. And since you do not know my Father, it is evident that you do not know who I am either. I do know the Father, and since I was sent by him, I do his will. Therefore you have no excuse for your disbelief. From the fact that I do everything according to the will of the Father, and from the things you perceive about me with your senses, you can ascertain that I am the Messiah. You can also tell this from the fact that in me there is something hidden that goes beyond your comprehension [. . .][47] because you also said that this is a sign of the coming of the Messiah."

[7:30] After he said this, they tried to arrest him, but no one laid hands on him—as if they were prevented by divine power—because the time had not yet come for his passion to be accomplished. It appears then that he could not be arrested by them if he did not want it so. But his words also were not without benefit, as the Evangelist said, because many believed that he was the Messiah. They said, "It is impossible that the one who should come would do greater signs than he." Yet the Pharisees, since they could not stand this opinion of the people, were consumed with envy and anger. Together with the high priests they sent their guards to arrest him. But they were prevented by divine intervention and could not do it.

Making it known that he would accept suffering when it seemed right to him, our Lord said to them, [7:33] *I will be with you a little while longer, and then I am going to him who sent me.* [7:34] *You will search for me, but you will not find me; and where I am, you cannot come.* "Why," he says, "are you eager to arrest me? Why are you trying to do something that is not in your power? If you can wait for a short while, I will give myself to you. Indeed, after my death, I am going to my Father. And when I depart to be with him, I will certainly withdraw from you. Then, I will be exalted over you so that, even if you look for me, you will not find me. And even though you want to, you cannot come where I am because I will be raised over you in glory and honor." But the Jews did not understand any of these words. And this is not surprising, because even the disciples, as we have already demonstrated many times, could not understand the words that were said at that time. It was only at the end that they learned these things from the facts.

Since they did not understand his words, they gave him a foolish answer by saying to each other, [7:35] *Where does this man intend to go that we will not find him? Does he intend to go to the Diaspora among the Greeks and teach the Greeks?* [7:36] *What does he mean?* So they were in doubt about his words because they thought about them in a human way.

[7:37] *On the last day of the festival, the great day, while Jesus was standing there, he cried out, "Let anyone who is thirsty come to me,* [7:38] *and let the one who believes in me come and drink. As the Scripture has said, 'Out of the believer's heart shall flow rivers of living water.'"* [7:39] *Now he said this about the Spirit, which believers in him were to receive; for as yet there was no Spirit, because Jesus was not yet glorified.* At the beginning of the festival he avoided going up. When the festival was approaching its middle stage, he did go up and began by speaking humbly and ascribing everything to the

---

[46]The editor J.-M. Vosté indicates a lacuna in the text here. See above [1:19] and CSCO 4 3:i-iv and 159. [47]The editor J.-M. Vosté indicates a lacuna in the text here. See above [1:19] and CSCO 4 3:i-iv and 160.

Father. Now, at the end of the festival, when the crowds were about to return home, he clearly drew everyone to faith in him. Clearly they referred the words, *As the Scripture has said*, to the sentence following and began to ask where the phrase, *shall flow rivers of living water*, is written. But the words, *As the Scripture has said*, must be referred to the previous sentence since in the Holy Scriptures there are many prophecies about the Messiah, as he had already said in another passage: "Those scriptures testify on my behalf."[48] Therefore he, looking to incite every person to faith in him, means, "Whoever follows the Scriptures and believes in me will be filled with grace." And this grace will not only be like a river that never dries up, but will also flow out of him so that it is not only sufficient for him but is beneficial to many others as well. Therefore, after the apostles had received the Spirit they proved of benefit to many others, thanks to the gift they had received. We also must understand that the term "Holy Spirit" often does not indicate the person of the Holy Spirit, but its works and grace. Here he evidently was talking about the grace that the apostles would receive and that would be transmitted to others through them. But this operation had not yet been performed. Indeed grace will begin in those who receive it, and will increase, and sometimes will decrease because of the sin of those who receive it. Therefore Paul too said, "Do not quench the Spirit."[49]

After hearing these words, some again said, [7:40] *This is really the prophet.* [7:41] *Others said, "This is the Messiah."* But the Scriptures did not intend to say that one is the prophet and another is the Messiah. And yet the crowd foolishly expected two persons because of the different names. *But some asked, "Surely the Messiah does not come from Galilee, does he?"* But where is he from? [7:42] *Has not the Scripture said that the Messiah is descended from*

David and comes from Bethlehem, the village where David lived? Therefore there was a great division among the people: some said this, others said that. Since they knew the place and the family where the Messiah would come from, what they had said above was evidently false, that is, that the place where the Messiah would come from was unknown. Therefore the Lord, with good reason, replied to them by saying, "You know me, and you know where I am from."[50] With the help of God, we have explained this in a previous passage.

Since the Pharisees could not accept the fact that the people had this opinion about our Lord, they wanted their subordinates to arrest him. But no one dared approach him. They were in fact prevented by the grace of God. And when these emissaries came back and were asked, [7:45] *Why did you not arrest him?* they said that he was teaching a new doctrine superior to any human doctrine.

Therefore once the Pharisees saw that those subordinates, along with the people, admired his words and neglected to do their duty, they said to them, [7:47] *Surely you have not been deceived too, have you?* [7:48] *Has any one of the authorities or of the Pharisees believed in him?* [7:49] *But this crowd that does not know the law—they are accursed.* These words are said by troubled men who oppress people with threats and force. They recalled how no doctor of the law believed.[51] They were ashamed of lowering themselves to the state of beginners, and so they cursed the people as if they were oblivious of the law, that is, those people who reached the truth with their simple minds.

After the Pharisees had said this, Nicodemus provides an appropriate reply, [7:51] *Our law does not judge people without first giving them a hearing to find out what they are doing, does it?* "You," he says, "unjustly condemn him because you have not yet heard the words the guards heard and admired." Since they had put

---

48Jn 5:39. 491 Thess 5:19. 50Jn 7:28. 51In the words of Christ.

forward their leaders and the law, Nicodemus's reply was suitable to [oppose] both [these arguments]. Indeed it is clear from Nicodemus's words that they accused Jesus of sinning against the law. It is similarly evident that not all the leaders approved of what they were doing, since one of the leaders was Nicodemus, who spoke against what they said.

Therefore they turned their anger on the ones they had sent saying, [7:52] *Surely you are not also from Galilee, are you? Search and you will see that no prophet is to arise from Galilee.* Since they realized that Jesus' words and deeds were beyond reproach and sufficient to convert everyone to faith, they refused any correct opinion and in their anger spoke against anyone who might rightly say something good about him. They did the same thing and offered the same reply to those whom they had sent and to Nicodemus. But Nicodemus, either out of weakness or fear of the leaders, did not reply to them when they wanted to diminish the words and works of Christ by mentioning Galilee.

When our Lord saw them arguing among themselves he approached them and said, [8:12][52] *I am the light of the world. Whoever follows me will never walk in darkness but will have the light of life.* They attacked the region of Galilee, considering it to be pagan. It was a fact, however, that in the prophet it was written, "Galilee of the nations, the people who walked in darkness have seen a great light."[53] These words make it clear that the people of Galilee were chosen, according to this prophecy, to receive an abundance of great gifts. Therefore he said to them, *I am the light of the world.* "Do you not recognize the words of the prophet," he says, "in the fact that the Galileans will enjoy a great light? I am that light, not only for them, but for everyone. Whoever remains close to me will not suffer. I am all the people need."

[8:13] *Then the Pharisees said to him, "You are testifying on your own behalf."* How is this possible? What does the Lord answer them? [8:14] *Even if I testify on my own behalf, my testimony is valid because I know where I have come from and where I am going, but you do not know where I come from or where I am going.* "Now," he says, "even though I testify on my own behalf, my testimony is not to be rejected. Indeed, I speak that which suits my dignity. I know in what state I will be after my ascension to heaven, and I am aware of the dignity abiding in me." He spoke here symbolically, according to his customary way of speaking, when he said, *where I have come from and where I am going.* He was making known the honor of his humanity and clearly also alluding to his divinity. "You ignore these things," he says. "They indeed are far beyond your comprehension."

And why did they not know you or believe your words?[54] He says, [8:15] *You judge by human standards,* that is, "Since you only judge these things by the flesh you see, you do not know the one who performs these miracles." *I judge no one.* [8:16] *Yet even if I do judge, my judgment is valid because it is not I alone who judge, but I and the Father who sent me.* When speaking to the Jews, he usually refers to himself in a figurative way, especially when he wants to reveal the dignity of his humanity. He then alludes to the nature of his divinity, which makes him a participant in all its dignity. We have said this before[55] and repeat it here as well. This is clear enough from these words, *I judge no one. Yet even if I do judge, my judgment is valid.* Now if [he says] *I judge no one,* what is the meaning of the phrase, *even if I do judge?* If he himself judges people, as is true, what is the use of saying, *I judge no one?* What therefore is meant by this? Since he said to them, *You judge by human standards,* he wants

---

[52]The section concerning the woman caught in adultery is missing. The most ancient authorities lack it, while others, more recent, add it here, 7:53–8:11, or after 7:36, or after 21:25 (that is, at the end of the Gospel of John). The passage is undoubtedly of Lukan origin, and is also included after Lk 21:38 with variations of text. [53]Is 9:1-2. [54]Theodore is addressing the Lord. [55]See comments on Jn 5:22.

them to know that it is not necessary for them to think that what he says about his humanity is out of the realm of possibility because they only see his visible nature. Why? Because, he says, the divine nature is hidden in him, and through it he is a participant in all those miracles. If the Jews could have understood what he was saying about his divinity, nothing would have prevented him from speaking those words openly and publicly. But since what he was teaching was well beyond anyone's comprehension, he chose to speak figuratively when proposing to teach such truths.

He had actually said above, in another passage, "The Father judges no one but has given all judgment to the Son."[56] This does not mean that all the responsibility for judging has been taken from the Father. However, since it is necessary that the face of those who must be judged falls under the gaze of the judge, this task is more appropriate for the assumed man—not because of the dignity of his nature but because God the Word abides in him through whom he communicates with the Father. Therefore he says, *The Father judges no one but has given all judgment to the Son.* He is saying, "judgment has been given to him," that is, to the one who is visible, which means that he also renders judgment as well. This is precisely what we demonstrated previously when we explained these words.[57] Therefore the purpose of what he said is namely this, that the divinity of the Only Begotten does not judge the world because God the Word is invisible to humanity just as the Father is—even though the responsibility for judging is not taken away from God the Word, just as it is not taken away from the Father either.

The phrase, *Yet even if I do judge, my judgment is valid*, refers to his human nature, which will come from heaven to judge everything. Therefore as soon as he said, *my judgment is valid*, he added, *for it is not I alone who judge, but I and the Father who sent me.* While it was necessary to say, *for it is not I alone, but also my Father who sent me*, he actually alluded again to his divinity by adding, *but I and the Father.* In a similar way, when the apostle speaks about our soul and body in the Epistle to the Romans and teaches us how the soul tends to virtue, while the body, because of the tendency of its mortal nature, tends more easily toward sin, he says, "So I find it to be a law that when I want to do what is good, evil lies close to me."[58] But the subject of the two phrases—"when I want to do what is good" and "evil lies close to me"—is not the same because not even the contradiction of terms can accept this, even though in both phrases he has used the pronouns *I* and *me*. Rather, "when I want to do what is good" refers to the soul; "evil lies close to me" refers to the body. Since he was discussing two natures and two different entities and yet was speaking about a single subject, it was most appropriate for him to use the pronoun *I (me)*[59] with each of the two different natures. Indeed he is talking about his own person, which possesses both of these elements because of the union of body and soul. And so our Lord too, when he spoke about his humanity and his divinity, referred the pronoun *I* to the common person. And in order to show that in all these passages he was not speaking about one and the same nature, he used different words. In one passage he said, *I judge no one*, and in another he said, *Yet even if I do judge, my judgment is valid.* He said the first in the sense that we have explained above. After saying to them, *You judge by human standards*, he wanted to ensure that no one doubted his own capacity to judge, and so he added, *I judge no one. Yet even if I do judge, my judgment is valid.*

This is similar to what he meant when he said, "The Father judges no one but has given all judgment to the Son."[60] Here too, he said,

[56]Jn 5:22.   [57]Cf. comments on Jn 5:22.   [58]Rom 7:21.   [59]Latin *mihi* in Vosté.   [60]Jn 5:22.

"Just as you should have no doubts about what is referred to my human nature, so you also must know that when I say, *I judge no one*, I am referring to my divinity. The [man Christ] is the one who judges all and comes to the judgment. Since he is the one those who must be judged will see, the judgment he renders must be valid and just. Indeed, since he participates in this dignity, he justly pronounces judgment for every person because he is not alone and does not do this on his own. Now, if he judged on his own, people would not believe that he could do such a thing because of his apparent weakness. But I, namely the divine nature, am with him. The Father is with him as well. And this is necessary, because what is connected with me is also with the Father." Therefore, if one comes to read that passage where he says, "The Father judges no one but has given all judgment to the Son,"[61] he will find a great similarity of meaning between this passage and that one. And here too he demonstrates his greatness through the words *I judge*. There should be no doubt about such words because there is another reason for their fulfillment.

Therefore it was appropriate that he added, [8:17] *In your law it is written that the testimony of two witnesses is valid.* [8:18] *I testify on my own behalf, and the Father who sent me testifies on my behalf.* Here he also clearly makes known that the testimony which he is said to offer with the Father concerns his divinity, and it is from both of these that the testimony of his humanity comes—from the Son by reason of his being joined together [with the humanity], and from the Father by reason of the close relationship [the humanity has with the Father] mediated by the Son.

After he said *You judge by human standards* and demonstrated the character and dignity of his human nature, he fittingly added, "Since the testimony concerning him comes from two [witnesses], he was thus worthy to have been believed by you, as far as everything that was said about him, even if those things said about him appeared to exceed his nature—and especially since your law states that any case about which there is doubt is settled if two testimonies are given. Therefore, according to the will of the law, there should be two witnesses besides the one about whom the testimony is given." If the Father and the Son testify in favor of the human nature of our Lord in regard to divinity, the rule of law is respected. But if he testifies by himself about all these things, the witness is one, not two. Therefore the rule of law clearly illuminates the meaning of our Lord's words, which had been spoken in a round about way because of his audience.

After this the Jews asked him, [8:19] *Where is your Father?* They meant this in a human way. And the Lord said to them, *You know neither me nor my Father. If you knew me, you would know my Father also.* "I know," he says, "that you ask about the Father without knowing what I am talking about. But you think the father I am talking about should be a human being. And is it any wonder, since you do not know him or me, although you think you do." This is similar to the words said to Philip: "Whoever has seen me has seen the Father."[62]

[8:20] *He spoke these words while he was teaching in the treasury of the temple, but no one arrested him*, even though they were very angry and wanted to arrest him. And so the Lord answered against their will and intentions by saying, [8:21] *I am going away, and you will search for me, but you will die in your sin. Where I am going, you cannot come.* "Why are you in such a hurry to arrest me when you cannot? Wait a little while, and I will give myself to you. For I must go to where I will greatly surpass you, a place where you cannot reach me; when your arrogance against me will be punished."

The Jews, however, said, [8:22] *Is he going*

---

[61]Jn 5:22. [62]Jn 14:9.

to kill himself? *Is that what he means by saying,* *"Where I am going, you cannot come"?* This remark is not only human but also foolish. If they considered his death in a human way, they would have certainly gone, like everyone else, to the place where he had to go after death, since this limit has been established for all humankind.

But our Lord said to them, [8:23] *You are from below, I am from above; you are of this world, I am not of this world.* [8:24] *I told you that you would die in your sins.* "You think," he says, "in a human way about my words. My death is not like that of all other human beings. After my death I will be in the highest glory when I ascend into heaven by means of the superior nature that is in me. But since you are only immersed in the things of this world, you only think about me in a human way. Therefore I have told you that you will suffer punishment for your arrogance against me because you did not want to believe what happened to me. And the just punishment you will receive will be commensurate with the dignity of these things that happened to me."

Then they said to him, [8:25] *"Who are you?"* Jesus said to them, *"Why do I speak to you at all"* [8:26] *I have much to say about you and much to condemn; but the one who sent me is true, and I declare to the world what I have heard from him.* "I must judge you people whom I address as totally unworthy since you are so impertinent and of ill will. Indeed, although I would have many reasons to rebuke you, by all rights you should not even be considered worthy of a word from me. The one who sent me to you never entrusted me with a single false word to say to you because he is true in everything and always rejoices in the truth. I would never say anything to you other than what he wants me to say. And, since I could justly reprove you because you oppose the truth, I should consider you unworthy of

my words." [8:27] *And they did not understand,* the Evangelist notes, *that he was speaking to them about the Father;* that is, they did not understand which father he was speaking to them about.

[8:28] *So Jesus said, "When you have lifted up the Son of Man, then you will realize that I am he, and that I do nothing on my own, but I speak these things as the Father instructed me.* [8:29] *And the one who sent me is with me; he has not left me alone, for I always do what is pleasing to him."* "I know," he says, "that you do not understand now what I say, and you do not know of what Father I speak. These things go beyond your comprehension. But in the cross you will know my power. You will understand that I do nothing against the will of the Father when you see the whole universe upset,[63] and the Father showing his anger—that Father, I mean who is now with me, and enjoys all that is said and done by me." Also here [Christ] shows that the words, *I do nothing on my own,* stand for, "I do nothing against his will." Then the Evangelist observed that many believed in him because of those words.

So the Lord said to those who believed [in him], [8:31] *If you continue in my word, you are truly my disciples;* [8:32] *and you will know the truth, and the truth will make you free.* Whatever human art we learn, we learn it because it is useful for us. Among human beings it is well known what art each [artisan] promises to teach those who want to learn the art of the carpenter or the blacksmith or any other art. Our Lord aptly defined the truth of discipleship as one who remains faithful, saying, "I teach the knowledge of the truth. There is nothing higher than this teaching. Its fruit is freedom from evil, and through this truth every blessing is given to humanity."

After the Lord had spoken these words to the faithful, the Jews thought that his words were a reproof against them. And so they said

[63]See Mt 27:51-53.

to him, [8:33] *We are descendants of Abraham, and have never been in bondage to anyone.* [8:34] *How is it that you say, "You will be made free"?* They were not speaking the truth. They had been freed from the bondage of the Egyptians, who were their neighbors, and from the Babylonians. And now, even while they were speaking, they were subjects of the Romans. But our Lord did not lower himself to rebuke them about this even though they were lying. Instead he offered a clear explanation of his words and revealed to them what was suitable in order to teach them. Therefore he said to them, [8:34] *Everyone who commits sin is a slave to sin.* [8:35] *The slave does not continue in the house forever. If the Son frees you, you will be truly free.* Among human beings it depends on the will of the master as to whether a servant stays in the house or not. The master drives them away whenever he wants. But the son is the heir and the master of the house. This is what he means: "The subject of my speech is not physical bondage. I am talking to you about real freedom. The master has the prerogative to drive away from the house the servant in whom he sees an evil will. He can subject him to any punishment he considers to be appropriate. But no master drives his son away from the house. In the same way, one who is a slave to sin and far removed from all divine goodness is given over to perpetual punishment. But one who has been made worthy of freedom and has been given status as a son always enjoys divine goodness and can never be removed from it. If you," he says, "are freed through me, and are made worthy of the title of sons, then you will possess true freedom."

He then reproves them because they boasted of their descent from Abraham. [8:37] *I know that you are descendants of Abraham; yet you seek to kill me because my words find no place in you.* "You are sons of Abraham. But I rebuke you because I see that you are not the sons of Abraham in what you do. You do not accept my words and even want to kill me,

although such an attempt is useless." Once he had shown that their will had nothing to do with Abraham, he mentioned the one with whom they did have an affinity, at the same time also revealing himself by way of comparison. [8:38] *I speak of what I have seen with my Father, and you do what you have heard from your father.* "Therefore from your works," he says, "it is clear whose sons you are. In the same way, from what I say and do, it is clear whose son I am even though you do not believe my words."

After the Lord had said, *I know that you are descendants of Abraham*, the Jews saw that he admitted as much and therefore added, [8:39] *Abraham is our father.* Then the Lord bluntly told them, *If you are the sons of Abraham, do the works of Abraham.* [8:40] *But now you seek to kill me, a man who has told you the truth that I heard from God; this is not what Abraham did.* "How can they be sons of Abraham," he says, "when their actions demonstrate they are anything but sons? He was also eager for them to know that he was not ignorant of what they were planning. You want to kill me—I who am your helper and who teaches you the truth." And then, concluding what he had said above, he said, [8:41] *You do what your father did.* "Your works themselves," he says, "prove that you have no part with Abraham and clearly proclaim who your father is."

The Jews thought he was saying their father was someone else. They, in fact, interpreted every spiritual thing he said in a human way. They replied, [8:41] *We were not born of fornication; we have one Father, even God.* The Lord could have objected that they were wrong in this regard too. Indeed, they had often mixed with the Gentiles and many were born of fornication. The prophets, in fact, frequently condemned them for this. But the Lord did not want to take this route. Instead he used their own words as a stern rebuke by saying, [8:42] *If God were your Father, you would love me, for I proceeded and came forth from God; I came* not of my own accord, but he sent me. "I came to you from God," he says, "and nothing I say to you is against his will. If God is your Father, as you have said, how is it that you do not accept him who speaks to you according to his will? Also here we understand that the words, *I came not of my own accord*, are evidently said to refute their opposition.

[8:43] *Why do you not understand what I say? It is because you cannot accept my word.* We need to read this sentence as a question. Indeed it means, "I say to you: why do you not understand my words?" And instead of saying, "Because you are inclined to evil," he checked his words to avoid an open reproof and said instead, *It is because you cannot accept my word.* Then, showing why they cannot accept his words, he added, [8:44] *You are from your father the devil, and you choose to do your father's desires. He was a murderer from the beginning and does not stand in the truth because there is no truth in him.* "Since," he says, "you made the devil your own father because your works are so much like his and you enjoy being with him, you are eager to do what he likes and seek to kill me. This is his work, and from the beginning he transgressed against God's command and killed Adam and through him all who would come [after him]. Therefore your affinity with him does not allow you to understand my words because he is inclined to falsehood. Your relationship with him is in proportion to your aversion for the truth." *When he lies, he speaks according to his own nature, for he is a liar and the father of it.*[64] "When Satan," he says, "speaks lies and similar words, he does not use those of others but his own. He is the father of falsehood because he birthed it and was the first to use it by speaking to Adam when he said certain things to him in place of others." The expression, *he is a liar and the father of it*, means, "he is a liar and the father of lies," that is, he brought lies into being since

he was the first one to introduce them and to use them.

[8:45] *But because I tell the truth, you do not believe me.* "So," he says, "since you enjoy lies, you do not accept the truth I speak." He connects these words to, *Why do you not understand what I say? It is because you cannot accept my word.* He notes the reason why they could not [accept his word], so that it appears that the expression "you cannot" refers to their will and not to their nature. And since they do not accept the truth of his words because they are inclined to evil and therefore do not even understand them, he adds, as a conclusion to his reproof, *But because I tell the truth, you do not believe me.*

And lest it be thought that what he said was a mere jest—namely, that they could not accept his doctrine because of their inclination to Satan—he confirms the truth of his words with his following remarks. He says, in fact, [8:46] *Which of you convicts me of sin?* "You have no reason to accuse me. Can you really find any good reason to blame my works? Are they not wonderful works? And all my words are directed to the glory of the Father."

Since they had no answer because they had nothing to say, he added, *If I tell the truth, why do you not believe me?* "If," he says, "you can raise no objection against me if what I said is true, why do you not believe my words? It is evident that you hate the truth because you love falsehood." After clearly demonstrating this point, he again uses this argument against them. The objection he had previously raised against them with the words quoted above—namely, that they could not hear his words because they were inclined to Satan—is once again evident from his remark, [8:47] *Whoever is from God hears the words of God. The reason you do not hear them is that you are not from God.* It is evident that anyone who is close to

---

[64]The Syriac text of the Peshitta reads "the father of it" instead of "the father of lies."

God obeys his words. "You do not accept what is said because you do not have communion with God. Since you have nothing to argue—my words are indeed truth—it is clear that because you love evil, you want to kill me, your herald of truth."

Since the Jews, then, could find no fault in these words, they moved on to insults. They called him a Samaritan and said to him, [8:48] *You have a demon.* The Lord made a modest reply and at the same time proved his reply by saying, [8:49] *I do not have a demon; but I honor my Father, and you dishonor me.* "I always do everything," he says, "in honor of the Father, as is clear from what I have said to you many times. It is up to you to judge if this is the work of someone possessed by the devil. And yet, instead of honor for the Father, I receive this insult from you as my compensation. This is what is evident from your words. See that you are not found to speak against the honor of the Father with those things you cry out against me." [8:50] *Yet I do not seek my own glory; there is one who seeks it and he is the judge.* "But," he says, "I do not reprove you because of that offense. Indeed the one whom I honor judges it, but you still are not ashamed to persecute me."

He then tells them that their disbelief would not remain unpunished, adding in good order, [8:51] *Very truly, I tell you whoever keeps my word will never see death.* "In truth," he says, "the believers' faith will not go unrewarded. They will always enjoy eternal life thanks to their love for me."

As they heard this, the Jews said to him, [8:52] *Now we know that you have a demon. Abraham died, and so did the prophets; yet you say that you will make those who believe in you immortal.* And so it would seem that you are exalting yourself over them.

Jesus said to them, [8:54] *If I glorify myself, my glory is nothing. It is my Father who glori-*

fies me, he of whom you say, "He is our God," [8:55] *though you do not know him. But I do know him; if I would say that I do not know him, I would be a liar like you. But I do know him and I keep his word.* He had said before, "If I testify about myself, my testimony *is not* true"[65]—even though in another passage he attributes to himself the very thing they were objecting to him in this discussion when he said, "If I testify about myself, my testimony *is* true."[66] He does the same here too. Since they were openly rebuking him and accusing him of exalting himself over Abraham and the prophets, saying, "Who do you claim yourself to be?" he made the apt reply, "If I spoke about myself, you rightly would not believe me." Clearly he did not mean the words, *If I glorify myself,* in the sense of, "If I make myself glorious," but, "If I spoke about my glory and the things that pertain to me, you would have good reason not to believe me because then I would be testifying about myself. But my Father revealed my glory when he testified about me," as he had said before, "The Father who sent me testifies on my behalf."[67] "You say, then, that you are from God, but you have no knowledge of him nor are you close to him because you do not obey his words. *I do know him*, and I do what suits his testimony about me. Even if I tell you something great about myself, I am saying nothing contrary to the previous testimony of the Father about me." This is what he wants to signify when he says, *and I keep his word. If I would say that I do not know him, I would be a liar like you.*

After saying, "If I speak about myself, I speak according to the testimony of my Father. What I do appears to be done by me according to the will of that witness," he says, [8:56] *Your ancestor Abraham rejoiced that he would see my day; he saw it and was glad.* "Therefore," he says, "after my Father's testimony about me has been explained, listen now to the things about

[65]Jn 5:31, emphasis added. [66]Jn 8:14, emphasis added. [67]Jn 8:18.

me that are in conformity with that [testimony]. I am certainly so superior to Abraham that he also wished and hoped to see the time when I would reform the world through my passion. And what he desired he saw, insofar as he was allowed to, and he certainly rejoiced. When he sacrificed his own son, he revealed his will and received from God the revelation of the future that, just as he accepted offering his son as a victim for God, so also God would give his Only Begotten Son for the salvation of the world."

[8:57] *Then the Jews said to him, "You are not yet fifty years old, and have you seen Abraham?"* [8:58] *Jesus said to them, "Very truly I tell you, before Abraham was, I am."* At a bare minimum he is referring here to his divine nature, which exists not only before all creatures but also, in its immensity and infinity that exceeds [their abilities to comprehend], is the cause of their very existence, which he gave to them.

Since the Jews could not stand these words, they [8:59] *picked up stones to throw at him, but Jesus hid himself and went out of the temple.* He passed right through them and left the place as if their eyes were closed by divine power, so that they might not know how he had removed himself from among them.

After he left there, he performed the miracle of the man born blind in order to confirm his words. The miracle that followed confirmed his words, and therefore the Evangelist [added], [9:1] *He saw a man blind from birth,* in order to show that immediately after leaving the midst of the Jews, he performed the miracle of the blind man. This miracle is connected to the other miracle. Indeed, according to his will, he hid himself and disappeared among people who could see, since he had closed their eyes. And, in a similar way, according to his will, he gave the miraculous power of seeing to a man who did not by nature have eyes capable of seeing.

End of the Third Book.

Book Four (John 9:1–10:42)

[9:1] *As he walked along, he saw a man blind from birth.* [9:2] *His disciples asked him, "Rabbi who sinned, this man or his parents, that he was born blind?"* It appears from this episode that it was usual for his disciples to ask this kind of question about all that was happening to the Lord as a way of improving their religious instruction. Indeed, since they had left everything and had given themselves completely to the Lord so that they might learn how to lead the best kind of godly life, they laudably sought help from him, taking the opportunity from what happened around them to ask him such questions. When they saw this man born blind—a man who had this disability before he could even sin since this defect of the eyes happened to him when he was still in the womb—they were upset when contemplating what this meant for their faith since they were looking at this event from a human perspective. They thought that there must be a just reason for this misfortune. They could not believe that such adversity could occur without good cause because they knew that God rules everything that has to do with human beings. With no other perspective, because of their human weakness, they could only attribute what had happened to the sin of the parents—or to the sin of the blind man himself. They could not attribute the injury to a sin he had already committed. Indeed, how could he sin if he was not born yet? Rather, since he would have sinned if he did not have this disability, God in his foreknowledge restrained him. They piously and rightly believed that human sins were the cause of all evils. But since their human weakness disabled them from understanding anything further, they thought this disability was caused either by the blind man himself or by his parents—as if the son had received this punishment for their sins, or as if he was the cause of his misfortune because he had received this punishment for his future sins.

Since this is what the disciples thought about the blind man, the Lord appropriately adjusted what he had to say to their disposition in his answer to them. And so, after they asked him *who sinned, this man or his parents?*—in other words, "did this happen to him because of the sins of his parents or because of his own sin?" as if no other possible cause existed—the Lord taught them that there are many reasons these kinds of things happen, but that they are certainly secret and unexplainable. Therefore we are always complaining about events whose causes we ignore. But then we learn that nothing happens in vain. This knowledge will be given to us in the future world because what is hidden now will be revealed to us.

So he said to them, [9:3] *Neither this man nor his parents sinned; he was born blind so that God's works might be revealed in him.* And from this event he confirmed that there were other occurrences like this one. The blind man benefited greatly from his healing because, when he was freed from this defect, he came to know the Only Begotten and through his eyes reverently received his teaching about the faith. In addition, many others also came to admire the power of our Lord through the miracle that had occurred and honored most of all the faith in him. But evidently none of them could have imagined this event turning out the way it did, and that his blindness would become the cause of so much good. And so through this one fact he confirmed the others. In other words, just as something great and wonderful happened—something no one could have previously imagined—through his [disability] thanks to God's providence, in the same way we must understand that there are other things too that happen whose causes are hidden and beyond scrutiny but which after a time will be revealed to help those who do not understand them.

Therefore the sentence, *Neither this man nor his parents sinned*, must not be understood as a precise definition of their circumstances. Rather, at this stage he chose not to go into detail on this point just as we also are accustomed to omit any number of words in proportion to the subject matter. It is not his intention to show that the blind man and his parents were without sin. In fact, the disciples themselves never asked whether they had committed any sin. Their concern was why this had happened to him and whether it had happened because of his sins or those of his parents. And it was to this that our Lord directed his answer since he wanted to teach them that there are other hidden causes for those things that, with the permission of God, happen to us. Therefore he said to them, *Neither this man nor his parents sinned*; that is, "Since you think this was the sole cause, let us consider the possibility that none of those causes you cite is the real one, and that neither he nor his parents sinned, but that he who does everything through his providence allowed this disability to occur so that his power might be revealed. Consider if in fact this turns out to be the case from what happened. If his blindness had been prevented, he would not have been born blind. And, if he had not been born blind, he would not have received this healing. And if this had not happened, the greatness of this miracle through which the blind man came to know me would have remained hidden. Now, instead, all those who have come to understand my power through what happened to him can no longer doubt what I say and hence derive great profit from their faith in me. You also need to recognize that there may be similar causes for events that at the moment remain inscrutable to you."

The phrase, *so that God's works might be revealed in him*, is Scripture's customary way of saying things. In other words, he was not made blind so that [God's] works might be revealed in him; rather, it was a birth defect. God's permission for this defect was, however, extremely useful because a miracle was clearly accomplished because of it. This expression is common in the Holy Scriptures, both in the

Old and the New Testaments. For instance, when it says, "So that you are justified in your sentence,"[1] this is not why the sinners sinned; rather, when they sin, God is shown to be just in punishing them because he does everything justly according to his providence. This usage is frequent in the Scriptures and there is no need for many words in order to have everyone agree with us.

Therefore, after he answered the disciples and not only solved their question but taught them by what he had to say, he added something that absolutely needed to be said when the blind man was about to be healed. [9:4] *I must work*, he said, *the works of him who sent me while it is day; night is coming when no one can work.* The Jews revealed their ungrateful mind in different ways against his accomplished miracles, as we have learned from previous encounters—especially after he had healed on the sabbath. Not only did they show no admiration for his miracles, but they even persecuted him as a sinful and impious man. When he was about to heal the man born blind, it was the sabbath. Therefore the Pharisees, who could say nothing against the miracle, condemned the action instead, saying, "This man is not from God, for he does not observe the sabbath."[2] But he was anticipating this and so he said, *I must work the works of him who sent me.* "I know," he says, "that the Pharisees will complain about the work I must do. They will forget all about the miracle and focus their concern instead on the day. They will use this as the reason to complain, calling me impious and a transgressor of the law, as if I was breaking the sabbath. They will present this as the reason for their righteous persecution of me. But let them say and do whatever they want: I must accomplish the works *of him who sent me*, by working his works."

This is certainly very similar in meaning to his statement, "My Father is still working,

and I also am working,"[3] which he had replied in answer to the Jews who had accused him of healing the paralyzed man on the sabbath. In that instance he had demonstrated that his and the Father's works were held in common, and therefore he must do what the Father also does. In the present instance he again says that he must perform the works of him who sent him, since the works that are done by him are also the works of the Father. "And so," he says, "even if a hundred thousand of them had complained about the things I was doing, I still would have needed to do them when it was the appropriate time to do so. There will come a time, in fact, when I must stop doing these things. Just as people distinguish between day and night, with the day being the appropriate time for work and the night being more appropriate for rest since no one can work then, so for me the time up to my passion is a time appropriate for miracles. Everything I do during this time must agree with the will of the Father and declare my own dignity. After the passion and the cross, however, I must stop doing all of these things since I will abandon my residency here on earth and my dealings with human beings. But up to that hour I must not desist from doing the miracles that need to be performed, and there is no use in your persecuting me for my signs. You cannot accomplish what you want before the time comes when, after fulfilling my duties, I will freely accept my passion, which comes at the end of the time in which I am performing signs among the human race."

Then he clearly demonstrates that he figuratively refers to *day* as the time of his presence [on earth] and *night* as the time following his passion and death by saying, [9:5] *As long as I am in the world, I am the light of the world.* In other words, "Just as the sun gives people the opportunity to work by bringing daylight into being, I too illuminate the world with my presence as long as I am in it." He said these words before performing the miracle and demonstrated to those who murmured against him that he was not about to stop doing his miracles, because his Father was pleased that these works were being accomplished. Therefore there was no profit for them in persecuting him, because he could suffer nothing before the set time. He would face his passion when the time the Father had fixed for him came. This is indeed what he wanted to illustrate through these words, as we have emphasized for the understanding of those who encounter this book.

Then, when he began his narration of the miracle, the Evangelist for this reason added, [9:6] *When he had said this, he spat on the ground and made mud with the saliva*, in order to show clearly that what he said before the miracle was preparatory to the miracle itself he was about to perform. He made some mud and spread it on the eyes of the blind man, but he did not heal his eyes immediately. Instead, he ordered him to go to the pool of Siloam so that after he had washed he might open his eyes and see. For, just as he frequently displayed his greatness with his words, he did the same with his works, that is, through the way[4] in which they were done. He used mud to restore his sight so that he who had received no sight from birth might receive it through that very element that was used in the beginning in forming the whole human nature. Through [all of] this, he was revealing himself to be the creator of the human race. For, by providing what was missing in the blind man's formation and in utilizing that [element] which the Creator had used from the beginning when he constituted [our] nature, he was clearly indicating that he was the author of creation and equal in his creative power with the Creator of the human race.

He did not heal him immediately. Instead he ordered him to go and wash. And only after he washed was he healed. This is how providence acts so that the accomplished miracle might escape no one's notice. Just as he ordered the paralyzed man to carry his mat on the day when this was not allowed[5]—in order that all those who complained that the law had been violated by the occasion of that miracle might be instructed about the greatness of the miracle—so he also ordered this blind man who was far away from Siloam to go there and wash. The whole crowd that was close to the Lord probably left him at this point and followed the blind man to see the miracle that was about to happen to his eyes. And as the blind man walked through the crowded streets of the town with the crowd eagerly following him, everyone who saw this began asking why they were in such a hurry and why this blind man had such a great crowd following him. And so they too, after attentively listening to the account, hurried to see what would happen. In the meantime, as more and more people found out, the crowd following him increased. This is how so many people saw the blind man come to Siloam to wash and miraculously regain his sight.

When he arrived at the pool and washed, he received grace. And yet his neighbors and those who were with him when he was begging did not all come to the same conclusion about him. There were some who said that he was indeed the blind man, but others, because of the miracle that had happened to him, said, [9:9] *"No, but it is someone like him." He himself, however, kept on saying, "I am the man"*—not because the event itself compelled him to but because he was eager to proclaim before everyone the miracle that had happened to him.

And so he told them that he was that blind beggar. Those who had not seen the events

---

[4]In my translation I accept the variant proposed by the editor who replaces *bzabno'*, "through the time" with *bzno'*, "through the way." See CSCO 4 3:187.   [5]See Jn 5:1-47.

transpire asked him what had happened to him and how he had regained his sight. Indeed those who *had* seen had no need to ask him what they already knew. And so he explained what happened and revealed who had healed him by saying, [9:11] *The man called Jesus made mud, spread it on my eyes, and said to me, "Go to Siloam and wash." Then I went and washed and received my sight.* "If you want to know how I received my sight, this is what I am telling you. If you want to know who did this, I'll tell you that too: The man called Jesus did this." After hearing this, they asked, [9:12] *"Where is he?" He said, "I do not know."* He did not know him because his eyes had not yet seen him.

They took him and brought him to the Pharisees. Here the Evangelist adds, [9:14] *Now it was a sabbath day when Jesus made the mud and opened his eyes.* Therefore the Pharisees asked him how he had come to see. He thought they already knew who had healed him, and so he only talked to them about how he was healed, which they had already learned from those who had brought him. After hearing the blind man's answer, there was again a difference of opinion among the Pharisees. Some said, [9:16] *This man is not from God, for he does not observe the sabbath.* Others said, "A man subject to sin cannot do these works." So, while they were discussing this, they again turned to the blind man—as if choosing him as their arbiter—and asked him, [9:17] *What do you say about him? It was your eyes he opened.* "Should he be admired for the work he performed? Or is he a sinner for violating the sabbath? So, about him *who opened your eyes* . . .[6] what do you say, or what is your opinion about him?" The blind man wisely answered their question by saying, *He is a prophet;* that is, "I hold him in such high esteem for what he

has done that I think this is what *must* be said about him."

When they saw that the miracle itself already testified to the power of the healer and that the blind man was so open with them about the grace he had received and about the greatness of his helper, they began to doubt whether this man who had been healed was really the blind man, or someone else. And so they were obliged to call his parents. After calling them, they asked whether he was their son who was blind from birth. And in addition they asked, [9:19] *How then does he now see?* expecting that the parents, not knowing how he was healed, would deny he was their son if there was any hesitancy in their reply.

They quite shrewdly avoided denying he was their son and, at the same time, acknowledged that he was born blind, but that [9:20] *We do not know how he was healed, or who healed him.* And, they added, "You should ask him since he is of age and can answer for himself." The Evangelist notes that they answered this because they were afraid of the Jews, [9:22] *For the Jews had already agreed that anyone who confessed Jesus to be the Messiah would be put out of the synagogue.* From this it appears evident that who had cured him and how he had been cured had also not escaped his parents' notice. But they were afraid and so they said, *He can speak for himself,* in order not to say anything that might upset the Jews.

They again called in the man who was previously blind and—without questioning him further because they knew that he said openly how he had been healed—said to him, [9:24] *Give glory to God! We know that this man is a sinner.* Since they could not deny the fact of what happened, they said to him, "Consider what happened to you as a benefit from God. You must believe [Jesus] is a sinner. We

---

[6]The editor J.-M. Vosté indicates a lacuna in the text here. CSCO 4 3:i-iv and 190. Also the relevant Greek fragment appears to have lacunae: See R. Devreesse, *Essai sur Théodore de Mopsueste,* Studi e Testi 141 (Vatican City: Biblioteca Apostolica Vaticana, 1948), p. 342; Theodore of Mopsuestia, *Commentary on the Gospel of John,* introduction and commentary by G. Kalantzis, Early Christian Studies 7 (Sydney: Saint Paul's Publications, 2004), pp. 71-72.

definitely know that he is." He who had been healed shrewdly answered, [9:25] *I do not know whether he is a sinner. One thing I do know, that though I was blind, now I see.* "I do not want to declare," he says, "what I do not know; but neither can I keep silent or hide what I do know. I really do not know whether he is like you say he is. The fact remains that I did not come to know him as a sinner. But I do know this: I was blind and against hope I received my sight. It is up to you to judge whether a sinner can do something like this because you are the ones who decide such things." He provided quite a prudent answer, weighing his words so that he might not appear to disagree with those who questioned him, but through his silence nonetheless suggesting that [Jesus] could not have done what he did if he really had been a sinner.

However, they asked him again, [9:26] *How did he open your eyes?* At this point he began openly mocking and reproving them and heaping scorn upon them, saying, [9:27] *I already told you, and you would not listen? Why do you want to hear it again? Do you also want to become his disciples?* The words, *I have told you already, and you would not listen,* were clearly a rebuke because they did not accept the truth. The words, *Do you also want to become his disciples?* mock them and heap scorn upon them.

Since the Pharisees did not like what he said, they reviled him by saying, [9:28] *You are his disciple, but we are disciples of Moses.* [9:29] *We know that God has spoken to Moses, but as for this man, we do not know where he comes from.* But they did not actually know that God had spoken to Moses either, since they were not present when he did so. Therefore he who was previously blind responded by [again] mocking them and confirming our Lord's account: [9:30] *Here is an astonishing thing! You do not know where he comes from, and yet he opened my eyes.* [9:31] *We know that God does not listen to sinners, but he does listen to the one who worships him and obeys his will.* [9:32] *Never since the world began has it been*

heard that anyone opened the eyes of a person born blind. "So he must be admired," he says, "as someone above human comprehension. Although you do not know where he is from, the accomplished miracle openly proves his power to me. Since you were unaware of who he was, you would have needed testimonies from others if there had been no clue of his power. But if his miracles display the greatness of the man and yet you still do not know where he is from and who he is, it is evident both from the greatness of his miracles and your own foolishness that he is beyond human comprehension.

"It seems clear from these events that he cannot be called a sinner either. Certainly God does not hear the requests of sinners but is accustomed rather to the voice of those who exhibit honesty and faithfully do his will. In addition, what has just happened is of no little importance and is not appropriate for someone who only shares a common virtue [with everyone else] that is heard by God. Indeed, he healed a man born blind and we know that this has never been done before—not even by Moses, whom you admire. It is obvious that he would not be able to do this if he did not do everything according to the will of God." Therefore we must not only admire the behavior of this healed man who showed a great love for his helper and took on the task of proving [Jesus'] power instead of neglecting the trust that was due to him—but we must also admire his wisdom and his ability to garner arguments against them on many different fronts as he did, for instance, when the Pharisees said, "We do not know him," and yet he presents Jesus as this great person. Or there was the accomplished miracle itself. There was also the fact that God does not listen to sinners but to his worshipers. And finally there was the fact that never before had such a miracle been performed by anyone. How great anything good or bad appears to us when we hear that someone has done it for the first time!

Since the Pharisees could not tolerate the

inference of his words but also could answer nothing in reply against his reproofs—indeed, he had spoken quite shrewdly and wisely to them—they resorted to insults, saying [9:34] *"You were born entirely in sins, and are you trying to teach us?" And they drove him out.* However, this did not bother him. In fact, he was pleased that he had been driven out because of the one who had helped him. When Jesus heard that he had been expelled by them—he heard about it because many had told him what was happening, because there was a large crowd present when these events occurred—and seeing from what he did that he was worthy, Jesus wanted to give him perfect knowledge in addition to what he had already given. [9:35] *And when he found him, he said, "Do you believe in the Son of Man?"* And he, recognizing his voice—he had not seen him yet—said, [9:36] *And who is he, Sir? Tell me, so that I may believe in him.* There was a good reason he thought that he who had given him sight beyond his expectations could also show him the Son of God. Our Lord said to him, [9:37] *You have seen him, and the one speaking with you is he.* He indicates himself not by saying, "I am," but *the one speaking with you.* He acted in the same way with the Samaritan woman. However, in her case, since he was speaking with her alone, he did not refuse to say clearly, "I am he, the one who is speaking to you,"[7] so that she might believe for herself. Here, on the other hand, since there were still many unbelievers, he revealed who he was indirectly. But when the healed blind man heard this, he worshiped him, demonstrating his faith by his action.

At this point our Lord began his regular teaching, something that he usually did after his signs when the greatness of what had occurred confirmed what he said. [9:39] *And Jesus said, "I came into this world for judgment so that those who do not see may see, and those who see may become blind."* In another passage he had also said, "God did not send the Son into the world to condemn the world."[8] But now [he says], *I came into this world for judgment.* The previous passage spoke about the purpose of his coming. The purpose of his coming was that all people might live, while here he talks about the outcome. You see, even though it is his will to save all people, unbelievers must still be condemned because of their evil intent. And here he indicates the consequences of these events. "As is evident," he says, "I have come to discern who is blind and who is able to see. Indeed, he who was believed to be blind twice received eyes to see. He received bodily eyes and, in the perfection of his soul, received religious insight. Those, on the other hand, who have been entrusted with the teaching of the commandments of the law think they see with bodily eyes, but appear to be blind in both regards: neither accepting the truth nor believing the works that they have seen with their own eyes."

After hearing these words, the Pharisees said to him, [9:40] *Surely we are not blind, are we?* They had previously done something quite similar. When our Lord was speaking to them about freedom from sins, they replied, "We are descendants of Abraham and have never been slaves to anyone,"[9] since they thought that he was speaking about physical bondage. Similarly here, when the Lord reproaches their spiritual blindness, they respond that their bodily eyes are perfectly capable of seeing. [9:41] *Your sin remains.* This is why he highlighted their sin of which they boasted, saying, "Why do you say you see? It would be better if you were blind. Then at least those of you who do not believe would have a partial excuse due to this. But now, even though you can see and have, in fact, seen with your own eyes that the one who was blind now sees, you still do not believe what happened. Therefore you have no excuse and incur condemnation for all to see because of your unbelief."

[Chapter 10] Once he had made his reply to them, he began to speak figuratively to them concerning the dignity that was due him as a teacher more than them. Since the scribes, the teachers of the law and the elders of the people—that is, in a word, the people in authority—had driven out the blind man, Jesus received him instead in order to show by his actions that the authority to drive away or to receive someone belongs to him, not to any of them. But he spoke to them by way of allegory so that he might not appear to ostentatiously usurp the dignity of the teachers. But since our Lord evidently said these things allegorically, it is necessary that we now relate the entire allegory. Then we will give a full explanation so our readers can understand.

This is what he said: [10:1] *Very truly, I tell you, anyone who does not enter the sheepfold by the gate but climbs in by another way is a thief and a bandit. [10:2] The one who enters by the gate is the shepherd of the sheep. [10:3] The gatekeeper opens the gate for him, and the sheep hear his voice. He calls his own sheep by name and leads them out. [10:4] When he has brought out all his own, he goes ahead of them, and the sheep follow him because they know his voice. [10:5] They will not follow a stranger, but they will run from him because they do not know the voice of strangers. [10:6] Jesus used this figure of speech with them, but they did not understand what he was saying to them.*

This is our Lord's allegory, the force of which the Jews did not understand. In order that these words might not be as obscure to us as they were to the Jews, let us prepare ourselves, with the help of God, to explain the meaning of this allegory for those who encounter this book. This is what the Lord means: A thief approaches the sheepfold from somewhere else in order to hide and steal. The

shepherd, on the other hand, does not look for an alternate entrance because he has the authority to enter through the gate and uses the ordinary entrance as he then leads them to pasture. And the sheep follow him because they know their shepherd. They run away from strangers whose voice they do not know; so now too [. . .].[10]

The sheepfold symbolically represents the teaching of the law, and the sheep are those who subject themselves to this teaching and have promised to live according to its precepts. The gatekeeper of this sheepfold is Moses, who established this sheepfold through the prescription of the law, so that those who live according to his will may be safe. The shepherd of the sheep is the one who is worthily endowed with the gift of teaching and uses the lawful entrance. In other words, he is the one who endeavors to live entirely according to the teaching of the law and thus enters the sheepfold exactly as he should. He then leads all the rest, like sheep, to the pastures of his teaching by showing them the food of his words, with which they must first nourish themselves. Once they have done so, he explains the power of those words and how they must be understood. He also points out to the sheep those teachings that others might deceitfully propose to them for their perdition but from which they should abstain.

Since this is what the shepherd is like, it follows that a thief and a bandit is the exact opposite. He does not use the lawful entrance, nor does he show respect for the precepts of the law. This is how he teaches the people given to him: he simply scales the fence and seizes the entrance as well as the office of teacher, because he has done nothing that would entitle him to such honor. He behaves inconsiderately and, by doing whatever he wants, does things that harm the sheep. Indeed, how can one who does not discipline

---

[10] The editor J.-M. Vosté indicates a lacuna in the text here. See CSCO 4 3:i-iv and 197.

himself in the precepts of the law be useful to anyone else? In other words, the Lord is saying, "Let us discern between you and me, if you like, who uses the lawful entrance; who diligently follows the precepts of the law; for whom Moses, the gatekeeper of the sheepfold, opens the gate; to whom [Moses] offers praise for completing his work and who he considers worthy to be declared shepherd because of what he has done.

"If, therefore, in his writings Moses praises the one who fulfills the commandments of the law, this fulfillment of the commandments will be found in me, not in you, because none of you [truly] occupies the office of teaching nor do you perform any useful function for the sheep—although you are quite eager to look out for your own interests. You have no authority to expel anyone and, as a result, even those you do expel end up harmed. I, on the other hand, am rightfully called *shepherd* because, in the first place, I diligently observe the law. I also use the lawful entrance, which the gatekeeper [Moses] has shown me. And, finally, I make sure everything is done that concerns the care of the sheep. Therefore, if I reject someone or other who is far from the truth, that person falls who was rejected. But if I receive someone or other who was expelled, such a person will not be outside truth because he was expelled by you; rather, he will be inside the law in the fear of God because he was received by me."

When our Lord presented this parable, the Jews did not understand anything he said. Our Lord, however, considered it appropriate to say these things in a parable in order not to appear arrogant. He could have boasted of his superiority over them and openly said, "According to the evidence, the office of teacher by right belongs to me, not to you." He did then proceed to talk primarily about himself. But this was not arrogance. He was only trying to show how he was superior in comparison to others—especially when speaking to those who were considered to be the leaders of the people and were held in great honor. Therefore, at this point, he began saying more openly that the rank of shepherd belonged to him, anticipating the reply they were about to give him and explaining it but also confirming what he had just said, even though he had only spoken figuratively when he declared his superiority to them by way of comparison. This is what we understand from his words.

After the parable he spoke in this way: [10:7] *Very truly, I say to you, I am the gate for the sheep.* But here he seems to contradict himself. Indeed, previously he had demonstrated that he had more authority to pasture the sheep because he had entered by the gate. Here, however, he says the opposite, calling himself the gate of the sheep. But in his previous discussion with the Pharisees, who were the leaders of the people in matters of the law, he was showing them how they had unjustly driven out the blind man. And, in offering an appropriate comparison of himself with them on the basis of the rules of the law, he demonstrated that he had fulfilled its requirements to the letter. Therefore he was the true shepherd of the sheep. It was appropriate for him then to say that he entered by the gate because he himself was subject to the law and therefore had to use the lawful entrance. Here he is not talking about the same issue. He calls himself the gate of the sheep because he is the primary access to the truth for everyone. His teaching is, indeed, unique, in that he has made it the instrument through which he issues his call to everyone. He is also the one who established laws as he saw fit so that people might live through them according to his will. He also is the reason [Logos] through which all might come to know the Father. Therefore we have abandoned the works of the law and have applied ourselves to obeying Christ's commandments instead. We have devoted our lives to the principles of the gospel and diligently seek to fulfill his laws. And so it was indeed appropriate for him to call himself the gate of the sheep, since it is otherwise impossible for us to reach the truth unless we first of all believe in our Lord and through his commandments approach the entrance of truth. We can then delight in the blessings we possess through him, thanks to his access to the Father.

There were, however, others before him who asserted that they too taught something new and useful. They enticed many Jews to follow them by deceiving them with great promises and became a cause of many calamities for those who followed them. We need only think of Theudas and Judas the Galilean,[11] whom Gamaliel also mentions in the Acts.[12] And so, when Jesus speaks to the Pharisees, it is probable that the Pharisees intended to bring up these same individuals in order to show by way of comparison that the promise of Christ was false because these same people had also seduced many with the hope of miraculous signs. Time, however, proved their promises to be empty and false. Therefore, anticipating what the Pharisees intended to do, he not only rejected the reply they were about to give but also illustrated with facts the difference between him and them. He said, [10:8] *All who came before me are thieves and robbers; but the sheep did not listen to them.* "Those," he says, "who came—indeed I know what a shameful accusation you are about to level against me—were only thieves and robbers. This is why the sheep did not listen to them." He does not call everyone *sheep*—we need to look closely at this—but only those who are inside the lawful sheepfold of his kingdom. Their entire

focus is on pursuing the truth, which is why they have become close with the Lord of truth.

Then what does he say? [10:9] *I am the gate;* that is, "I am not like them; they are thieves. I am the true door." *If anyone enters by me, he will be saved, and will go in and out and find pasture.* "Those who come to me will receive truth through me. They will enjoy true life and safely graze in the truth, being filled with delight by the teaching of the divine law." The words, *he will go in and out and find pasture,* refer to what happens among sheep that derive great delight from his doctrine of truth.

But how can it be ascertained that they are the thieves and you are the shepherd of the sheep? Since what he had said could not be verified by words only, his words also had to be confirmed by evidence. And so he added, [10:10] *The thief comes only to steal and kill and destroy; I came that they may have life, and have it abundantly.* He confirms his argument by citing those actions that are typical of thieves. "Thieves exist to steal, kill and destroy for their own greed. I am so far removed from these actions that I, in fact, do the exact opposite for those who obey me. In other words, I give them life—and not just any life, but eternal life." This is what he meant when he said, *and [they] have it abundantly,* alluding to the resurrection he will give to the human race.

And so, after providing the evidence derived from these facts, he said to them, [10:11] *I am the good shepherd.* "Therefore, if I take action against thieves, not only am I *not* the cause of perdition for those who obey me, but I even invite them to enjoy eternal life. Thus my actions themselves reveal me as the shepherd because I bring about so much good for

---

[11]Theudas, mentioned in Acts 5:36, was a rebel who opposed Roman authorities around A.D. 6. Judas the Galilean was a Jewish leader who promoted a rebellion against Roman authorities at the same time as Theudas (ca. A.D. 6-7), and is mentioned in Josephus (see *Jewish Antiquities* 18.1.1-6; 20.5.2; *Jewish Wars* 2.8.1; 2.18.8-9; 7.8.1). However, it seems that Theodore is confusing the Theudas of the Acts with a later Theudas who was a pseudo-messiah living in the mid-first century A.D. (ca. 44). He promised to lead his followers through the Jordan, whose waters he would divide with the mere power of his words (see Josephus *Jewish Antiquities* 20.5.1), but was arrested and then beheaded by the Roman consul Cuspius Fadius. [12]See Acts 5:34-37.

the sheep." And he proves his argument even more accurately so that he may not appear to be vainly testifying about himself as the good shepherd. Therefore, using various arguments and facts, he continues, *The good shepherd lays down his life for the sheep.* "If," he says, "the good shepherd is the one who accepts suffering for every affliction on behalf of his sheep, then this testimony is no doubt about me since I will die for the salvation of the whole world. *I am the good shepherd.* Indeed, if the thief kills, not only do I not kill, but I give new life to the human race after taking death from them. So, in every respect, I appear to be the good shepherd according to these facts."

Having shown that he is neither a thief nor a robber like them, he now wants to demonstrate that he is not a hired hand either, like those who lead the sheep to pasture but are not themselves the owners of the sheep that they feed. This is what he declares in comparing himself with the Pharisees and the scribes and all those who were leaders in the law. They did not consider themselves thieves and robbers because they appeared to possess authority over the people according to the traditional order. And yet they did not pasture their sheep like owners but like hired hands, hired by the owner of the sheep for a period of time. So then, he adds, [10:12] *The hired hand who is not the shepherd and does not own the sheep sees the wolf coming and leaves the sheep and runs away—and the wolf snatches them and scatters them.* [10:13] *The hired hand runs away because a hired hand does not care for the sheep.* He demonstrates through this argument that the shepherd is not like the hired hand. Why? Because when the hired hand, who does not own the sheep, sees the wolf coming, he leaves the sheep and only worries about saving himself. After all, since he is only a hired hand, he has no interest in endangering himself for those who don't belong to him.

[10:14] *I am the good shepherd. I know my own, and my own know me,* [10:15] *just as the Father knows me and I know the Father. And I lay down my life for the sheep.* "I am not a shepherd like him [the Father]," he says, "but I do the work of the good shepherd because I die for the sheep and accept death for their salvation. I have drawn them close to me once and for all, and therefore I willingly accept death on their behalf." The words, *I know . . .* refer to his closeness, as in the sentence, "The Lord knows those who are his."[13] Evidently he is signifying differing degrees of knowing according to different persons. He does not say, *I know my own,* in the same way as he says, *my own know me.* How could he have said that he was known by his sheep in the same way that he himself is close to them when he was the one who brought the human race into an intimate relationship with himself? Rather, he means, "I brought them into a close relationship with me by virtue of their goodwill, and they in turn are rewarded by receiving careful attention from me. Those who know me, know me as their master." And this is why he added, *just as the Father knows me and I know the Father.* He is referring here to his human nature, as the context clearly shows. In other words, "Just as I have a close relationship with the Father that never ends, which makes it impossible for me to be alienated from him because I am his Son through my union with God the Word, and I know him as Father and cannot deny my close relationship with him—in the same way, I also draw my sheep into a close relationship with me as my own, and they too know me as their shepherd, nor do they deny my dominion over them as though oblivious of the help I have given them." Nor is it any surprise that the Lord talked about himself as a man. Through his union with God the Word, he has communion with all things.

After demonstrating that he was not a thief

---

[13] 2 Tim 2:19.

like some or a hired hand like others—but that he was a shepherd who would never leave his flock but always serves as their leader and shepherd through his union with God the Word—he now predicts something that was still unknown before the event but would later be revealed by the facts themselves. He says, [10:16] *I have other sheep that do not belong to this fold. I must bring them also, and they will listen to my voice. So there will be one flock, one shepherd.* This sentence alludes to those among the Gentiles who would come to faith because many among the pagans as well as many among the Jews were destined to gather together into a single church and to acknowledge one shepherd and one lord who is the Christ. And this actually happened. But just as at that time the miracles confirmed the words, now the fulfillment of the words confirms the miracles accomplished then, even though it was not apparent at the time. For there were two kinds of things he did: miracles and predictions. But his predictions were fulfilled among those who later saw their results, while his miracles confirmed [the faith] of those who saw them at the time. In this way, whatever each person saw would lead him without hesitation to believe those things which he had not seen.

Since he had spoken at length about his passion—mentioning that he would give his life for his sheep and thus proving he deserved the title of shepherd and that he was not a thief or a hired hand—he did not want his hearers to falsely conclude that the esteem in which they had held him was now diminished because the greatest and most wonderful feat that was to be found in him was actually death. Therefore he wanted to explain at this point that his death would not be like that of any other human being, but that there was a great difference between him and them in this regard. In fact, since everyone else is necessarily obligated to die, they undergo

death out of necessity and can expect nothing else after their death. He differs from them and is superior to them in this respect for two reasons: in the first place, because he accepts death voluntarily and when he wants. The second reason is because he knew that his stay in the tomb would be short-lived and that death would be defeated. And when his soul returned to his body, he would have an imperishable and immortal life that was better than before.

And so he begins his approach to the argument by saying, [10:17] *For this reason the Father loves me, because I lay down my soul in order to take it up again.* He appears to relate allegorically all the things he says about himself, as we will demonstrate in the course of our commentary—especially those that will happen later, such as his resurrection, ascension and the like. Therefore, these things cannot be understood from the context. Instead we have to interpret them in light of their intended result. We see this, for instance, when he says, "No one has ascended into heaven except the one who descended from heaven";[14] or "What if you were to see the Son of Man ascending to where he was before?"[15] These verses suggest a certain power of their own, but the words themselves are unclear. And this occurs with many other expressions, as we have already shown in the course of our commentary, with the help of God. Our present verse [10:17] is similar to these. Certainly one may laugh at the idea that he could lay down his soul in order to take it up again and that this is why the Father loves him. It would have been more reasonable if his Father loved him because he laid down his soul—not in order to take it up again—but because of his love for the sheep. But he referred the words, *For this reason the Father loves me,* to the previous context,[16] and added to them, *I lay down my soul in order to take it up again.* Since

---

[14]Jn 3:13. [15]Jn 6:62. [16]Jn 10:16. [17]Jn 9:3.

he wanted to show that his passion would be absolutely glorious, he started with the most admirable aspect of his passion, the one that his Father would appreciate the most and that aspect that would most draw the attention of his Father's love to him. So he declared that he lays down his life so that he may take it up again in his resurrection, when it will be returned to the body. He did not say, *in order to take it up again*, as though this was the reason [for his sacrifice]. He did not, in fact, die in order to be resurrected. Rather, according to the usual idiom of Scripture, he announced what was going to happen as if this were the reason. For example, "so that God's works might be revealed in him," and so forth.[17] He had also previously presented the result of what happened as the reason, but he did not say that this was the reason for his blindness.[18]

After demonstrating that his passion was great and admirable in these two respects, when he said, *For this reason the Father loves me*, he certainly meant that his passion was pleasing and well received by the Father. Since he would be immediately resurrected after his passion to an imperishable life, being the first one among the entire human race, he demonstrates this again by saying, [10:18] *no one takes it from me, but I lay it down of my own accord*. "I am not obligated to undergo death like everyone else, as if by decree. However, since no one can take [my life] away from me by force, I lay it down whenever I want." And in order to underline even more the sense of these words, he says, *and I have power to lay it down, and I have power to take it up again*. And since this assertion appears to go a great deal beyond his visible nature, he adds, *I have received this command from my Father*. "If what I say to you seems extraordinary and beyond the limits of nature, it nonetheless is the command of the Father's will. Therefore you must believe even

though my words seem to be extraordinary and beyond the possibilities of nature." The words, *I have received this command*, mean this is how he wanted it to happen. He did not order him to die and be resurrected. It was certainly not, in fact, within the power of a man to resurrect himself by observing this command. Rather, he asserts that this was the will and the command of the Father.

If, on the basis of his humanity, he asserted that he has the power to lay down his soul and to take it up again, this is not at all surprising. Indeed, if Enoch was taken,[19] and Elijah was lifted up,[20] how much more did it suit him not to die—he who was more excellent than any other man. However, this is not what I am saying, but only that he has the power to do what is beyond his [human] nature because of his union with God the Word. Just as this assumed man is adored by all creatures, as the truth itself requires—although this act of [worship] has nothing to do with his nature—so does he himself also participate in the act [of resurrection] because of his union with God the Word. Therefore, he has either the power not to die if he does not want to or the power to die when he wants to, according to what appears to him to be the most beneficial for our salvation. But he also has the power to raise himself after his death because he participates in this power on account of his union with God the Word. This is clearly evident because he said, "Destroy this temple, and in three days I will raise it up."[21] Since the Word is obviously God, he promised on the basis of his own strength and power that he would raise up the temple in three days after it had been destroyed. Therefore, if it is characteristic of divinity to resurrect, it is clear that he through his union with divinity has the power to die when he wants and, through the same power, to take

---

[18]See Jn 9:1-8. [19]See Gen 5:24; Sir 44:16; Heb 11:5. [20]See 2 Kings 2:1; 1 Macc 2:58; Sir 48:12. [21]Jn 2:19; see also translator's introduction, esp. quotation from Norris, p. xxvi.

up his soul by returning it to his body against the laws of nature.

Because of these words, [the Evangelist] says, a new debate arose among the Jews. Some of them said, "He has a demon," and so they reproached those who listened to him. Others said, "These are not the words of someone who has a demon. But from the miracles that he has done, his wisdom appears to be far superior to any other human wisdom. Therefore his words must be believed, especially because of his wonderful miracles. A man possessed by the devil," they said, "cannot open the eyes of a blind man."

We must express amazement at those heretics who do not accept that our Lord assumed a soul,[22] when our Lord, in many passages above, talks in detail of his soul. But they raise the objection that it also says that God possesses a soul. Then again, they do not understand that God is also said to possess eyes, hands, feet and any other limb. But this is no reason to deny that our Lord also assumed them. Here, when something like this is said, we understand these words to refer to the [human] nature that was assumed by God the Word, while in the previous context above it only refers to the [divine] operation and will. So *my soul* is said here about the [assumed human] nature. Above, it is referred to the will of *God*, which is inclined to action, because the will of *our* soul can be swayed by either good or bad intentions. In either case, rational thought is characteristic of the nature of the soul.

They also raise the objection to us that the blessed Simon said, "I will lay down my soul for you."[23] I think that this sentence can be used instead to support our argument. Indeed, Simon said, "I will lay down my soul," as a man composed of soul and body, just as our Lord did. It was not the divine nature that spoke about the soul but the human nature, just as

Peter also promised that he would lay down his soul, since it is evident that the soul is a part of man. They have many other objections we could talk about, which we would have to reject, one after another. But there is no time now. Our intention is to explain the text, not to refute heresies. The fact that we have faced these objections is not surprising. Indeed the order of the exposition would have been affected if we had not said something. We had to refer to these objections in order to show that the intended sense of the words was that which we reported in our explanation. In other words, we wanted to show that he was actually speaking about the soul and not intending to express merely a name so that we could think of dreaming up alternate meanings. Just as the interpreter believes that it is useless to introduce many words extraneous to his exposition, so he must also report those which are against the true sense of the words—either because of evil intent or because of the incapability of the other interpreter. And he must also pick the right occasion to resolve the issues. I think that this is necessary for the accurate instruction of those who encounter this book. Therefore I do not take into consideration the heretic Asterius who, in the extreme arrogance he demonstrates in his interpretation of this Evangelist, shows that he did not want to provide any interpretation at all. He only used the excuse of interpreting this Gospel as an opportunity to write about the abominable doctrine of his sect. If someone made the effort to compare the words that he writes in his commentary with those concerning his heretical sect, he would find that barely one out of ten is actually an interpretation. Then, if we eliminate from his words all the insults that he lavishes, nothing else would remain.[24] If someone wants to know how these things should be understood and wants to set out on a pious scien-

---

[22]He refers here to the heresy that has been identified with Apollinaris, who taught that the human soul of Christ was replaced by the divine Logos. [23]Jn 13:37. [24]See preface n. 1 (pp. 1-2). [25]See Book 1 n. 37 (p. 16).

---

tific investigation with a mind that desires to be taught, he must look for the volume that we wrote on the humanity of our Lord, and through that he will understand the truth of what we are saying. Indeed we have accurately refuted his arguments and offered an attentive discussion against all of them.[25]

After these statements the Evangelist said, [10:22] *At that time the festival of the dedication took place in Jerusalem.* He is referring to the dedication of Jerusalem itself—not because the city was founded at that time but because it had been often destroyed by its enemies and in the end was totally devastated by Antiochus. After the enemies had been driven away by the Maccabees, the city regained its ancient magnificence with the help of God. And so every year they celebrated the day in which they had won, and they called it the *Enkainia*[26] of Jerusalem in memory of the victory obtained beyond any hope.

Then, since everyone was gathered together on that day of celebration, Jesus walked in the temple in the portico named after Solomon. As the Jews approached him, they surrounded him and kept him in the middle, saying to him, [10:24] *How long will you keep us in suspense? If you are the Messiah, tell us plainly.* They clearly asked him this question deceitfully. If they really wanted to believe, their faith should have been shown toward the things he had done rather than those that he said. But they intended to question him in order to get him to declare clearly, "I am the Christ." Then they could accuse him of pride as one who openly testified about himself. They did the same thing in the passage mentioned above. Indeed, after he said, "I am the light of the world,"[27] they raised the objection against him, "You are testifying on your own behalf; your testimony is not valid."[28] He saw through their evil intention and therefore did not say, "I am," in order not to give them an opportunity to accuse him.

Instead he said to them, [10:25] *I have told you, and you do not believe. The works that I do in my Father's name testify to me.* [10:26] *But you do not believe, because you do not belong to my sheep.* "If you want to learn about me from my words," he says, "I have already spoken many words to you, and you did not believe. However, why do you want to learn about me from words when my works themselves can better testify on my behalf? Since I refer all my works to the Father, there are two reasons you should be embarrassed before these works: first, because of the magnitude of what I did, and second, because of the glory that ascends to the Father because of them. But you show no respect for either of these because, as I have often told you, my teaching is foreign to you and you can have no communion with me because of your evil intent."

And then, since he wanted to show them that he could foreknow in his inscrutable knowledge who would believe and who would not believe, he said, [10:27] *My sheep hear my voice. I know them, and they follow me.* "Where you're concerned," he says, "I know that you do not belong to my flock. Therefore I believe it is useless to talk to you. However, I do know my sheep, and I consider them to be mine because they hear my voice and obey my words. This is why I prefer talking to them." But he does not identify what their obedience is or how they are obedient.

[10:28] *And I give them eternal life;* that is, "As a reward for their obedience I give them eternal life." He emphasizes this further by adding, *and they will never perish.* In other words, "My gift is so powerful that those who accept it will continually enjoy eternal life, because there is no way they can perish and die after receiving the gift of my grace." And he further tells them that even though there are many deceivers, *No one will snatch them out of my hand.* "It would be impossible—even

---

[26]That is, "dedication" or "inauguration": the term is attested both in the LXX and the Greek New Testament.   [27]Jn 8:12.   [28]Jn 8:13.

if there were ten thousand enemies striving against them—for someone stronger than me to snatch them from my hands. And this is what separates you from my [followers]: you do not believe the words that you heard or the miracles you saw, while even though they may suffer ten thousand afflictions, they will never recede from my presence. This is why they will receive eternal life as the reward they deserve for their goodwill." Since he said, *No one will snatch them out of my hand*—that is, "They cannot separate them from me"—he wanted to clarify these words to his audience by saying, [10:29] *What my Father has given me is greater than all else, and no one can snatch them out of the Father's hand*. He referred the cause of all of this to the Father in order to establish his statement as beyond doubt even to those who did not believe. And since his statement, *No one will snatch them out of my hand*, could appear to be quite ineffective because he had said it, he introduced the power of his Father and his outstanding greatness by adding, *no one can snatch them out of the Father's hand*, because the Father is greater than all. And he also establishes why the words, *no one can snatch them out of the Father's hand*, are necessary to confirm his statement when he says, [10:30] *The Father and I are one*. And so, after saying, "No one can snatch [them] out of my hand, nor out of my Father's hand, because he is greater than all," he appropriately added, *The Father and I are one*. In other words, Jesus says, "I am superior to all just like he is, because I, like him, am the author of creation and I created with him. And so I am equal to him in power. He and I are one in greatness and power. No one can snatch what is mine from my hand or from my Father's hand either."

[10:31] *The Jews* could no longer tolerate his words, so they *took up stones again to stone him*. The heretics, however, are even worse than the Jews in trying to corrupt the evident

meaning of these words by saying, "Now, in another passage he says, 'I ask not only on behalf of these, but also on behalf of those who will believe in me through their word, that they may all be one, as you, Father, are in me and I am in you.'[29] Therefore," they say, "we do not believe that they are equal to God in power or nature." We will clearly show, with the help of God, what these words actually mean when we reach them because they too demonstrate the equality of the Son with the Father. I say this now, in order not to introduce more superfluous words outside the order of the commentary since those words must be explained at their appropriate place.

The term *one* means agreement, similarity and many other things. When, for instance, we read, "Now the whole group of those who believed were of one heart and soul,"[30] it is clear that *one* refers to the unanimous agreement of souls. And again, when we read, "For in one Spirit we were all baptized into one body,"[31] *one* indicates the similarity of our common nature, because we are all transformed into one another through one spiritual regeneration, and each of us is made a member of Christ as we are all gathered into one body. We are all one body according to nature. Adam is the head of us because he was the beginning of our nature. Therefore we are also called the one body of Christ because we were born through the Spirit to an incorruptible life. We declare in the symbol of the resurrection that our head is Christ because he was the first to rise from the dead. It is well known that baptism is a symbol of death and resurrection. The blessed Paul clearly asserts this when he writes, "Therefore we have been buried with him by baptism into death, so that, just as Christ was raised from the dead by the glory of the Father, so we too might walk in newness of life."[32] Since it is quite clear that the term *one* is used in a number of different ways, it was unneces-

---

[29]Jn 17:20-21. [30]Acts 4:32. [31]1 Cor 12:13. [32]Rom 6:4.

sary to inquire whether it occurs somewhere else with a different meaning. In one place it means similarity, while in another place it means agreement. Therefore, what must be ascertained now is how and in what sense it is said here. Does it mean equality or something else? The context of the narrative indicates the answer, and we must refer to it in the explanation of [Christ's] words. He was certainly using the word *one* with regard to strength because [his strength] is greater and more powerful than anyone else's. And this is evident from the interpretation of the words since the Jews did not use the stones they took up because clearly our Lord with his hidden strength calmed their fury after they had picked up the stones.

[10:32] *Jesus replied, "I have shown you many good works from the Father. For which of these are you going to stone me?"* It was beautiful the way he said, *from the Father,* since this magnified their shame because they believed that miracles belonged to the Father. Therefore they had no pretext to accuse him of sin. [10:33] *The Jews answered, "It is not for a good work that we are going to stone you, but for blasphemy, because you, though only a human being, are making yourself God."* Since they could not refute him because of his works because his works clearly appeared to be admirable and beneficial, they reproached him by using the pretext of blasphemy. *You, though only a human being, are making yourself God,* which was indeed an accurate statement. He who said, *The Father and I are one,* makes himself what the Father is. How does our Lord answer? He did two things simultaneously: he put a stop to what they were saying,[33] and he demonstrated that the accusation of the Jews was groundless through a comparison with something inferior. Indeed, usually when you compare something

to its inferior, it causes the value of that thing to increase. What did he say then? [10:34] *Is it not written in your law, "I said you are gods?"*[34] [10:35] *But if they are called "gods" because*[35] *this word came to them—and the Scripture cannot be broken—*[10:36] *can you say that the one whom the Father has sanctified and sent into the world is blaspheming because I said, "I am God's Son?"* "Now, in your law, it was said to the human race, 'You are gods.'[36] Even if we allowed the plain sense of the word spoken to them, they were not in fact transformed into the divine nature, but have received this name by the grace of God. And even though this statement is absolutely sound, I nonetheless seem to you to be blaspheming because I said about myself, *I am God's Son.*" Now, according to the context he should have said, "You say, 'You are blaspheming,' because I said, 'I am God,'" since this was their objection to what he had said. This was also the logical conclusion required by our Lord's words. For the one who says, "If those . . . were called 'gods,'" in good order should have added, "You say, 'You are blaspheming,' because I said, 'I am God.'" But because the word was only spoken to them,[37] he himself said, "The Father and I are one." For there is a great difference between this and that.[38] He uses a comparison in order to demonstrate that it is blasphemous to call a human being by the name of God. Thus, when we compare [calling human beings "gods"] with the phrase, "We are one," there appears to be quite a difference. He also did not want them thinking that when he used the term *one* he was indicating that he had no beginning like the Father. Therefore he appropriately added, "I am God's Son." This indicated that even though he says he is one with the Father, he is not at all saying that he is without beginning like the [Father] who is himself without

---

[33]The Syriac text reads "he stopped his word," *wlmelteh tkas,* but we think it can be easily emended to "he put a stop to what they were saying" according to the context. [34]Ps 82:6; Ex 7:1; 22:28. [35]Theodore's text allows a causal element here. [36]Ps 82:6; Ex 7:1; 22:28. [37]And not to Jesus. [38]That is, between them being called "gods" and Jesus referring to himself as God.

beginning. Rather, like a son with his father, he has perfect similarity with him through his generation.[39]

And so he showed them that his words must not be doubted, and cautiously indicated the deficiency of the comparison—otherwise someone might believe that he could be called God and God's Son in the same way as the rest of humanity. And so he added, [10:37] *If I am not doing the works of my Father, then do not believe me.* [10:38] *But if I do them, even though you do not believe me, believe the works.* "Do not doubt what I say when my works clearly proclaim my greatness. If I do things that do not suit God, do not believe me. But if they are suitable to the Father and are in accordance with his will and power—indeed, all of these things are admirable and profit humanity— even though you raise objections against me, you must blush before the power of my works." And he declared what they must believe on the basis of these facts, saying, *So that you may know and understand that the Father is in me and I am in the Father.* In other words, "In order that you may know and believe that the Father and I are really one." This is what he said above when the Jews argued with him. He settled their complaints by persuading them to believe his words and by saying, *I am in my Father and my Father is in me,* because he knew that the same power was in them both. For he means, "Even though you do not believe my words, at least believe what I am saying through my works." The sentence, *the Father is in me and I am in the Father,* evidently indicates their natural similarity because he appears in the Father, and the Father appears in him, which is the same as saying, "The Father and I are one."[40]

When the Jews began to understand that he had brought them back to his previous words by way of comparing himself with hu-

man beings in order to confirm his speech, [10:39] *they tried to arrest him again, but he escaped from their hands.* [10:40] *He went away again across the Jordan to the place where John had been baptizing earlier, and he remained there.* Many gathered around him there, especially those who had embraced the faith through his words, including those who said, [10:41] *John performed no sign, but everything that John said about this man was true.* And to these words the Evangelist added, [10:42] *And many believed in him there.* Evidently those who gathered around him there were confirmed in their faith by the things that they saw him doing later or that they heard him teaching.

With these words the Evangelist now introduces the episode of Lazarus.

The End of the Fourth Book.

Book Five (John 11:1–12:50)

[11:1] *Now, a certain man was ill, Lazarus of the village of Bethany, the brother of Mary and Martha.* If he had just wanted to speak about the miracle, [the Evangelist] would have said concisely, "There was a certain man named Lazarus who was ill, and Jesus raised him after he had died." But the people would not have believed this if it had been said in such a simple way. So, after he added all the other details and related all of these accurately by indicating from which village he came and whose brother he was and what had exactly happened in the course of events, he was able to corroborate his account for those who might come to read this story. For it would have been impossible to make up this whole story in its entirety. But the Evangelist does not merely want to relate the miracle. He knows that there are many other things in his book beneficial to his readers and records them all in good order.

First of all the description of the women was

---

[39]Being generated, or begotten, is the typical characteristic of the Son, as is maintained by Gregory of Nazianzus *Orations on the Holy Lights* 39.12 (PG 36:348B). [40]Jn 10:30.

useful for instruction in virtue. This is why we
see him accurately describing their behavior
in other areas by first noting, [11:2] *this is the
one who anointed him*, and then saying, [11:5]
Jesus loved them. And so this sign too was ef-
fective in proving the modesty of the women.
The faith and chastity of these women is also
truly revealed through the words they spoke
to our Lord both before and after the death of
Lazarus. The Evangelist thought that all these
details had to be reported for the instruction of
those who would read this story. He relates the
miracle in chronological order, knowing that a
great benefit will result from his words because
this story is full of profound teaching.

So a certain man named Lazarus was ill. He
was from the village of Bethany from which
Mary and Martha came—actually he was their
brother. The Evangelist then emphasizes that
she is the same Mary who anointed the feet of
Jesus with perfume and wiped them with her
hair, clearly showing that he wants to briefly
report the virtue of the women. Therefore he
reports this action of Mary, which shows her
deep love for our Lord because she anointed
him with abundant perfume and wiped his
feet with her hair.[1] So she chose to devote
herself totally to the comfort of the Lord. But
this happened after the events concerning
Lazarus. And the Evangelist demonstrates this
by narrating that fact later. Since the Evangelist certainly wrote his book after this event,
and was about to relate the same event in the
order in which it happened—in view of giving
greater importance to his story and of present-
ing the identity of the woman about whom
he writes—he anticipates this fact by saying
that she is the same woman who did this and
whom he mentions now in the story of Lazarus. Without this addition, someone might
have thought that it was the same name but
different women, as frequently happens among
people.

[11:3] *So the sisters sent a message to Jesus,
"Lord, he whom you love is ill."* There is a great
demonstration of faith in these words. They
knew that the Lord had such great power that
they were amazed that one whom he loved
might be taken ill. The words, *he whom you
love is ill*, are certainly said with great modesty.
But they also demonstrate great faith. Therefore our Lord said, [11:4] *This illness does not
lead to death; rather it is for God's glory, so that
the Son of God may be glorified through it.* "Do
not even entertain the thought," he says, "that
he will die because of this illness. There is
now a short hesitation on my part for the one
whom I love, so that, after accomplishing this
great miracle for him, there may be a sound
demonstration of my power and an occasion
of greater glory for God." He said, *rather it is
for God's glory, so that the Son of God may be
glorified through it*, because this event equally
effected both his glory and that of the Father,
as if he were saying, "So that the Father and
I may be glorified." If someone would like to
consider that Jesus referred the term "God's
[glory]" to himself, we will not discuss this
argument here. And no one must be amazed
if our Lord, even though Lazarus was dead,
said, *This illness does not lead to death.* There
was no real death for the one he was going to
raise shortly thereafter. To this the Evangelist
adds, [11:5] *Jesus loved Martha, and Mary and
Lazarus.* He recalled his love for them in order
to highlight their virtue and the agreement of
their wills. Indeed it would have been impossible that all of them were loved by our Lord
if they had not all been equal in their feelings
and love for him.

After our Lord heard that Lazarus was ill,
as the Evangelist reported, and after providing
his answer,[2] he remained where he was for two
more days. [11:7] *Then after this he said to the
disciples, "Let us go to Judea again."* [11:8] *The
disciples said to him, "Rabbi, the Jews were just*

Book Five [1]See Jn 12:3. [2]To the messenger sent by Lazarus's sisters.

now trying to stone you, and are you going there again?" Since the disciples were still thinking in a human way, they wanted to hold him back in order to save him even though many had accepted the evident proof that nothing could happen against his will. This proof was not only indicated from the things he said but also from the fact that a few days earlier he had miraculously escaped, against all odds, from the hands of those who wanted to arrest him.

What is our Lord's reply to this? [11:9] *Are there not twelve hours of daylight? Those who walk during the day do not stumble because they see the light of this world. [11:10] But those who walk at night stumble because the light is not in them.* "You do not seem to know me yet," he says, "and you do not know that it is impossible for me to die against my will. How can you tell me to run away from Judea so that I may save myself from my enemies? Therefore I say to you: As the day is made of twelve hours and he who walks during the day travels safely and without troubles, whereas he who walks at night is in danger because his steps are uncertain in the darkness—so is it impossible for anything to happen to me against my will. Indeed I have the light of knowledge and, since I know everything, nothing happens to me against my will. Therefore I do not need to protect myself, because I know everything perfectly."

He said these things and then added, [11:11] *Our friend Lazarus has fallen asleep, but I am going there to awaken him.* Our Lord called death "sleep" because of what he was about to do, thus indicating how easy it would be for him to raise Lazarus. Earlier he had said something similar: *This illness does not lead to death.* Because the disciples did not understand, they said, [11:12] *Lord, if he has fallen asleep, he will be all right.* "If he sleeps, he also necessarily will wake up: this is human nature." Since they had not understood that he referred to death as "sleep," he openly said to them, [11:14] *Lazarus is dead. [11:15] For your*

sake I am glad I was not there, so that you may believe. But let us go to him.* In other words, "It is not a question of sleep. Still, I am glad for your sakes that this has happened. The fact that *I was not there* is useful in confirming your faith. Because, in fact, if I had been there, I would have cured his illness and my miracle would have been only a minor demonstration of my power. But since I was away when death came, now I will go there to raise him so that you may be all the more confirmed in your faith, seeing that I can even raise the dead, who are already rotting. Let us go to him, for the time is now at hand."

[11:16] *Thomas, who was called the Twin, said to his fellow disciples, "Let us also go, that we may die with him."* Since the disciples wanted to keep him back, fearing that something bad might happen to him among the Jews—but he would not stay there—Thomas quite aptly gave this reply, which, even though it revealed an unstable faith, nevertheless showed a deep love for the Lord. "It is impossible for him to avoid an ambush by the Jews if he goes back to those from whose hands he just escaped. This much is evident. It would be better for him if he could be persuaded to remain here and stay away from his enemies. However, since he has chosen to go, *Let us also go, that we may die with him.* It is better to share in his death than to be deprived of our teacher in order to be safe."

When Jesus arrived, he found that Lazarus had already been in the tomb for four days. Indeed if you add the two days of the journey to the two days they spent in the place where they were before, you have four days. [11:18] *Now Bethany,* where Lazarus had died, *was near Jerusalem, some fifteen stadii away,* that is, about two miles, as we say. The proximity of the place provided ample opportunity for everyone to hear reports of the accomplished miracle. [11:19] *Many of the Jews had come to Martha and Mary to console them about their brother,* and their presence was quite useful as well so that they might be witnesses to the miracle. [11:20] *When Martha heard that Jesus was coming, she went and met him, while Mary stayed at home.* Mary had not heard that the Lord was coming, as appears from the words that follow.

[11:21] *Martha said to Jesus, "Lord, if you had been here, my brother would not have died."* This is consistent with the words explained above, *He whom you love is ill.* In the same way that she thought illness would not touch those who are loved by the Lord, she also believed that the Lord's presence would be able to prevent death. She then amplifies her speech by saying, [11:22] *But even now I know that God will give you whatever you ask of him.* Up to this point they were still addressing him as an admirable man who could do many things through his power. But at that time before the crucifixion not even his disciples had a perfect understanding of him as God the Word who is the cause of everything—an understanding that the Evangelists and the apostles later proclaimed. Therefore they did not understand many things that they were told, as we have demonstrated above from the words of the Evangelist. And this clearly appears from the words that follow. This will become obvious to those who examine in detail the entire Gospel.

What did the Lord say to her? [11:23] *Your brother will rise again.* [11:24] *Martha said to him, "I know that he will rise again in the resurrection on the last day."* It is clear from this statement that, even though they believed somehow in the power of the Lord, they were still in doubt because of the formidable nature of the task. Since [Martha] had said, *I know that God will give you whatever you ask of him,* the Lord replied, *Your brother will rise again,* because, on the one hand, she had no doubts about his promise, but on the other hand, she considered the task superior to human power—indeed, we said above that they still

[believed] they were speaking to a man who does everything through his own power. This is why she said to him, "I know that he will rise again on the last day." What does our Lord say in reply to her? [11:25] *I am the resurrection and the life.* "If you believe the first [resurrection you mentioned], have no doubt about this one either. No one but me will be able to accomplish this. I am the cause of the resurrection for the entire human race. The one who will raise everyone is not so weak that he cannot raise one individual."

He extends his speech at this point in order to teach, saying: *Those who believe in me, even though they die, will live,* [11:26] *and everyone who lives and believes in me will never die. Do you believe this?* "Therefore, since I am the one who will do this,[3] all those who believe in me will live even though they die." Therefore through his promise they receive death in the blessed hope of what will be in the future; that is, "Whoever lives in me in faith will never die. Even though he may in fact seem to die, he is not dead but lives by reason of the promise with which he receives the law [that governs] the dissolution of [human] nature." After saying this, he quite appropriately added, *Do you believe this?* That is, "Believe firmly what is for your benefit and for the benefit of all those who have this same idea about me in their own true faith."

What did Martha say after this? [11:27] *Yes, Lord, I believe that you are the Messiah, the Son of God, the one coming into the world.* Since he had said, *I am the resurrection and the life*— they were expecting that these things would be done by the Messiah who would rise up from among them for the sake of the human race— it was only right that she made this statement to him, *Yes, Lord, I believe that you are the Messiah, the Son of God,* whom we expected to come into the world according to the words of the prophets. She said these things when

---

[3] That is, who will cause the resurrection of all.

she still had no perfect knowledge of him. Indeed, the most excellent and virtuous men are also called "prophets of God" or "anointed" [i.e., messiahs] in the law. She said this, then, since they expected that the Messiah would be a man far above anyone else. In the course of events we realize that she said those things without perfect understanding, as we also learn from this book. We know this because not even the apostles knew [Christ] perfectly before his resurrection. And even after his resurrection they still had many doubts in their minds as to whether he had truly arisen, as we have learned from Scripture itself.[4]

[11:28] *When she had said this, she went back and called her sister Mary, and told her privately, "The teacher is here and is calling for you."* Nowhere in the Gospel do we read that the Lord told her to call her sister. But we can surely know that this was said to her, even though the Evangelist omitted it since he only expressed what was necessary. Because the Jews were present, she acted with caution when she privately called her sister. She knew that the mere mention of him could be disturbing to them.

[11:29] *And when she heard it, she got up quickly and went to him.* [11:30] *Now Jesus had not yet come to the village, but was still at the place where Martha had met him.* When the Jews who were there to console her in her mourning saw that Mary had suddenly gotten up and gone out, they thought that she was going to the tomb to weep. And so they followed her as if she, being overwhelmed by her sorrow, might be about to do something which it was their duty to prevent. Ordered by divine providence, then, and not under their own volition, they went there and became witnesses of the miracle that was about to occur. When Mary came to Jesus, she immediately fell at his feet, repeating what Martha had said, [11:32] *Lord, if you had been here, my brother would not*

have died. There is no record of Martha actually falling at his feet, but only that she came to him. This is why many think that Mary had a greater love for the Lord. This also appears from the fact that Martha was intent upon serving the Lord when he was at their house, while Mary, because of her great love, sat at his feet because she did not want to be separated from her teacher for even a brief period of time.[5] Therefore the Lord exalted her in his praise more than Martha.

[11:33] *When Jesus saw her weeping, and the Jews who came with her also weeping, he was greatly disturbed in spirit and deeply moved.* [11:34] *He said, "Where have you laid him?"* The fact that he was disturbed was a sign of anger. The Lord demonstrated his anger ahead of time in order to highlight the unbelief of the Jews, even after they had witnessed the miracle. This is why the Evangelist commented that *he was greatly disturbed in spirit.* Jesus asked, *Where have you laid him?* not because he had no idea—how could the one who said that [Lazarus] was dead while he was still far away be ignorant of this?—but because he wanted to show he did this miracle according to a certain order and not merely to show off. *They said to him, "Lord, come and see."* [11:35] *And Jesus wept.* And yet, since he was about to raise him, it was useless to weep. Nonetheless, he established a rule for us and through his tears taught us the right measure of mourning as to what was sufficient so that we might not be oppressed by grief beyond proportion. When some of the Jews saw Jesus weeping, they said, [11:36] *See how he loved him!* Others, however, said, [11:37] *Could not he who opened the eyes of the blind man have kept this man from dying?* It is typical to try to undercut what someone does by citing what he or she did not do, just as the Jews dealt with Moses, "Even though he struck the rock so that torrents overflowed, can he also give us bread?"[6] Therefore the

---

[4]See Mk 16:11; Lk 24:11-49; Jn 20:9. [5]See Lk 10:39. [6]Ps 78:20.

Evangelist added, [11:38] *Then Jesus, again greatly disturbed, came to the tomb.* He was disturbed because he was angry at what they were saying since he could see that they despised the signs he had already done. And even then they did not accept the fact that they had received what they had asked for once it had been granted.

Since Lazarus was placed in a cave and a stone enclosed its entrance, [11:39] *Jesus said, "Take away the stone."* The stench offended Martha when they removed it. She said, *Lord, already there is a stench because he has been dead four days.* These were the words of a woman who doubted. But her words also highlighted the enormity of the miracle about to be performed. Indeed, the more they knew that his body was putrefying and in a state of natural decay, the more extraordinary the miracle appeared to be for Lazarus. This is why the Lord also reproved her saying, [11:40] *Did I not tell you that if you believed, you would see the glory of God?* From this it is evident that doubts still lingered in her mind, even when she said what she did above, where she seemed to admit that it was possible and believed.

[11:41] *So they took away the stone.* Then Jesus lifted his eyes upward in order to show that he deferred to the Father in all the work he did so that the Jews might have no excuse for their unbelief. *Father, I thank you for having heard me.* But it was too great a thing to thank his Father for complying with a request he has not yet made. Therefore, what is the purpose for him saying this? [11:42] *I knew that you always hear me, but I have said this for the sake of the crowd standing here, so that they may believe that you sent me.* Even though he speaks from a human point of view, he nonetheless shows that he has omnipotence, which he has received from God the Word through his union with him. This is what the phrase, *you always hear me*, means. Therefore he revealed why he said what he did for those present in order that they might have no excuse for their disbelief, as though he were acting against the will of the Father since, on the contrary, everything he does is referred to the Father. It is abundantly clear that God the Word would never need to make a request through a prayer in order to obtain power to raise from the dead. Indeed the Creator of all needs no prayer to raise the dead. He openly said this with reference to the temple, "In three days I will raise it up,"[7] attributing to himself all the will and power for that task. [11:43] *When he had said this, he cried with a loud voice, "Lazarus, come out."* He said this with a loud voice, not because he needed a loud voice in order to resurrect someone, but in order that he might show to those present that he called the soul from a long distance and that he did not raise the dead as if the soul was still in the body.

[11:44] *The dead man came out, his hands and feet bound with strips of cloth, and his face wrapped in a cloth*, that is, in the apparel in which he had been buried according to human custom. All these things were admirable, namely, the fact that he came alive and then rose with his hands and feet bound, and came out with his face wrapped—in a word, anyone who wants to examine these things will see how admirable and great they all were. It is not necessary for the sake of the interpretation of the text to add anything else about the extraordinariness of this event.

Our Lord ordered them to unbind him and let him go, as was his custom. The Jews who were present had different opinions about what had happened. Some believed in him because of the miracle that he had performed. Others, on the contrary, were so far away from believing that they went to the Pharisees to denounce him as if he had done something unlawful. But even what they did out of hatred and evil intent contributed to making the ac-

---

[7]Jn 2:19.

complished miracle well known to everyone.

After hearing this, the chief priests and the Pharisees gathered together and called a meeting where they said, [11:47] *What are we to do? This man is performing many signs.* Since they could not disavow this fact, they believed the miracles were evil and therefore said, [11:48] *If we let him go on like this, everyone will believe in him, because of the miracles.* And what will happen as a consequence? *The Romans will come and destroy both our holy place and our nation.* They invented a reason to justify their evil. They said this because they were under the tribute of the Romans, under whom they were registered and to whom they paid tributes as they were ordered. "If now everyone believes in him, and follows him by considering him a king and a leader, the suspicion will arise among the Romans that we are planning a rebellion and endeavoring to become a nation again to free ourselves from their domination. Then they will become angry with us, destroy us and annex our region." And this actually happened to them because of their arrogance toward the Lord. This need not have happened, however. Our Lord did not incite rebellion among those who believed in him. He provided the Romans no cause to think this and kill the Jews as enemies and rebels. On the contrary, if the Jews had believed, those very Romans themselves who accepted faith in Christ with great love would have held the Jews in honor because the Lord Jesus was born among them.

[11:49] *But one of them, Caiaphas, who was high priest that year, said to them* at the meeting, [11:50] *It is better for us to have one man die for the people than to have the whole nation destroyed.* He puts a slightly different interpretation on what they said above.[8] John refers to him as the *high priest that year.* In other words, he was high priest at that time and for that year. Indeed the high priesthood was no longer

passed on for posterity from one generation to the next but was given to those whom the Romans desired. And after they had served for a certain amount of time in the dignity of the high priesthood, they were removed and immediately replaced by others who were entrusted with this duty. The Evangelist adds, [11:51] *He did not say this on his own,* but since he had the rank of high priest, he began to foretell future events without knowing what he was saying. What did he say? That Christ would clearly die for the people and would undergo his death for the common good. He added, [11:52] *and not for the nation only, but to gather into one the dispersed children of God.* The death of our Lord is not beneficial only to them but also to those among the Gentiles who would believe and later be converted by the apostles to the fear of God. [11:53] *So from that day on they planned to put him to death.* [11:54] *Jesus therefore no longer walked about openly among the Jews, but went from there to a town called Ephraim in the region near the wilderness; and he remained there with the disciples.*

After the Evangelist related what had happened, he digressed at this point before describing the passion of our Lord by reporting what was said and done by our Lord before his passion, as well as what he himself said about his passion. No other Evangelist had addressed all of these topics. But the blessed John thought that all these things needed to be related because they were useful to his purpose. Indeed he wanted to tell what had been omitted by all the others.

Therefore he says, [11:55] *Now the Passover of the Jews was near.* In order not to overly extend our work by quoting well-known sentences and interpreting them again, we will now do what we did elsewhere concerning the previous sentences, that is, we will relate what the Evangelist recorded without following the entire course of the narrative. At the same

---

[8]See Jn 11:48.

time, we will keep the order of the sequence that will enable us to treat single sentences while avoiding an overabundance of words.

Many went up from the country to Jerusalem in order to purify themselves before the Passover according to what the Law commanded because if they did not purify themselves, they would not have access to the mystery of the Passover due to some impurity they had contracted by chance. They gathered together in the temple and discussed among themselves whether our Lord would come [to Jerusalem] out of respect for the festival, or would avoid coming in order to protect himself from the ambushes of his enemies. This is what those who wanted to see him were discussing since, as one would expect, the crowd was interested in him because of the miracles he had performed. [11:57] *Now the chief priests and the Pharisees had given orders that anyone who knew where Jesus was should let them know, so that they might arrest him.*

[12:1] *Six days before the Passover Jesus came to Bethany*, to the village of Lazarus, Martha and Mary, where he had raised Lazarus from the dead. As usual, they received him with great affection and prepared a meal for him while Martha waited on them. Lazarus was also at the table with him. And Mary took a small vase of very good and expensive perfume and anointed his feet, then wiped his feet with her hair. When Judas, who was going to betray him, saw this, he complained as if this woman were trying to keep the scent of the body of our Lord on her flesh. He could not appreciate the faith and love this woman displayed through the things she did to honor the Lord—even to the extent of using her own hair. Indeed, since she was always eager to be by his side, she obviously did this out of love. In fact, even when he happened to be far away, she believed even then that he was always with her.

And yet Judas reproves this woman as if she were guilty of being extravagant, saying, [12:5] *Why was this perfume not sold for three hundred denarii and the money given to the poor?* The Evangelist not only reports what he said, however, but also explains his motives by adding, [12:6] *He said this not because he cared about the poor, but because he was a thief; he kept the common purse and used to steal what was put into it.* And what the Evangelist said is confirmed by facts. One who was supposed to care for the poor out of compassion[9] could never have honored the poor more than the teacher of all mercy. And so our Lord, in order that he might not leave the woman under accusation—and so that he might not appear to prefer himself [over the poor]—modestly and with kind words excused the woman while implicitly uncovering at the same time the motives of the one who appeared to accuse her.

This is also why he spoke to him in such an obscure way. And what did he say? [12:7] *Leave her alone. She bought it so that she might keep it for the day of my burial.* [12:8] *You always have the poor with you, but you do not always have me.* Even though he could have employed more severe words against Judas by reproaching his intention for saying those things and accusing this woman who showed such a great love for him, Jesus chose not to do so. Judas, in fact, was quite bold in blaming her when he actually should have been praising her if she cared so much for the teacher. Jesus excused the woman and issued a veiled rebuke to Judas. And yet, at one point when he was talking about his passion, he sternly called the blessed Simon "Satan,"[10] even though Simon appeared to express with great love the words, "God forbid it, Lord. This must never happen to you."[11] But Jesus only employed harsh words when it was clear that his rebuke would have some benefit for those whom he reproached. When he knew that it was useless, he spoke with moderation and refrained from saying anything that would

[9]That is, Judas. [10]Mt 16:23. [11]Mt 16:22.

have been superfluous anyway.

Therefore he says, "Why do you rebuke her for doing this when you should rather praise her for what she did and for her love for me which should be pleasing to you? Even if nothing else happened that might persuade you to admire what this woman did, you should have at least exhibited some human sympathy since I am approaching my passion, realizing the great honor due a man who is about to die. Even enemies frequently reconciled with those who were dying and gave up their hatred for them. Since I will soon taste death, realize that she, according to human custom, poured that perfume for my burial. Or do you think that I am unworthy of this kind of care for my burial? Therefore, since she will not be able to do these things for me—indeed there will be no opportunity for her to do anything at the time of my burial, nor to find the dead body in the tomb on the third day to take care of it according to custom[12]—realize that through what she has now done she has fulfilled the ritual that is due and leave the woman without rebuke. This is what he means when he says, *Leave her alone. She bought it so that she might keep it for the day of my burial.*

[12:8] *You always have the poor with you, but you do not always have me.* "If," he says, "you really desire mercy for the poor, there is still much time left for you to benefit them; there will never be a shortage of them in this world. But it will not always be easy for you to perform a service for me. I am staying with you for only a short time, and then I will leave." With these words, he purified the woman from blame by modestly suggesting that a greater honor should be attributed to him than to the poor because he was staying with them for only a short time. He also offered an indirect rebuke of Judas's motives since Judas was not at all concerned for the poor, nor had he reproached the woman because of the perfume she had poured.

In relating these events the blessed Matthew is extremely concise.[13] He did not identify the woman who anointed with the perfume. Instead, he simply omitted the name and said it was a certain woman. He also did not identify Judas as the one who complained but simply indicated these were the words of all the disciples, since his purpose was not to accuse but simply to relate the story in a simple way. The blessed John, on the other hand, demonstrated the power of his own great love for Christ by what he related. He had no desire to omit the name of this woman who demonstrated her love for our Lord through what she did, nor did he decide to denounce and openly refute the intention of the betrayer. In this way, he made them both well known to future generations by mentioning her for her work of virtue and by reproving him for his evil intention. We still must notice this detail, that is, that Matthew said that she poured the perfume on his head, while John tells us she anointed his feet and wiped them with her hair. It is evident from this that she did both: she anointed his head and feet. The blessed Matthew related [the story] concisely and therefore only spoke about the head. John, since that [detail] had been reported already, omitted it because there was an even greater demonstration of love for Christ in the fact that she anointed his feet and wiped them with her hair. He thought that it was fitting to relate this fact.

The Jews discovered that Jesus was again in Bethany and was living with Lazarus and his sisters, and was with them at that moment. Many came, [12:9] *not only because of Jesus but also to see Lazarus, whom he had raised from the dead.* Maybe they expected to hear something extraordinary from him, like someone who comes back to civilization from a strange and remote land. For this reason the chief priests, when they saw that the crowd was also greatly attracted by the desire to see Lazarus, planned

---

[12]See Mt 28:1-10; Mk 16:1-7; Lk 24:1-12; Jn 20:1. [13]See Mt 26:6-13.

to kill Lazarus together with Christ. They were obviously thinking that the crowds would not confine themselves to seeing Lazarus but rather, when they saw him, would be led to faith in Christ—as if he who had raised him from the dead once would not be able to bring him back to life again.

When Jesus was about to enter Jerusalem for the festival, the crowds [12:13] *took branches of palm trees and went out to meet him, shouting, "Hosanna! Blessed is the one who comes in the name of the Lord—the King of Israel."* The blessed Matthew[14] mentioned that even the children spoke these words of praise. This is why the chief priests and Pharisees murmured and found fault with our Lord, as if he was the cause of this event. Therefore he reminded them of the words of the prophet, "Out of the mouths of babes and infants you have established praise."[15] The implication is that, when they saw the deeds and the outcome of the prophecy, they should not blame him for something that had been predicted then and fulfilled here. John, on the other hand, did not mention these events. He only relates how the crowd went out to meet him and reports what they said, omitting all the other details already reported by the blessed Matthew. Matthew also relates that these two events did not happen at the same time; rather, after the crowd went out to meet him and welcome him, then the events with the children occurred, that is, after his entry into the temple.[16] It also seemed appropriate to John to relate his entrance into the temple, both for the order of the events and in order to show the reason why this happened, since it appears later[17] that the reason the crowds were motivated to go out to meet him was the greatness [of his miracle].[18]

Therefore John briefly records that [12:14] *Jesus found a young donkey and sat on it*, in order to manifest clearly the fulfillment of this prophecy, while omitting all the other details because they had been sufficiently reported by Matthew. Then he added in his narrative for the sake of accuracy, [12:16] *His disciples did not understand these things at first; but when Jesus was glorified, then they remembered that these things had been written about him and had been done to him.* [He added this] in order to demonstrate to those who would read his book that the disciples understood nothing of what happened before his resurrection. Also, above he seems to allude to this in the words that our Lord said about his resurrection.

After describing how his entry occurred in which he sat on a donkey so that he might confirm the words of the prophecy, and after alluding to the fact that the disciples understood nothing of what happened at that time but only received such grace of comprehension after his resurrection in order to perfectly understand everything—after including these further supplemental details, he finally included the reason that incited the crowds to go out to meet him, [12:17] *So the crowd that had been with him when he called Lazarus out of the tomb and raised him from the dead continued to testify.* [12:18] *It was also because they heard that he had performed this sign that the crowd went to meet him.* For, through Adam death had entered and brought all under subjection, but through the prophets they had heard and believed that death would be defeated.[19] When they saw that this had indeed been done by our Lord, who raised a man that had been dead for four days, they took branches of palm trees and went out to meet him as the victor over death which oppresses the human race, and extolled him with appropriate songs of praise. Since this was unacceptable to the Pharisees, they began arguing among themselves because they had set traps against [Jesus], but to no avail, since all the people were going after him.[20]

---

[14]See Mt 21:15. [15]Ps 8:2; Mt 21:16. [16]See Mt 21:1-16. [17]See Jn 12:18. [18]That is, the resurrection of Lazarus. [19]See Hos 13:14. [20]See Jn 12:19-22.

Accompanying these words, the Evangelist also adds that in Jerusalem there were some Gentiles who, according to custom, had come up for the festival in order to worship God. Because of the miracles that God had always performed among the Jews, the temple in which God was worshiped was held in great honor. And many Gentiles, even though they did not perfectly observe the precepts of the law, went up to worship God and to participate in the festival, as much as they could. They were there at this time and had heard that some signs had been done, as well as seeing other signs as they occurred. This is why they approached Philip, because they desired to see our Lord in order to fulfill their desire through him and through his disciples. Philip, however, did not believe that he had the permission to inform our Lord about them because he would have had to speak to him about Gentiles, with whom, according to the law, Jews were not allowed to communicate. And this is even more the case because our Lord himself, when he sent them to Judea, had ordered them not to go the way of the Gentiles,[21] because at that time he wanted to arrange things in this way. At any rate, [Philip] talked to Andrew, and both approached our Lord, informing him that some Gentiles wanted to see him. What did our Lord say to them?

He foretold the future in order to let them know that he was not hearing anything new or extraordinary from them, and that things greater than those which they planned on saying to him would be happening. He said, [12:23] *The hour has come for the Son of Man to be glorified.* "The time for my glorification before everyone is quite near; the time when I will be elevated to honors that are higher than my nature is very close." He uses the title *Son of Man*, as we have shown in various passages, to refer to the man who before the cross took on all the characteristics of humanity but

who, after the resurrection and ascension into heaven, is worshiped by all creatures because of his union with God the Word. Because he was promising something entirely new and wonderful, this could have appeared to be in conflict with his future passion. Therefore he added, [12:24] *Very truly, I tell you, unless a grain of wheat falls into the earth and dies, it remains a single grain; but if it dies, it bears much fruit.* "However," he says, "my death must not upset you. As indeed a grain of wheat is just a single grain before falling into the earth, once it has fallen and has decomposed, it sprouts forth in great glory and produces a double increase of fruit, displaying the abundance in its ears before all and the spectacle of its beauty to those who are looking. This is how you should think about me. At the moment, I am alone and considered to be no more glorious than all the other obscure mortals. But when I undergo the passion of the cross, I will rise in great honor and bear much fruit. Then everyone will know me—not only the Jews, but the entire world. And they will call me their Lord, and not even the spiritual powers will refuse to worship me."

After he made this prediction about himself, which was fulfilled by ensuing events, our Lord openly exhorted his disciples to imitate him, saying, [12:25] *Those who love their life lose it, and those who hate their life in this world will keep it for eternal life.* "Therefore," he says, "not only must you not be upset by my passion or doubt my words because of it, since events will confirm what I have said, but you must also be prepared for this [suffering], so that when you suffer what I suffer, you will also enjoy what I enjoy. Whoever appears overly concerned with his life here and does not want to submit to testing will lose it in the life to come. Whoever hates his life and in this world exposes it to the afflictions that sometimes befall him gathers much fruit for himself." He does not say this as if the soul actually suffers something here.

---

[21]Mt 10:5.

Rather, he simply calls the "love of the soul" that idea which prevails among us where we believe we are defending our soul and serving it if we protect our body from any possible danger. So he incites them with modesty by saying, [12:26] *Whoever serves me must follow me.* "If someone wants to be my servant, he must show through his works that he follows me." And what is the benefit for those who suffer with you? He answers, *And where I am, there will my servant be also. Whoever serves me, the Father will honor.* "Whoever participates with me in tribulations," he says, "will also participate with me in honor. And in the age to come he will be with me eternally and will rejoice with me in the kingdom of heaven. The Father will reward such honor to those who have faithfully served me."

After exhorting them by his example and confirming them in his teaching, he illustrates his experience again by saying, [12:27] *Now my soul is troubled. And what should I say—* *"Father, save me from this hour?" No, it is for this reason that I have come to this hour.* "The things that happen to me," he says, "are an example for you. Even if my soul is troubled in anticipation of the passion, what should I ask of my Father? To be freed and rescued from suffering? But this would not be right, and therefore this is not what I ask at all. On the contrary, since I know that it is good to undergo trials on behalf of the truth, this is the expectation I have as I wait. Even though passion afflicts, what is better prevails. What this is, I do not say. Instead I say, [12:28] *Father, glorify your name.*" "I ask for that which brings greater glory to God," he says. "Therefore do not fear death or be frightened by trials and tribulations. Instead do what is pleasing to God and glorify him more before everyone so that they all may know him through the trials inflicted upon you."

As he spoke these words, a voice from heaven came to confirm even more for the disciples what he had said: *I have glorified it,* *and I will glorify it again,* that is, "I have glorified myself already through the miracles I have done, and will further reveal myself through those which still must be done." The things experienced by the assumed man revealed, then, the nature of God the Word dwelling in him and how great the dignity was of him who is the cause of all these events—as well as the [dignity of] the Begetter himself who begat such an excellent and admirable nature. The crowds had different opinions about the voice that came. Some said that it was thunder; others said, [12:29] *an angel has spoken to him.* It is evident that that voice itself was indistinguishable, stupefying those present by its mere sound. But the disciples, to whom these words of our Lord were addressed, came to know what had been said through divine revelation.

But our Lord said, [12:30] *This voice has come for your sake, not for mine.* "I did not need this voice," he says, "to know that I would be glorified. Indeed I already knew this would happen. Therefore I had no need to ask for what I knew would certainly happen. This voice came so that you would learn the identity of the one who has come, because the one who speaks to him is in heaven. It also confirms that my words are true concerning what will happen to you and me at the end if you want to be a part of this."

After our Lord received such a great and irrefutable confirmation in the presence of his disciples—indeed, they could not fail to believe what was spoken to them from this point on— he tells them that his passion will bring about much good in the world so that they need not believe it was useless for him to suffer. Therefore he adds, [12:31] *Now is the judgment of this world; now the ruler of this world will be driven out.* [12:32] *And I, when I am lifted up from the earth, will draw all people to myself.* "Whatever happens occurs on behalf of the world," he says, "for now the entire world is judged by me. You see, when the first human being was created, he withdrew from God out of disobedience and was subsequently condemned to death. He became subject to Satan, along with all of his descendants, who, because they were evil, greatly increased in their iniquity and established Satan as their harsh and tyrannical lord. And because of this, they became even more wicked as their sins multiplied, establishing more and more a kingdom of death for themselves. There was no human being capable of attacking this tyrant. Therefore I came for every person, both for those who lived previously and for those who would come afterward. I do not trust in my own power, however. Instead, I hope to fulfill this through the help of the nature dwelling in me.

"The world, therefore, is judged by me, that is, through me against Satan. Indeed, sin and iniquity gave him dominion over the human race, and he bound everyone in the fetters of death. However, since I have lived perfectly and have paid the tribute to the law established by God, and have done everything according to his will and desire—even though I can find no reason why I should deserve death—I will not flee, like Elijah[22] or Enoch.[23] I do not want to be the only one to profit from this. Instead, I will accept death—not out of necessity as though I deserved it, but in order that before God, the Lord of the universe, I may condemn him who brought death into the world. God the Word, who assumed me and united me to himself, has confidently given me the victory of judgment. He made me his own once and forever when he assumed me, and it is evident that he will never leave me, lest I do something rash. When the Lord of the universe hears our judgment and sees that [Satan] has unjustly and undeservedly brought death to me by abusing me with his tyranny, he will order me to be released from the chains of death so that I may thereafter have the certainty of offering prayers to God on behalf of the children of my race, so that those who share the same nature with me may participate in the resurrection as well. And thus, there will be grace for all when they are all freed from condemnation through the victory of my judgment. The tyrant who has iniquitously ruled over them in this world will be deposed from his throne. The chains by which he first bound the human race and then subjected them will be snatched from him. Humans made mortal through their punishment used to be easily inclined to crime, and the tyrant, allied with the multiplication of sins, dominated them more and more. However, when everyone is delivered from his bondage after being healed through the resurrection, they will return to their Lord, because after the cross, death, and resurrection I will draw all of them to me and will bring them to life in me."

It was appropriate that he said, *I will draw*, indicating how he snatches them away from the one who holds them. He draws everyone because he has given them all the hope of the resurrection, in which they will participate afterward, and because he generously endowed many with the knowledge of the truth in this life. He delivered the human race from great iniquity and through his commandments removed them from various deeds of wickedness. He will give them all perfect [knowledge of the truth] after the resurrection. Through the words, *I will draw all people to myself*, he means that all will be united to him through his resurrection—not only because he delivers them from death and draws them close to himself but also because he generously gives them his perfect knowledge.

The Evangelist explains the phrase, *when I am lifted up*, observing that, [12:33] *He said this to indicate the kind of death he was to die.* The crowd objected to what he said: [12:34] *We have heard from the law that the Messiah remains forever. How can you say that the Son of Man must be lifted up? Who is this Son of Man?*

---

[22]See 1 Kings 17:2-5. [23]See Gen 5:21-23; Sir 44:16; Heb 11:5.

It is clear that the Jews thought highly of the Messiah since they say, *He remains forever*, instead of, "he will not die." They expected that he, like Elijah, would remain immortal. It is not surprising that the Jews held various opinions about the Messiah, however, since they quite frequently disagreed about what these prophecies meant before the events themselves occurred that had been prophesied, since they each heard the words of the prophets in different ways.

What did our Lord say? [12:35] *The light is with you for a little longer. Walk while you have the light, so that the darkness may not overtake you. If you walk in the darkness, you do not know where you are going.* [12:36] *While you have the light, believe in the light, so that you may become children of light.* By way of example, he declared that he would experience death but would not remain dead. He called himself *light*. "This light," he says, "is like the light of the sun after it sets, which appears to be extinguished to those who do not see it; but it is neither extinguished nor destroyed. It continues to exist in its nature and reappears at the proper time. This is how you should think of me. I do not remain dead when I die since my body will not be subject to corruption. Instead, after the soul departs for a short time, the body will soon be resurrected and the soul will remain incorruptible. Therefore, at the proper time, I will reappear from heaven in the sublime glory that I have above everything else from my union with God the Word, and I will reveal my dignity to all."

It was quite fitting that he said, *The light is with you for a little longer.* Through the phrase, *is with you*, he signified that the light would not cease nor would it be extinguished. Instead, it would simply depart from them. "So, this is how you should think of me. Do not fear that death will completely destroy me. Rather, take confidence in my teaching, be en-lightened by the light of my words and receive the knowledge I give, so that through your faith in me error may not catch up with you and nothing may happen to you that befalls those walking in darkness who have no idea what to do or how they should act. But since you are with me as my children, this light will always be in your soul when by faith you become familiar with my teaching so that, even if it seems as though I am absent, I may be close to you through the words of my teaching. Then you will always be enlightened by the truth, and no one can deprive you of this as long as the memory of my words remains in you."

[12:36] *After Jesus had said this, he departed and hid from them.* Evidently, as was proper, he was preserving himself for the day of his passion, which was the day of the Passover, in which he would create a new Passover[24] by offering himself as a lamb endowed with reason for the sins of the world, instead of the lamb of the Jews, thus protecting himself so that nothing might happen to him before the proper time, he decided to leave this dangerous situation with the Jews before the day in which he would suffer according to the divine plan.

To these words the Evangelist added, [12:37] *Although he had performed so many signs in their presence, they did not believe in him.* [12:38] *This was to fulfill the word spoken by the prophet Isaiah, "Lord, who has believed our message, and to whom has the arm of the Lord been revealed?"*[25] He does not mean this was the reason for their unbelief. Indeed how could their mind be forced to not believe against their will in order to fulfill the prophecy? The fact that the Jews did not believe the things that happened [in their midst] is nothing new. In fact, this had long been predicted and was well known. He quoted the prophet Isaiah because Isaiah had foretold that it would be difficult to find believers among the Jews.

[24]Namely, Easter. [25]Is 53:1.

Then he adds another testimony to confirm what he said. [12:40] *He has blinded their eyes and hardened their heart, so that they might not look with their eyes, and understand with their heart and turn and I would heal them.*[26] He further adds, [12:41] *Isaiah said this because he saw his glory and spoke about him.* Indeed, when he saw the Lord of the armies sitting upon the high and lofty throne along with the Seraphim who were praising him and proclaiming him "Holy," the Lord then said to him, "Go and say to this people, 'Keep listening, but do not comprehend; keep looking, but do not understand.'"[27] Here the blessed John says that the glory of the Christ was seen by Isaiah. In the Acts the blessed Paul said that he saw the Spirit, as he said to the Jews, "The Holy Spirit was right in saying to your ancestors through the prophet Isaiah, 'You will indeed listen, but never understand,'" and so forth.[28] What did he see? In the spiritual vision, in the revelation of the divine nature, which is incomprehensible, Isaiah saw the glory that is common to the Father, the Son and the Holy Spirit, since Scripture cannot establish precisely whether it is the glory of the Son or the Holy Spirit. Therefore neither the Evangelist nor the apostle is in contradiction in saying that it is the glory of the Son or of the Holy Spirit. We might also notice that when the blessed Paul in the Epistle to the Romans[29] wanted to demonstrate that the unbelief and reproach of the Jews had already been revealed by the prophets, he made use of these same testimonies just as the blessed John did for the same purpose. After relating what Isaiah said, John added these words to confirm the reproach that occurred because of the disbelief of the Jews.

Then the Evangelist said, [12:42] *many among the authorities who believed in him hid their opinion about him because of the Pharisees, as they feared they might lose their privileged* positions, and [12:43] *because they valued the glory of men more than the glory of God.* What did our Lord say? While some believed, others did not even accept the accomplished miracles. And there were also others who only came to know the truth through the miracles, but hid their opinion because of their fear of the Pharisees since they were pursuing human glory. This is why he cried and spoke aloud in words that would confirm his own [glory] while at the same time closing the mouths of his adversaries.

Therefore the Evangelist recorded, [12:44] *Jesus cried aloud, "Whoever believes in me believes not in me but in him who sent me."* How is it that he who believes in him does not believe in him? But since above and elsewhere they endeavored to persecute him as if they were protecting God and the law, he said, *whoever believes in me believes not in me but in him who sent me,* in order to reject their alleged reasons and to resolve the doubts of those who believed in him. "I am raising you up to God. This is why I say what I do. Therefore, whoever believes in me knows the Father through me. Do not think that this reason you offer may excuse your disobedience. [12:45] *And whoever sees me sees him who sent me.* What was said before seems to contradict this. Indeed what was said previously indicates a great difference [between Father and Son]; here there is a perfect similarity. Whoever sees that One [i.e., the Father] through this One [i.e., the Son] is clearly led to such a vision through their similarity. But since he had said those words to remove the reason of their pretext, in order not to lower himself to excessive humility, he indicated his similarity by adding, *whoever sees me sees him who sent me.* Through both statements he revealed that he was not separating them from the Father. The earlier statement was directed toward the unbelievers, while the present statement now elicits more precision.

---

[26]See Is 6:9-10. [27]See Is 6:1-9. [28]Acts 28:25-26. [29]See Rom 10:16.

For knowledge of their true similarity was evidently granted to the entire assembly of believers and was certainly not meant to remove them from the Father.

What did he say then? [12:46] *I have come as light into the world, so that everyone who believes in him should not remain in the darkness.* "Through my advent, I fulfill the role of light for you so that I may instruct you about myself and the Father, just as the light, as soon as it rises, is seen and enables all things illuminated by it to be seen as well." [12:47] *I do not judge anyone who hears my words and does not keep them, for I came not to judge the world, but to save the world.* "If someone," he says, "does not hear my words or, even though he seems to hear them does not keep them, he is not judged by me. I indeed have come to save him, and this is the purpose of my advent." What else? [12:48] *The one who rejects me and does not receive my word has a judge.* Who is he? *On the last day,* he says, *the word that I have spoken will serve as judge.* And who is the word spoken by you that will judge? [12:49] *I have,* he says, *not spoken on my own, but the Father who sent me has himself given me a commandment about what to say and what to speak.* [12:50] *And I know that his commandment is eternal life. What I speak, therefore, I speak just as the Father has told me.* Many words seem to contradict one another if they are examined separately from their context and by themselves.

In the first place, he says, *I do not judge.* How does this not oppose his statement, "[The Father] has given all judgment to the Son"?[30] How does it not contradict the statement, "I came into this world for judgment"?[31] In the same way, how can the word that he has spoken judge when it has no personal subsistence? How is this possible when he[32] does not sit in the place of judge? Rather, he judges because he leaves no excuse for unbelievers. Again, we must inquire as to the identity of the judge who leaves them no pretext because through their foolish words and opposing will they did not believe what was said to them and thus rightly are condemned to extreme punishment. Who is he then? Clearly he is the one who received all judgment, as he had said. But now he says, *I do not judge.* Therefore, as we have already observed many times, he uses metaphors due to the unbelief of the Jews. He employed them both when speaking about his glory and when he was accusing them because they did not receive the authority of the words spoken to them. Here we find the same situation.

For this reason we need to consider the purpose of the words. Indeed he means, "I came for the salvation of everyone. You who do not believe will be condemned, but not by me. This is not what I wanted, and it is contrary to why I suffered. Because of your [evil] mind you will be condemned instead by my own words, which will leave no excuse to unbelievers on judgment day. These are the same words that I said many times. In other words, that I want nothing that is against the will of the Father, nor do I intend to establish a following for myself alone. I always referred you all to him in what I said, noting that I was sent by him and from him received the command to tell you what was right. Therefore I spoke words that were in agreement with his will, and I testify in the same way before you now: By those same words you will be condemned. Indeed you will be unable to offer any pretext as though you were defending the honor of God, because I always referred you to him." Also here he uses the phrase, *I have not spoken on my own,* as we have explained in other passages, when addressing his opposition, which means, "I said nothing that was only mine and foreign to the Father or outside of his will, as if I wanted to avert you from the Father and bring you into my own gathering."

Finally we must also notice that after the

---

[30]Jn 5:22. [31]Jn 9:39. [32]Here Theodore is speaking about Christ both in his role of Son of Man and God the Word.

Evangelist had said before, "After Jesus had said this, he departed and hid from them,"[33] he added the words that we have now explained, and reported them as if they were said by Jesus to the Jews. But if he was hiding, how could he speak these words to them? Evidently, then, he said them before he went into hiding. Since the Evangelist had completed the subject of his speech and, in a sense, personally blamed the Jews, because "although," our Lord "had performed so many signs, they did not believe in him," he first related the words of the prophecy to confirm his speech and then added the words spoken by our Lord to them as a valid demonstration of their ungrateful mind so that their unbelief might have no excuse. We recall here what we have already said in the description of the argument, that is, that [one of the] purposes of the Evangelist was to accuse the unbelief of the Jews throughout his book.

End of the Fifth Book.

Book Six (John 13:1–17:26)

[13:1] *Now, before the festival of the Passover, Jesus knew that his hour had come to depart from this world and go to the Father.* From here the Evangelist passes to the story of the passion. Here also, as far as possible, he is careful in saying nothing that has already been related by the other Evangelists, unless the course of the narrative obliges him to do so and it would be impossible to construct an accurate sequence of events without reporting part of the facts already related by his fellow Evangelists. When he reports things done and said by our Lord to his disciples that we do not find mentioned by the others in their books, he wants to make clear that our Savior did not undergo his passion unknowingly or unwillingly, but that he did so by his own free will. He tasted death when he wanted to. When he writes that Jesus said, "I have power to lay down my life, and no one takes it from me, but I lay it down of

my own accord,"[1] he reveals that Jesus was not forced to suffer. And again, when in the story of Lazarus he records how the disciples were afraid that he would be killed by the Jews if he left [for Judea] and that therefore they tried to hold him back with the ominous warning, "The Jews were just now trying to stone you, and are you going there again?"[2] he relates how our Lord answered, "Are there not twelve hours of daylight? Those who walk during the day do not stumble, because they see the light of this world."[3] Through these words he reveals that our Lord knew ahead of time when his passion would occur and only suffered when he chose to do so. In the same way here, by writing, *Jesus knew that his hour had come to depart from this world and go to the Father*, he means that he knew exactly the time of his passion and everything that would happen to him.

He says this about the assumed man since he is the subject of John's narrative, as we have demonstrated above. He calls his resurrection and ascension into heaven his departure from this world to the Father. Since at this stage he no longer lived according to human limitations or suffered according to the rules of nature since he was united with the God the Word and through him obtained access to the Father, he should be highly honored by everyone since we know now that he must be worshiped by both men and spiritual powers, as the apostle says, "Therefore God also highly exalted him and gave him the name that is above every name." And what is this name? "So that at the name of Jesus every knee should bend, in heaven and on earth and under the earth, and every tongue should confess that Jesus Christ is Lord to the glory of God the Father."[4] But it is necessary that we quote the entire section, so that the meaning may be explained more clearly.

[13:1] *Now before the festival of the Passover, Jesus knew that his hour had come to depart*

---

[33]Jn 12:36.   **Book Six** [1]Jn 10:18. [2]Jn 11:8. [3]Jn 11:9. [4]Phil 2:9-11.

from this world and go to the Father. Having loved his own who were in the world, he loved them to the end. [13:2] *The devil had already put into the heart of Judas son of Simon Iscariot to betray him. And during supper,* [13:3] *Jesus, knowing that the Father had given all things into his hands, and that he had come from God and was going to God,* [13:4] *got up from the table, took off his outer robe, and tied a towel around himself.* [13:5] *Then he poured water into a basin and began to wash the disciples' feet and to wipe them with the towel that was tied around him.* Humility is the principle of all virtues. It removes any conflict, division or dissension among people, planting peace and charity among them instead. And through charity humility grows and increases. Our Lord frequently desired to teach this to his disciples through his words and his works.

Thus, when he was approaching his passion, he wanted to teach them humility as the greatest and most sublime commandment, and to show them how great his love was for them. Therefore, he first taught humility through his actions and then proposed the following admonition: [13:14] *So if I, your Lord and Teacher, have washed your feet, you also ought to wash one another's feet.* [13:15] *For I have given you an example that you also should do as I have done to you.* The Evangelist wants to teach all of us how excellent humility is by focusing in on what our Lord did. [The Evangelist] relates how the human being of our Lord[5]—for he is the one who washed the feet—even though he would soon be in an exalted position where he would reveal the greatness and imminence of his honor and that he is the Lord of all—indeed his conjunction with God the Word granted him all these things—his mind did not become arrogant because of his dignity.

He had come from God and was going back to God, that is, even though he knew he had

been destined by God for the kind of dignity that would be his after his passion, he did not become proud. Since he had repeatedly shown his love for his disciples, although Judas had already conceived his bitter intention of betrayal, he gave them evidence of his love with sublime humility by washing their feet and by tying a towel around himself to wipe them. He felt no shame in doing the task of a servant nor was he ashamed of his immodest attire. The Evangelist provides a detailed account in order to portray more clearly Jesus' love and humility in light of both his greatness and the intent of the betrayer. For instance, even though he knew what Judas was planning on doing, Jesus did not refuse to wash his feet. This is all the more amazing when one considers the act itself—there is nothing more vile than washing feet—and ultimately the way in which he performed it, that is, by tying a towel around himself. Now it is necessary that we examine the meaning of the words and consider their order. Words, in fact, are not placed and precisely coordinated in divine books. All these words have been interposed because of the extended narrative.[6]

The following is a summary of this passage's meaning: Before the festival of the Passover, during supper, he stood up, took off his garments, took a towel and tied it around his waist, and so on. All the other things were expressed between these events in order that the Evangelist might portray how, even though Jesus knew everything and was already aware of the intention of the betrayer, he nevertheless washed the feet of all the disciples and of the betrayer too.

[13:6] *He came to Simon Peter,* but Peter did not want his teacher to wash his feet. Our Lord said to him, [13:7] *You do not know now what I am doing, but later you will understand.* In other words, "Through what I am do-

---

[5]The human nature of our Lord. [6]Theodore seems to be justifying the length of his own extended exposition as well as the fact that he has not followed the order of John's narrative, which itself, he maintains, is also not given in the order in which the events occurred.

ing here, I want to teach you that you are to love and serve one another deeply." Peter did not understand that this was the purpose of what Jesus had done. Therefore, since Peter was still resisting, our Lord once again said to him, [13:8] *Unless I wash you, you have no share with me.* Peter, however, thought that he was being washed in place of baptism and that he would obtain his share with the Lord from this washing. Therefore he asked that all of him be washed if this was so. This is why the Lord corrected his error by saying, [13:10] *One who has bathed does not need to wash, except for the feet, but is entirely clean. And you are clean, but not all of you.* Then the Evangelist explained the words of our Lord, adding, [13:11] *For he knew who was to betray him; for this reason he said, "Not all of you are clean."* In speaking to Simon, our Lord meant, "This is not the baptism for the remission of sins. You already received this once and do not need a second baptism because you were made clean by the first baptism you received. Now it is only necessary that your feet be washed, and soon you will know the purpose of this action." Certainly the disciples had received the baptism of forgiveness from John, which the teaching of our Lord confirmed in them even more by exhorting them to virtue. The Spirit which descended upon them later would then perfect them.

[13:12] *After he had washed their feet, put on his robe and returned to the table, he said to them, "Do you know what I have done for you?* [13:13] *You call me teacher and Lord—and you are right, for that is what I am.* [13:14] *So if I, your Lord and Teacher, have washed your feet, you also ought to wash one another's feet.* [13:15] *For I have set you an example that you also should do as I have done to you."* These words that he said taught them the purpose behind his washing of their feet. After saying above to Simon, *later you will understand*, he appropri-

ately asks here, *Do you know what I have done to you?* In other words, "Learn the reason and the purpose for my action. I washed your feet so that what I did might be an example for you so that you might do the same thing for one another. If I whom you rightly call Lord and Teacher deigned to wash your feet, how much more must you do the same for one another without shame or timidity?"

And he confirmed his words even more by saying, [13:16] *Very truly, I tell you, servants are not greater than their master, nor are messengers greater than the one who sent them.* "It is evident," he says, "that you, my servants and messengers, cannot be greater than I, your Lord who sent you. Indeed a servant, as long as he is a servant, is inferior to his lord. And the one who is sent, until he plays the role of envoy, cannot be equal in honor to the one who sent him." But these other words cause great embarrassment too, [13:17] *If you know these things, you are blessed if you do them.* It is not sufficient just to know, you must also put into practice what you know.

Then, in order to explain that his speech is not addressed to just anyone, but only to those who believe, he says, [13:18] *I am not speaking of all of you; I know whom I have chosen. But it is to fulfill the Scriptures, "The one who ate my bread has lifted his heel against me."*[7] "I do not say these things," he says, "to all of you because I know that one of you will betray me so that what was written in the Scriptures may be confirmed: 'The one who eats bread with me will conspire against me and will deliver me to strangers.'" This testimony was not spoken about him as in prophecy, but because the circumstances themselves made it suitable to the betrayer. He then gives the reason why he predicted these things: [13:19] *I tell you this now, before it occurs, so that when it does occur, you may believe that I am he.* "I could not reveal," he says, "what would happen. However,

---

[7]See Ps 41:9 (40:10 LXX).

in order that you might not believe that I did not know the thoughts of those who follow me and that, being unaware, I was striving in vain because of my sense of shame because of the things that were happening to me, I foretell the facts before the event so that, when they happen, you will know who I am."

After he said to the disciples, *servants are not greater than their master, nor are messengers greater than the one who sent them*; and after he added, *If you know these things, you are blessed if you do them*, and finally, showing himself to be cautious in his speech so that it might not be believed that he carelessly declared his teaching to all people, he inserted as an addition, *I am not speaking of all of you*, and so on. Now in good order he adds with regard to the things he had said above, [13:20] *Very truly, I tell you, whoever receives one whom I send receives me; and whoever receives me receives him who sent me*. "Do not believe," he says, "that you are contemptible and vile because I said that you are inferior to me. Do not think that the task I gave you is insignificant and weak. Even though you are inferior to me as my envoys, nevertheless you are great because I sent you. And just as the purpose for everything that happens to me is always referred to the Father, so also the honor of those who are sent is common to me and them. I understand that I am personally received when one of them is received."

[13:21] *After saying this Jesus was troubled in spirit, and declared, "Very truly, I tell you, one of you will betray me."* Just as in the episode of Lazarus, he said that he was troubled in spirit because he foretold what was going to happen, and that he was angry in order to show that he had knowledge of the things that still had to happen as if they had already happened—so here too he says that he was angered because of Judas's betrayal, and that he was astonished by the viciousness of his will." The Evangelist also used here the words, *Jesus was troubled in spirit*, because through the operation of

the Spirit which was in him he foreknew the future.

The disciples were amazed by these words and looked around at each other. The blessed John, the same who wrote the Gospel, was reclining on Jesus' breast; that is, he was very close to him. The blessed Simon Peter nodded toward him, as toward one who was closer to Jesus, so that he might quietly learn from Jesus the identity of the one who would betray him. He therefore reclined next to our Lord, not in order to question him openly, but to learn from him. Our Lord said to him, [13:26] *It is the one to whom I give this piece of bread when I have dipped it in the dish*, since he wanted to point him out through an act so that he might be known to all the other disciples as well. Thus he gave Judas the bread in accusation, because although Judas participated with him in the bread, he felt no shame even before human law but agreed instead to betray his Lord without cause to his enemies.

Then the Evangelist adds, [13:27] *After he received the piece of bread, Satan entered into him*. What Judas believed was hidden in the ruminations of his own mind was disclosed when he received the bread and was then made known to all the disciples. He was so far removed from admiring the power of the one who knows our inner thoughts that— even though he should have felt ashamed and embarrassed because of this public rebuke—he instead confirmed even more inside himself the will of his sin. And since he was offended by this rebuke, he prepared to execute his crime at once. The Evangelist rightly called this thought the entry of Satan, attributing to Satan the confirmation of his will. Then he adds, [13:30] *So, after receiving the piece of bread, he immediately went out*. Nevertheless, we still need not take into consideration the fulfillment of his passion so much as the will of his enemies and his betrayer.

Already under the impulse of the same Satan, those who hoped to destroy him had secretly decreed to kill him without knowing the power and the wisdom of him who was inside the one who would undergo the passion. But our Lord, who knew this, said to him, [13:27] *Do quickly what you are going to do;* that is, "Since this is what you intend to do, and you are eager to execute your treachery against me, it would not displease me if, after hearing my word, you promptly brought your wickedness to its fulfillment." But the disciples did not understand what was said. They thought that our Lord was telling him to buy something for the festival or to give something to the poor, because he had the common purse. The reason why they did not understand what he said was due to the fact that his inner thoughts were hidden to them. So Judas hurried to do his will; and while it was night, he went out to accomplish his malice.

After this, since the passion was getting closer, our Lord began to tell the disciples what he thought should be heard by all of them before his passion. Therefore he said, [13:31] *Now the Son of Man has been glorified, and God has been glorified in him.* "The time is near in which the Son of Man who was assumed will be glorified in an amazing way, and in which, above all, God will be revealed before everyone through the things that happen to him." The events that happened at the time of the crucifixion—the earth shook, the light of the sun was hidden and darkness covered the earth, the tombs opened and the rocks were broken—all of these demonstrated how great he already was, and how great the magnificence of the one who had been crucified would become. At the same time, these events were also the reason why people admired God who had made the Son of Man worthy of such an honor. [13:32] *If God has been glorified in him, God will also glorify him in himself and will glorify him at once.* "Evidently," he says, "as much as God is glorified by those things

which happened to him, so much greater will God himself glorify him. God would not have been glorified if the things that happened to him had not themselves been great. And these things," he says, "were not given to him only after a long time, but had in fact already been given to him."

After revealing that the passion was not shameful, but on the contrary was in line with a wise and powerful providence, he addressed his speech to the disciples by saying, [13:33] *Little children, I am with you only a little longer. You will look for me; and as I said to the Jews so now I say to you, "Where I am going, you cannot come."* He says, *only a little longer,* with reference to the time up to his passion. When he tells the Jews "you will look for me," he adds, "and you will not find me,"[8] because they would not see him anymore after his passion. But to his disciples he only says, *You will look for me.* They did indeed look for him and, being led by devotion in their search for him and seeing themselves deprived of the care of their teacher, they found him, because they saw him after his resurrection and lived and ate with him until he ascended into heaven.

"However," he says, "just as I said to the Jews that they could not come where I go, *so now I say this to you.*" Notice that he added *now.* When he said that they could not come where he was going, he meant that they still could not face death like him. They did, in fact, all run away. And Simon even denied him with oaths. But he added *now* to indicate that afterward they would disregard suffering and trials. In fact, after the descent of the Holy Spirit they even enjoyed suffering for Christ since they were fully confirmed in their faith in him and in the promise of the future. "Therefore," he says, "even though your love leads you to look for me—I know you do this because you love me—you nevertheless cannot now prove your love by your actions because

---

[8]Jn 7:34.

your natural weakness inspires you with fear. Therefore this is how it has to be, and it cannot happen in any other way. What I am teaching you to do now in earnest is something you can observe if you want. It is useful even now and will prove useful later as well."

[13:34] *I am giving you a new commandment, that you love one another.* How is it new? *Just as I have loved you, you also should love one another.* What is new is the manner of how we are to love. In the law it was commanded that everyone should love his neighbor as himself.[9] But the voice of our Lord wants our companions in faith to be loved even more than ourselves because he is ordering us to imitate his love for us. In the words that follow he shows what this looks like. In fact, he even amplifies the greatness of this commandment by saying, [13:35] *By this everyone will know that you are my disciples, if you have love for one another.* "You must observe this commandment so well that it will be clearly evident as a sign that you are my disciples."

After these words were spoken by the Lord, Peter questioned him about the expression, *you cannot come*, by asking, [13:36] *Where are you going?* The Lord told him the same thing, *Where I am going, you cannot follow me now; but you will follow me afterward*; that is, "When you receive in the future the power to resist temptations." But even though the blessed Peter should have believed the word of the Lord that this could happen in no other way, he nevertheless said, [13:37] *Why can I not follow you now? I will lay down my life for you.*

What did the Lord answer him? [13:38] *Will you lay down your life for me? Very truly, I tell you, before the rooster crows, you will have denied me three times.* Some think that this contradicts the words of Mark who writes, "Before the rooster crows twice, you will deny me three times."[10] But there is no conflict between these two versions, if they are understood correctly. Since it was useless for Peter to discuss with our Lord his claim that he would not deny him and that he would, in fact, die with him if necessary, the Lord caused the rooster to crow, knowing that Peter certainly need to be reproved because of his denial so that it might appear evident that he had argued in vain with regard to his pretence [of fidelity]. Then, after hearing the rooster crow once, in order that Peter might not believe that it had happened by chance or that he had not really heard it, our Lord caused it to crow again, and Peter gave his first words of denial. And after he had denied our Lord three times, it crowed again as if to testify to the truth of the prediction. This alone was what the Evangelists were concerned to convey. The other Evangelists say, "before the rooster crows, you will have denied me three times,"[11] meaning, "Since you argue and think you know better than I what will happen, the rooster will put an end to our discussion. It will not crow according to the law of nature until it testifies with its crow to your denial, proving the truth of my words and blaming the arrogance of yours." [The Evangelist] says the words, *before the rooster crows, you will have denied me three times*, in this sense: On this occasion it did not crow twice according to the course of nature, but according to the will and command of the Lord in order to reproach the words of Peter. Later it crowed according to the course of nature.

Mark, following the desire of Peter himself,[12] described these events very carefully and recorded how many times the rooster crowed in the course of Peter's denial. Indeed the blessed Peter wanted the correction of his fault to be reported in the Scriptures.

After our Lord said these words to Peter, the prince of the apostles, all the others—having no doubts about what he had said—

[9]See Lev 19:18. [10]Mk 14:30. [11]Mt 26:34; Lk 22:34. [12]This tradition that sees Peter as the direct inspirer of Mark's Gospel dates from the time of the apostolic and early church fathers: see Eusebius *Ecclesiastical History* 2.15, who quotes Papias and Clement of Alexandria.

were chastened by a great fear as if they could expect nothing better for themselves because they thought that they would be excluded from all the blessings that were to come because of the denial. Jesus wanted to dispel this fear, and so he shifted his speech from the person of Peter to all by saying:

[14:1] *Do not let your hearts be troubled*; that is, "Do not lose hope because of the things I just now said, and do not let your expectations fall short concerning the blessing that is yet to come." What else? *Believe in God, believe also in me.* "Follow your faith in me and in God, and you will receive the blessing that is expected to come along with the remission of those sins that occurred because of your weakness." [14:2] *In my Father's house there are many dwelling places.* "With my Father there is such an abundance that he can provide everyone with the delights of eternal happiness." He calls the *dwelling places* the perennial rest because in his houses we have only rest and happiness.

If it were not so, would I have told you that I go to prepare a place for you? "Otherwise," he says, "would I have said to you, 'I leave to prepare a place for you'?" He mentions this here since the custom among us, when space is scarce, is to reserve a place to stay in advance. This is why he says, "Would I perhaps have spoken to you in this way, as is customary among us, if a great blessing were not already prepared and reserved for all those who want it—provided that there is no one who is preventing these blessings from being given to them?"

[14:3] *And if I go and prepare a place for you.* This seems to be contrary to what had been said previously. In fact, he had spoken previously as if there were no need for any preparation: *If it were not so, would I have told you that I go to prepare a place for you?* Here, on the contrary, he says, *And if I go and prepare a* *place for you.* What he says has the following meaning: "There is no need for me to prepare an abundance of blessings since the Father, according to his foreknowledge, has already made preparations for the eternal enjoyment of those who live their lives in perfect virtue; but you, nevertheless, need to show goodwill. In any case, I prepare these blessings for you and invite you to enjoy them because I will be the first to rise from the dead, and after my ascension I will give my followers a share in them."

What does he say next? *I will come again and will take you to myself, so that where I am, there you may be also.* [14:4] *And you know the way to the place where I am going.* He says in effect, "When I have given you the occasion to expect all these blessings through my ascension into heaven—so that it may be revealed to you who the source for all of these things is—I will come again." Here he is referring to his second coming from heaven. "And taking you with me, I will ascend again into the heavens so that you may be with me where I am, and may enjoy the same blessings. This is also what Paul said, "If we endure, we will also reign with him."[13] And in another passage he says, "If, in fact, we suffer with him so that we may also be glorified with him."[14] We will not reign or be glorified like him, but we will participate in his happiness as much as possible.

When he says, *And you know the way to the place where I am going*, he means, "You will always be with me just like those are who are accustomed to walking along the same path. For the more they persevere along that path, the more they come to know the way." Since these things were still beyond their comprehension, he spoke figuratively.

Since no one among his disciples understood these words, Thomas answered, saying, [14:5] *Lord, we do not where you are going. How can we know the way?* What did the Lord say? [14:6] *I am the way, and the truth, and the*

---

[13] 2 Tim 2:12.   [14] Rom 8:17.

122

life. "You do not need to work at knowing the way. Get to know my teaching so that you may come to an understanding of the truth through me. Then you will receive eternal life and enjoy eternal blessings. I will be your way so that through me, as through a leader leading you along the way, you may reach the fullness of those blessings." He further establishes what he is saying by adding, *No one comes to the Father except through me.* "You cannot know the Father except through me," he says, "nor can you be rewarded with his friendship in any other way." And since Thomas said, "We do not know the way," he wanted to show him and the others that they still did not know accurately and correctly what they thought they knew—in other words, they knew neither him nor the Father. Therefore he added, [14:7] *"If you know me, you will know my Father also,* but now you do not know my Father or me. Both things are necessary for you, that is, to know me and through me to receive knowledge of the Father."

Then, since he had talked about what was going to happen, he consoles them [by hinting at] the events that would happen later, saying, *From now on you do know him and have seen him.* "The time is close," he says, "when by faith you will know the Father, as far as it is possible." He is talking about the time when the Spirit would descend, from whom they would receive all knowledge.

Therefore, after hearing what Jesus had said from a human perspective, Philip said, [14:8] *Lord, show us the Father, and we will be satisfied.* What was the Lord's reply? Since Philip, by saying this, inquired about the words said to them, Jesus answered him,[15] [14:9] *Have I been with you all this time, Philip, and you still do not know me?* "Thus," he says, "was it be-cause there was insufficient time for the Father and me to teach you that you think you may still be able to see him? If you knew me, you would know the Father through me, and would not think that he can be seen with bodily eyes." Since the expression, *you still do not know me,* seemed not to fit in with the words, *show us the Father,* he clearly explains this by saying, *Whoever has seen me, has seen the Father. How can you say, "Show us the Father"?* "There is no difference" he says. "Whoever sees me sees the Father himself. The perfect similarity between the two of us shows the Father himself in me."

He rightly asks, *How can you say?* This expression of amazement confirms what was said above. "How can you ask me," he says, "to show you the Father unless you are completely ignorant of me? Therefore what I said is true: 'You neither know my Father nor me; if you had known me, you would have known him too,' because our perfect likeness would have made him known." And since they were even more in doubt, not understanding his words, he reproved Philip by saying, [14:10] *Do you not believe that I am in the Father and the Father is in me?* Among all the words spoken so far, these are the clearest evidence that he is talking about their likeness. Indeed, when he turns the discussion toward him and the Father he reveals the perfect likeness of nature inasmuch as, just as the Father exists in him and he in the Father, their perfect likeness is capable of revealing each in the other.

Then he proves and confirms what he has just said: *The words that I say to you I do not speak on my own.* "If you do not believe what I am saying," he says, "you should know that the conformity of our natures, ideas and power is so perfect that there is no difference in our words either. Whatever I say is common to us

---

[15]According to the editor of the Syriac translation (see Vosté CSCO 4 3:268) the text of the Greek fragment appears to be more suitable to the context: "Like one who with his words—those words that the Lord had addressed to his disciples—had sufficiently demonstrated this to Philip, he answered him." See PG 66:775; R. Devreesse, *Essai sur Théodore de Mopsueste,* Studi e Testi 141 (Vatican City: Biblioteca Apostolica Vaticana, 1948), p. 389 (fr. 124,1); Theodore of Mopsuestia, *Commentary on the Gospel of John,* introduction and commentary by G. Kalantzis, Early Christian Studies 7 (Sydney: Saint Paul's Publications, 2004), p. 115.

both, and I am not only speaking on my own." *The Father who dwells in me does his works.* He could have taken the opportunity to add, "my Father speaks," to the words, *I do not speak.* But he had [already] said above, *The words that I say,* and he says here, *the Father does his works,* in order to show that their nature as well as the words and the works were all held in common. From this it is evident that when he said, *I do not speak on my own,* he was not indicating anything inferior but was expressing a perfect communion and an inseparable union. This is especially apparent from the context. And it is not all that surprising that when the one who was in him was being prepared for suffering and had already said many things as a man, he proceeded to speak about things that were suitable to his divine nature. These words necessarily had to be said to the disciples so that later, when they recalled what he had said to them and eventually understood what he meant, they might come to possess perfect knowledge in their minds. This is what happened with the resurrection. First, they did not comprehend what they had heard him say, but later they understood. There was also another reason why he told them these things. Naturally, he wanted to show his disciples that they were still very far away from understanding the mysteries, since they still did not know him, even though they believed they did. And he could only demonstrate this through words about his divinity, which was still hidden from their minds.

Therefore he says the same thing here, [14:11] *Believe me that I am in the Father and the Father is in me; but if you do not, then believe me because of the works themselves.* "If," he says, "this likeness about which I talked to you appears to be too lofty to you to be credible, at least allow the greatness of my works and the way in which I did all of them for the benefit of humanity to convince you about what I said

to you." But how could they prove his likeness with the Father, or the fact that he was the creator of heaven and earth and the entire universe? What he is saying is this: he is pointing out to them the likeness of his divine nature with that of the Father. The assumed man, in fact, could not be said to be like God the Father. The miracles performed by the man, however, evidently overcame the nature of the one who did them. "If," he says, "I attributed such great power to him, consider then who lives in him as to whether he is not perfectly similar to him who does anything he wants and as he wants through his own innate power."

And so he extends his discourse further by saying, [14:12] *Very truly, I tell you, the one who believes in me will also do the works that I do and, in fact, will do greater works than these.* "Do not be amazed," he says, "when you see him do these things. Even those who believe in him will now receive the power to do greater works than these." And he declares how this occurs, saying, *Because I am going to the Father.* [14:13] *I will do whatever you ask in my name, so that the Father may be glorified in the Son*—because, he says, "he[16] will receive union with the Father through me after my passion." We said above that the phrase, *I am going to the Father,* is referring to this. After obtaining this union, [the assumed man] will have the power to give everything to those who ask him because when they ask him they ask because of the greatness dwelling in him, which is how he is able to give. The surpassing wonder and superiority of the Father is then recognized in the Son. Therefore their mutual likeness and greatness becomes known through the things that happened to the man and, through him, will happen to all the rest. This likeness indicates the glory of the Father, who generated such an admirable nature that is similar to him. When discussing either the divinity or the humanity, in both cases he uses the pro-

---

[16]The assumed man.

noun *I* so that the meaning of the words must be ascertained through the *context*, while the difference of the natures is discovered through the different words used. Through the fact that, in both cases, he speaks about himself as about a single person, he reveals the union of the person. If this were not true, there would be no honor for him who was assumed, since he evidently has a part in everything because of the one who dwells in him.[17]

Assuring them further concerning what he had just said, he adds, [14:14] *If in my name you ask me for anything, I will do it.* "You should have no doubts about this," he says. And, instructing them again how to ask and how to receive, he says, [14:15] *If you love me, you will keep my commandments.* [14:16] *And I will ask the Father, and he will give you another Paraclete*[18] *to be with you forever.* [14:17] *This is the Spirit of truth.* "In the first place," he says, "it is appropriate for you to ask because you love me and demonstrate your love by observing my commandments. And, because you are so disposed, I will confer the grace of the Holy Spirit so that you may always have it with you to teach you the truth." He says *another Paraclete,* that is, another instructor, referring to him as the *Paraclete,* meaning the comforter who will teach in times of tribulation, because the Spirit, through his grace, will lighten the sufferings inflicted upon them by humanity as he consoles them, through his gifts, and enables them to endure their afflictions, which is what actually happened. Indeed the more his disciples feared death previously, the more they rejoiced in tribulations after the descent of the Spirit. He calls him the *Spirit of truth,* because he teaches nothing but the truth, since he is never inclined toward truth's opposite that might otherwise cause him to teach anything different from the truth. He also refers to the Spirit as *another* because while he [Jesus] was among them, he certainly filled this same role for them as well. In addition, they received from the Holy Spirit the confirmation of all those things that he had taught them when he was present, as our Lord also indicated, "But you will receive power when the Holy Spirit has come upon you; and you will be my witness in Jerusalem, in all Judea and among the Samaritans, and all nations."[19]

It is worth observing that the expression, *I will ask,* is used as if he were saying, "Through me you will receive grace." He had no need to ask for them to receive what God had evidently already prearranged to happen for our benefit. And this had already been promised as well, because our Lord had also told the apostles to expect the promised Spirit about which they had heard.[20] If the gift had already been promised, the request for the promise would have been superfluous. Therefore what he says is quite clear. It was also quite appropriate and fortunate that he recalled the gift of the Spirit. Indeed, when he said, *the one who believes in me will also do great works,* he also taught them how this would happen, declaring, "After my resurrection I will receive perfect union with the Father. You also will receive the gift of the Spirit through your faith and love for me. And because this has been given to you, you will do many great miracles."[21]

Therefore, in highlighting the greatness of the gift to be granted to them, he says, [14:17] *[This is the Spirit of truth] whom the world cannot seize,*[22] *because it neither sees him nor knows him. You know him because he abides with you and will be in you.* He says, in effect, "The gift of the Spirit that you are about to receive through me is so amazing that the entire world, even if everyone banded together, would never be able to take it if it did not freely

---

[17]See translator's introduction, esp. quotation from Norris, p. xxvi. [18]Syriac *prqlyt',* which is a transliteration of the Greek *paraklētos.* [19]Acts 1:8. [20]See Acts 1:4. [21]Jn 14:13-14. [22]The Syriac text of this quotation from John reads *lo' mešca' lmasabeh,* "cannot seize him (i.e., the Spirit)," instead of "cannot receive him," which is the standard reading of the Greek or the Syriac Peshitta.

descend upon them." Notice, he didn't say, *whom the world cannot* "receive," but *whom the world cannot* "take." In other words, "No one can take hold of it, not even the entire world together, unless by his grace it freely descends upon those who are worthy, according to either his will or that of the Father."[23] For there is no difference in either case, because instances of both are recorded in the Holy Scriptures. The apostle, in fact, declares, "All these are activated by one and the same Spirit, who allots to each one individually just as the Spirit chooses."[24]

Therefore, establishing what he has just said even more, he continues, *because it neither sees him nor knows him.* "How could something above sight and intellect, whose nature is hidden and incomprehensible to the mind of created beings, be expressed by their knowledge? But you will know and receive what is incomprehensible, through me." He did not say, "You will also *see* him," because this is impossible.

And since the time to confer the Spirit was still far away, he says, [14:18] *I will not leave you orphaned; I am coming to you.* [14:19] *In a little while the world will no longer see me, but you will see me; because I live, you will also live.* The outcome of the event itself will demonstrate the order and the truth of the words. "Do not fear," he says, "that I will leave you without care for any time in between.[25] I myself will come to you and, as I said, the world—that is, all the other human beings—will see me only for a short time, but you will see me again after my resurrection so that this vision of yours may testify that I am living again. And you will not only see *me* living, but the same thing will happen to *you.* When you too are resurrected after your death, at the appointed time, you will live and will participate in a second life." He does not say, *because I*

live, casually; that is, "You will see me because I live." Rather, he means, "You will see this event and when you see it you will know that I am resurrected from the dead and live, and that I did not remain subject to death, as many believe."

[14:20] *On that day you will know that I am in my Father, and you are in me, and I in you.* "At that time," he says, "you will learn that what I said to you was true when I spoke with you about these very events about which you currently have doubts. When I said, *I am in my Father,* I was speaking about the equality of our natures and their inseparable connection that will then become apparent. And the phrase, *and you are in me,* means that you will receive communion with me through your faith in me and love through the gift of the Spirit. *And I in you* is said with reference to what the union will cause, when, after being regenerated by the power of the Spirit, you are with me in the body and I am with you in the head, as it is written, "[We must grow up in every way into] him who is the head, into Christ, from whom the whole body, joined and knit together by every ligament with which it is equipped, as each part is working properly, grows with a growth that is from God."[26]

After saying these words to the disciples—words that were not only for them, but for all those who would believe in him through faithful love—he wanted to ensure that they would not believe that the gift of the Spirit was reserved for them only, especially since he would only appear to them after his resurrection. Rather, in order to show that this was not the reason why they were worthy of a more excellent gift—as if those who did not see him after his resurrection would be deprived of this gift—he says, [14:21] *Those who have my commandments and keep them are those who love*

---

[23]Theodore, in his commentary, appears to consider both the readings "to receive" and "to take," or simply to play with the distinction between the Greek *dechasthai,* "to receive," and *labein,* "to take."   [24]1 Cor 12:11.   [25]Between the death and the resurrection of the Lord.   [26]Eph 4:15-16; Col 2:19.

me; and those who love me will be loved by my Father, and I will love them and reveal myself to them. In other words, "Whoever loves me and keeps my commandments will enjoy my love and that of the Father. In addition he will gain an understanding of who I am and will not be disadvantaged by the fact that he did not see me in body—even though he will also enjoy that vision at the proper time when he sees me coming down from heaven."

But since Judas (not the betrayer) had not understood what Jesus was saying, he said to Jesus, [14:22] *Lord, how is it that you will reveal yourself to us, and not to the world?* According to Jesus' words, Judas thought all but the apostles would be deprived of the blessings that were to come. Therefore our Lord explained what he meant, [14:23] *Those who love me will keep my word, and my Father will love them, and we will come to them and make our home with them.* "I have already said," he says, "that no one who is willing will be deprived by me of the reward for virtue. It is in fact possible, for anyone who wants to, to enjoy the blessings to come. Whoever indeed loves me and observes all of my commandments not only will not be deprived of the vision of my revelation, but will even enjoy our love: I and my Father will come and remain with him and will diligently take care of him."

[14:24] *Whoever does not love me does not keep my words.* In other words, "Whoever does not love me does not keep my commandments." The context required that he add, "And he will not enjoy any blessing," but he refrained from saying this and omitted it because it could be inferred from the context of the speech. And since he had said, "Whoever keeps my words will be loved by the Father, and he and I will come to him," he confirmed the truth of what he was saying by adding, *And the word that you hear is not mine, but is from the Father who sent me.* How is it possible that the words he spoke

were not his? But by saying that they were not his, he meant that they were not foreign to the Father. They were common both "to me and to the Father. Therefore we both will give him a gift at the same time."

The following is the sequence of that reflection: The phrase, *Whoever does not love me does not keep my words*, is placed in the middle, indicating that he wants to say something else to those present. He said this in the middle, among everything else he said, because he did not want to make it too blatant due to the harshness of the words that he was obliged to pronounce against the unbelievers. And therefore, before the end of his speech, he in a sense alludes silently to the future judgment because he did not think it was an appropriate time to speak about it in detail.

[14:25] *I have said these things to you while I am still with you.* [14:26] *But the Paraclete, the Holy Spirit whom the Father will send in my name, will teach you everything, and remind you of all that I have said to you.* "I have been telling you these things so that you would know what you needed to do, as long as I am with you. When I ascend into heaven, and you receive the grace of the Spirit, then you will learn through the agency of the Spirit many things that you did not yet know." Even though he talks about sending the Spirit upon them, he does not refer to the nature of the Spirit. In fact, it was not going to come upon human beings as though it existed outside the world. Rather, he describes the grace of the Spirit and its operation toward the believers in such a way that it either increases or altogether ceases when those who receive it do not remain worthy of it, as the apostle said, "Do not quench the Spirit."[27] This is not said [by Paul] in reference to the nature of the Spirit, because human sin cannot diminish the nature of the Spirit. But if [Christ] were to revert to words more in line with the Spirit's nature, he would

---

[27] 1 Thess 5:19.

be justified in doing so in order to show the Spirit's greatness, which he could not reveal in any other way but by using words in harmony with its nature. This is similar to what he did when, in speaking about himself as a man, he moved to speaking about his divine nature in order to clearly demonstrate his greatness.

Therefore, he in effect asks, "What am I eagerly looking for you to do?" [14:27] *Peace I leave with you; my peace I give to you. I do not give to you as the world gives.* "Possess this [peace]," he says, "and take care of it so that you may not be divided. Instead, let a consensus toward what is good reign among you. This is my peace. It is not like that which the rest of humanity possesses, who eagerly help one another do evil."

Therefore, since they were sad because they heard him speaking about his passion and their separation without knowing what would happen to him and them in the entire plan of salvation, he said to them, *Do not let your hearts be troubled, and do not let them be afraid.* But how was it possible for them not to be troubled by what he was saying? [14:28] *You heard me say to you, "I am going away, and I am coming to you."* "You did not only hear me say, *I am going away,* but also, *I am coming again.* So, if the separation that death brings saddens you, the promise, *I am coming again,* which will be fulfilled for you after my resurrection, should make you happy." "But," the [disciples] might say, "if you appear to us after a short time, then you will leave us again forever." "*If you loved me, you would rejoice* in this too," Jesus says. "Since you love me, it is all the more fitting that you rejoice. Sadness over my departure is in no way an appropriate response. Rather, you should be ecstatic because I am ascending into heaven and great things are going to be happening to me there."

How and in what sense does he say, *The Father is greater than I?* "If," he says, "I were

humiliated after being separated from you, my departure from you would be a proper cause for sadness. But if as a result of ascending into heaven I achieve greater glory in my union with the Father, there is no reason for sadness. Instead, you would rejoice if your love for me was real."

Concerning the heretics[28] who want to prove on the basis of this passage that the nature of the Father is greater than that of the Son, the context itself is sufficient to meet their objection and to show that he is referring here to the assumed man, because his death saddened the disciples, just as the dignity that would soon be his was a sufficient reason for their joy. In point of fact, the nature of God the Word did not suffer the torment of the cross, nor would it be affected by anything new after the passion that might fill the hearts of the disciples with consolation.

And in order that it might not appear that there was a cause for sadness because he had in vain predicted those things before they happened, he added, [14:29] *And now I have told you this before it occurs, so that when it does occur, you may believe.* "Therefore," he says, "it is not right that you are sad, because I am telling you what will happen before it occurs. Expect that those events will happen so that you will not be sad when they do occur. Instead, rightly and with good reason admiring the truth of what I predicted, know that what I faced did not happen against my will." And in order to prove the certainty of his foreknowledge, he says, [14:30] *I will no longer talk much with you.* "I know," he says, "that the time of the passion is approaching."

He then emphasizes one aspect of his passion in particular in order to provide even greater consolation for his disciples. He says, *The ruler of this world is coming. He has no power over me;* [14:31] *but I do as the Father has commanded me, so that the world may know*

---

[28]Again Theodore refers to the Arians. See also preface n. 1 (pp. 1-2).

that I love the Father. Sin was the cause of our death, and Satan, by leading all into transgression, worsened our condemnation. Therefore, he says, "Now [Satan] incites the Jews against me because through their malice he wants to bring death to me even though he cannot find in me a proper cause for death. However, I could avoid tasting death altogether if I wanted to. Nevertheless I accept it. Because of the amazing things that are going to happen to me in the course of my passion and the things that will happen to those who believe in me after my passion—for instance, the casting out of devils with a mere word, the healing of sick people, the various signs they will perform, the removal of any human tribulation through a command in my name, the various punishments that will befall sinners—because of all these things, I say, it will be evident that I was unjustly executed. However, because I love the Father, I will accomplish his will for the salvation of all. My defeat of death, which will occur according to justice and through the intervention of the Omnipotent One, will be the destiny for the entire human race by grace."

After providing such encouragement, he fittingly concludes, *Rise, let us be on our way.* "Therefore," he says, "since this is how things will be, there is no reason for us to feel sad and fear death. On the contrary, we should be ready and willing to hand ourselves over to those who would kill us." That this is what he intended to say when he was getting ready to leave is confirmed by the fact that, when he had not yet left, he continued his discourse with the words that follow.

Urging them to love him, he says, [15:1] *I am the true vine, and my Father is the vine grower;* and, a few lines below, [15:5] *I am the vine; you are the branches.* Since these phrases are already quite clear, we can avoid explaining their meaning in order not to expand our treatise with useless repetition.

His previous words of comfort addressed the sadness they felt after hearing what he had said about his passion. He first spoke about the coming glory that would be his after his passion, and then added that he was not facing death against his will or unawares, but freely and fully aware of what he was doing. He had not, in fact, committed any sin that might cause someone to believe that he was dying justly. Rather, he accepted his passion in view of the great things that were going to happen through him according to divine providence, and taught them to strive for his love after getting rid of their sadness, because it would benefit them more than anything else. Even as he comforted them because of their afflictions, he was also teaching them through much-elevated discourse, confirming through many arguments his exhortation to love, and demonstrating why love, should be preserved with the greatest care as the highest virtue. This assumed man had indeed received the grace of the Spirit, which was like an anointing for him, and the Spirit through its intercession provided him his union with God the Word. Therefore, all those other believers who followed, being regenerated through the power of the Spirit, were made the body of Christ so that they received union with him. Therefore he used the example of the vine, so that he might teach them at great length to practice charity for him.

"As," he says, "the vine planted in the soil has its own life, which it received at one time from the soil—while the branches that it produces give fruit as long as they remain in it but cease from living and giving fruit when they are cut off—consider me in this same light as your vine because I received all the grace of the Spirit first. You are like my branches because you received union with me through spiritual regeneration. Just as the branches produce fruit as long as they are in the vine—but after being cut off become useless because they immediately wither and are abandoned to a dry and unproductive existence—so you too, as long as you remain in my love, will necessarily produce an abundant yield of virtue by producing spiritual blessings with overflowing abundance. However, if you depart from my love, you will undoubtedly be deprived of any virtue whatsoever. Just as the vine grower examines the usefulness of his branches and makes those more fruitful that he sees are beautiful and capable of bearing fruit—whereas those that prove unsatisfactory or unfruitful to the vine grower are thrown into the fire—so also when the Father examines the mind of each person, he cares for those whom he sees united with me in their love, and grants them a wealth of spiritual blessings. Those he sees that have abandoned my love, however, he reserves for the future judgment."

Therefore he makes known here that they must love him a great deal—in the first place so that by uniting with him spiritually they may have a mind worthy of union with him; in the second place so that may produce abundant fruit by relying on these virtues; in the third place because, if they despise these virtues, they will rightfully incur punishment; and finally, because they will be a cause of great glory for God. Indeed, in admiring their virtues, the human race also admires the one who is the cause of these virtues. This is why he says, [15:8] *My Father is glorified by this, that you bear much fruit and become my disciples.* Both the variation of times and the arrangement of words are placed in the Holy Scriptures simply, without any pretence. He urges them to be diligent in their love for him, repeating what he had said above, that is, that their love would be tested to see if they were eager to keep his commandments. Once he has concluded all this instruction concerning their love for him, he says, [15:11] *I have said these things to you so that my joy may be in you, and that your joy may be complete.* "I said all this," he says, "in order to persuade you to possess what I enjoy most about you, so that, because

of your love for me, spiritual blessings may overflow from you and you also may rejoice over the gifts that are your delight because you will receive the reward of your love for me."

He then urges them to mutual love for one another, saying, [15:12] *This is my commandment, that you love one another as I have loved you.* He calls it "his commandment," not "the commandment of love" since this commandment had, in fact, already been given previously.[29] Here, rather, he is speaking about the manner of love. Therefore, he explains what it is by saying, *as I have loved you.* Then he adds, [15:13] *There is no greater love than this, to lay down one's life for his friend.* "This is the kind of love I have," he says, "and who has cared more about his friends than myself, the one who accepted death for their salvation?" And, in order to indicate who these friends are, he says, [15:14] *You are my friends if you do what I command.* However, lest they get the idea that the name of *friends* was only restricted to them, he does not say, "You yourselves are my friends," but simply, *you are my friends,* that is, "You are among my friends," and then adds, *if you do what I command you,* making it clear that keeping and doing his commandments should occur with them as much as it does with everyone else so that their love for him may increase.

And he adds an even better reason for why he thought the name of friends should be given to them, [15:15] *I do not call you servants any longer, because the servant does not know what the master is doing; but I have called you friends because I have made known to you everything that I have heard from my Father.* Evidently this is also said in a figurative way, like many other things. In fact, if we consider these words carefully, they do not even appear to be true. Everything a master does, does not remain hidden from the servant. Sometimes, in fact, the servant knows a little and, sometimes,

---

[29]See Lev 19:18.

even quite a bit about his [master's] business, especially if he loves his master. And Jesus himself did not reveal to them everything he knew—at least if we assume that the words, *everything that I have heard from my Father*, are referred to knowledge. Rather, this is what he means: "Servants are not introduced to secrets like those who are free. Even though they learn something when they are engaged in their duties, they are still ordered around by their masters. Those who are friends, when they share their blessings, come to know the secrets of their friends. So you must not be called servants, but friends, because you will hear everything about me and, as much as possible, you will later participate in the kingdom reserved for me." By the words, *I have made known to you everything that I have heard from my Father*, he means, "I made you a participant in every blessing that I received," symbolizing through his words what had actually happened.

And highlighting the greatness of his love in order to encourage his disciples even more, he adds, [15:16] *You did not choose me, but I chose you.* "I was not received by you," he says, "so that I might participate in these blessings; rather, I accepted you to participate in my blessings. Therefore I did not love you for the sake of a reward; rather, I began to bestow upon you the reward and the gift." In order to clarify what he was saying he added, *And I appointed you to go and bear fruit, fruit that will last, so that the Father will give you whatever you ask him in my name.* He means, "I gave you my blessings not so that, after tasting them for a short time, you might be deprived of them, but so that, by eternally producing spiritual fruits, you might abundantly enjoy the blessing that comes from the Father." He calls *fruit* the grace that they would receive from the Holy Spirit and from his blessings because, through the participation of the Spirit which they received, they were to him[30] like the branches [of the vine], according to the parable of our Lord.

After showing the greatness of his love for them—first with regard to how he loved them because he loved them more than himself, and then with regard to the gifts because he gave them his blessings—and after also showing that he first began to love them and that he gives an endless abundance of blessings—after all this, I say, he adds in good order, [15:17] *I am giving you these commands so that you may love one another.* "I say these things, not because I would like to celebrate my love for you, but in order to persuade you to love one another." And he said those words quite appropriately. First he urged them not to feel sad when they heard him talk about his passion. Then he offered them his teaching that persuaded them to love him. And, finally, he incited them to love each other deeply.

At this point he begins to teach them not to fear the afflictions that their adversaries will inflict upon them, by saying, [15:18] *If the world hates you, be aware that it hated me before it hated you.* It was appropriate for him to say this in order to arouse modesty in them. "If," he says, "the hatred of your adversaries upsets you, consider their hostility against me and know that you are no better than I. Therefore do not complain about the hatred of your enemies."

He further adds another reason, [15:19] *If you belonged to the world, the world would love you as its own. Because you do not belong to the world—but I have chosen you out of the world—therefore the world hates you.* "Consider who you are," he says, "now that you are regenerated by the power of the Spirit. You are quite different. Your life is in heaven, not on earth. Do you want to be loved by those with whom you have nothing in common? Or are you amazed that you are hated by them? Is this not shameful?"

Then, turning to the previous words, he says, [15:20] *Remember the word that I said to*

---

[30]To Christ.

you, "Servants are no greater than their master."
If they persecuted me, they will persecute you;
if they kept my word, they will keep yours also.
"It is time for you to remember that there is a
great difference between you and me," he says.
"Therefore it is not proper for you who are
servants to expect something better than what
I have received. Rather, you should want these
same things that I endured. When you see
happening to you what happened to me, accept
it joyfully as people worthy of my same destiny." And then, in order to arouse in them an
even greater modesty, he says, [15:21] *But they*
will do all these things to you on account of my
name, because they do not know him who sent
me. "Even though you seem to suffer this because of me, know that the Father also shares
the offense brought against me—indeed, they
offend him by not believing what I say. Therefore these incidents must not be considered serious, especially when you see that the Father
himself is despised by them."

Then he turns to accuse those who are
disobedient. When it became apparent that he
was clearly right in blaming them, the disciples
would then understand even better that they
suffered their tribulations because of their
virtue. [15:22] *If I had not come and spoken*
to them, they would not have sin; but now they
have no excuse for their sin. "They had no sin
when they were ignorant of the nature of the
Son—there was, in fact, a time when they
had not yet heard about him—but now, after
I have preached to them, I have left no excuse
for their unbelief." [15:23] *Whoever hates me*
hates my Father also. "On the contrary, they are
now reproached as enemies of the Father even
though they think they are defending him.
They should have believed the extraordinary
nature of the words I was speaking, but since
they did not believe them, it is clear that there
is no point in thinking they can defend the
Father." [15:24] *If I had not done among them*

the works that no one else did, they would not
have sin. But now they have seen and hated both
me and my Father. [15:25] *It was to fulfill the*
word that is written in their law, "They hated
me without cause."[31] "If," he says, "I had spoken
to them without performing miracles, they
would have thought they were prudent in not
accepting the extraordinary things I was saying
to them. But since I also performed miracles
and wonders when I spoke in order to confirm
my words, they must stand accused because
they have hated my Father and me and did not
accept my words. Evidently, according to the
word of the law, they hated me without just
cause."

After thus emphasizing the accusation directed against his enemies—because they had
heard what they were supposed to learn and
saw the signs—and also because he honored
the Father wherever he spoke about him and
clearly directed them to his [Father] in everything he taught—[after all this, I say,] he adds
a valid confirmation of all he has said. [15:26]
When the Paraclete comes whom I will send
to you from the Father, the Spirit of truth who
proceeds from the Father, he will testify on my
behalf. "Through the descent of the Spirit," he
says, "there will be a confirmation of what I
have said, that is, that they committed a serious offense against me and my Father. When
signs occur in my name through the power
of the Spirit, then the truth of my words will
become known. It will be evident that the Father was despised along with me because of the
iniquity of my enemies."

He further emphasizes their fault on the
basis of the person who will testify, *who pro-*
ceeds from the Father, that is, "the one whose
essence is from the very nature of the Father."
If, in fact, a natural procession is not understood by the word *proceeds* but, for instance,
some other external sending, there would be
uncertainty about which spirit he is talking

---

[31]Ps 35:19 (34:19 LXX).

about since many spirits are sent on missions, as also the apostle Paul said, "Are not all angels spirits in divine service, sent to serve?"[32] But here he mentions him as something unique, sufficiently revealing the one who alone proceeds from the Father and who properly is referred to by the name of "Spirit" in the Holy Scriptures.

And, just in case they might not believe the testimony he was about to give only on the basis of his words, he added, [15:27] *You also are to testify because you have been with me from the beginning.* In other words, "[The Spirit] will testify through you because you are always with him. Since he is always with you, your testimony will be confirmed before your audience. When you speak, the Spirit, through his testimony, will confirm your words by clear signs, as the apostle also said, "My speech and my proclamation were not with plausible words of wisdom, but with a demonstration of the Spirit and of power."[33] The signs that happened through the power of the Spirit in the name of the Lord showed the greatness of the one who underwent suffering and, at the same time, the foolishness of those who dared to crucify him. Previously he had persuaded them not to grieve when they heard about his passion by telling them why he predicted the event so that they might admire him even more after it was fulfilled, knowing that he was aware of everything that was happening to him and that his passion had a purpose, and thus dispelling and removing their sadness. He does the same here. He issues numerous pleas urging them not to despair because of their tribulations but to stand firm and resolute. And then, after revealing how sinful their enemies would be, thus persuading them even more to remain strong in the face of adversities—especially if they know they are suffering because of their

own virtue and godliness—he tells them why he predicted these things. It was certainly in order to teach them how to remain resolute, saying:

[16:1] *I have said these things to you to keep you from stumbling.* "I have predicted these things for you," he says, "so that when sudden, unexpected tribulations occur, your mind will not vacillate and falter but will instead be trained by these difficulties by continually focusing on what to expect." [16:2] *They will put you out of the synagogues. Indeed, an hour is coming when those who kill you will think that by doing so they are offering worship to God.* "Not only will you suffer expulsion by them from the synagogues," he says, "but know that there will even come a time when they think they are offering a sacrifice to God by your suffering and death, considering your murder as an act of piety."

And these actions were not only committed by Jews, but by Gentiles as well. Many from the sect of Simon Magus,[34] accustomed to being mixed in with the Christian church and treacherously feigning to follow its doctrine—up to this very day, in fact, they still appear to do the same but are now called Borborians,[35] and the faithful find it difficult to refute them—many of these were at times arrested by the Gentiles, I say, because of the foul wickedness they committed. And because of those who were arrested, the opinion then spread among many pagans that everyone in the church also committed these same crimes—as if they married their mothers and ate their children[36] and did all the other filthy acts that the [followers of Simon] did in secret, believing that this was the law of the church! And this is why believers were tormented with countless afflictions by the pagans who thought that the world had to be purified by exterminating them.

---

[32]Heb 1:14. [33]1 Cor 2:4. [34]See preface n. 5 (p.2). [35]The Borborians were radical Gnostics whose doctrine led them to live an extremely immoral life. Their name derives from *borboros*, that is, "mud." An imperial decree was promulgated against them in 428. See *Codex Theodosianus* 16.5.65. See also Epiphanius *Refutation of All Heresies* 26.3. [36]A typical accusation of the Gentiles against the Christians. See Tertullian *Apology* 2.

There is also a letter sent by a brother from Gallia to a bishop in Asia that relates how many afflictions befell the Christians at the time of king Verus because of this opinion. It even quotes this passage [in John] as if it had actually been fulfilled. Eusebius of Caesarea also reports this fact in his *Ecclesiastical History*.[37]

After he told them what would happen, he comforted them again by saying, [16:3] *And they will do this because they have not known the Father or me.* "But be comforted," he says, "about what will happen to you. Consider why this is happening and who it is who has a share with you in your contempt, namely my Father and I. This should be enough to let you know what kind of blessings you will enjoy because of these occurrences."

Then he clearly declares again why he is predicting these things to them, that is, in order to strengthen them to face their tribulations. [16:4] *But I have said these things to you so that when their hour comes you may remember that I told you about them.* "If I had not predicted these things," he says, "you might have lost your courage because these afflictions would have befallen you unexpectedly and you would have been unprepared. But if instead I predict what will happen to you, then, after it has happened, you will have to admire the power of the one who made the prediction, which is why you should have no doubt about the blessings I promised you."

After revealing the purpose of this prediction to them, he then indicated why he had not said these things to them previously. However, it seems that he had already spoken many times about his passion and the afflictions that they would suffer. In fact, at one time he had said, "The Son of Man must undergo great suffering on the part of the chief priests and the scribes, and they will crucify him and kill him."[38] And in another passage he had said,

"They will hand you over and flog you, and you will be dragged before governors and kings because of me."[39] But it is most likely that since he had said these things in an allusive way, they did not understand his words because they could not yet endure the severity of what he had to say. What did he say then? *I did not say these things to you from the beginning, because I was with you.* [16:5] *But now I am going to him who sent me.* "It was not necessary," he says, "for me to say these things to you before. Indeed, while I was with you, it was not a pressing matter for me to go into detail about what would happen to you since my presence among you was sufficient. But now, since I am about to leave you, all those things must be fully predicted for you so that you may have within you the support of my warning." As the Lord was saying these things, the disciples were overwhelmed with sadness. The longer he waited to say these things, the more they were grieved. Therefore, in order to encourage them and to persuade them to cast off the weight of their anxiety, he said, [16:5] *Yet none of you asks me, "Where are you going?"* [16:6] *But because I have said these things to you, sorrow has filled your hearts.* "There was a time," he says, "when you heard me say, 'I am going away,' and you asked me 'where?'" But now you do not question me at all. This is how far you have all fallen into grief."

And he comforts them again by saying, [16:7] *Nevertheless I tell you the truth: it is to your advantage that I go away.* "Even though you are sad, the truth demands this. None of these blessings can come to you if I do not suffer and if I am not at the place where I will be after my passion."

But what will happen to them after your passion? He answers, *If I do not go away, the Paraclete will not come to you; but if I go, I will send him to you.* "This indeed is how things must happen so that when I first am glorified,

---

[37]See Eusebius *Ecclesiastical History* 5.1 (PG 20:415-16).   [38]Mk 8:31.   [39]Mt 10:17-18.

you then who hope to participate in this glory may receive the grace of the Spirit. Therefore, if I go, you will also necessarily receive through the gift of the Spirit participation in the blessings that I enjoy. But if I do not enjoy them first, you cannot expect them either." And, in order to show them that he would invite them to share in these blessings once he had left, he proves in many ways that the gift of the grace of the Spirit is great. And this is only right since the Spirit provides all these blessings given to the human race.

[16:8] *And when he comes, he will convict the world about sin and righteousness and judgment,* [16:9] *about sin, because they do not believe in me;* [16:10] *about righteousness, because I am going to the Father and you will see me no longer;* [16:11] *about judgment, because the ruler of this world has been condemned.* "Because he is so great and powerful," he says, "so awesome is the descent of the Spirit that when it descends upon people it will reveal the *sin* of those who made an attempt on my life, because they planned to kill one who was worthy of such honor and greatness. The gift of the Spirit, which those believing in me receive, will clearly reveal this.

My *righteousness* will also be revealed by the words I preached among them with great integrity and the works I performed with such equity. The divine plan for my passion, in addition, will become evident from all of this because my suffering was not useless or in vain, but was for the condemnation of Satan. Indeed, when the sick are healed, the dead are raised and the demons are exorcised through the power of the gift of the Spirit; then, through all these works, Satan's condemnation will become self-evident. If I committed evil or taught false doctrine, I would justly be punished according to my actions and would be all the more despised after my death. And my disciples would also necessarily share with me in this same contempt. But when the presence of the Spirit through the accomplished mira-

cles evidences the contrary, and when it also elevates my disciples in great glory, then the condemnation of Satan will be known and the manifestation of my glory will become evident. The sin of my enemies, on the other hand, will be punished."

After referring all these actions to the Spirit in order to reveal his nature and power through the feats he was to accomplish, he added something even more excellent to confirm what he was saying: [16:12] *I still have many things to say to you, but you cannot bear them now.* [16:13] *When the Spirit of truth comes, he will guide you into all truth.* "More than anyone else," he says, "you will experience the power of the Spirit. Things that you now cannot even hear because you would be unable to understand them if they were spoken to you—those very things, I say, you will understand when you receive the gift of the Spirit because you will receive the whole truth from him. And you not only will be able to hear but will also understand everything that was said. Then you will know the nature of the Father, the dignity of the Son whose birth is beyond comprehension, the communication of his essence and the perfect similarity of his nature in the divine plan worked out among humanity. [You will also come to know] the great dignity that has been conferred upon him and the identity of the one who is in him, and what the conjunction is between him and the one who—notwithstanding the difference of the natures—could exist in him through the power of the one who made it so. Then you will also come to know the dignity of the Spirit whose work among the human race is so powerful that it can communicate God the Word. Then you will have a firm resolve about what is yet to come when you truly believe in the resurrection; then you will accept the tribulations you are given because you despise everything that is visible since you hope for the good that is to come." The words, *he will guide you into all truth,* mean, "The Spirit will give you an accurate understanding of all the things that you did not know before." In fact, the Spirit did not instruct the disciples through speech but communicated to their souls the revelation of the doctrine through an ineffable mystery and gave them a deeper sense of the truths. Therefore, after the descent of the Spirit, they were easily able to understand the things they had heard from the Only Begotten and had [previously] not understood, especially when he spoke about his nature.

Then, in order to confirm that the Holy Spirit could guide them into all truth, lingering on this subject of the Spirit contrary to the flow of his argument, he adds, *for he will not speak on his own.* Here again he does not use the phrase, *[not] on his own,* to refer to some defect but to a perfect harmony, as we have already shown many times. Indeed this means, "Do not think that the Holy Spirit is weak in power. Rather, he can do these things because nothing exceeds his knowledge, and he differs in no way from my Father and me. Because of his perfect union with the Father, he never acts on his own or apart from the Father. Instead, being in no way separated from the Father, he does everything with him because he is equal in nature, in operation, in knowledge and in will with both my Father and me." *But he will speak whatever he hears.* This does not mean that the Spirit learns what we humans have to learn. In fact, when the apostle said, "The Spirit searches everything, even the depths of God. For what human being knows what is truly human except the human spirit that is within? So also no one comprehends what is truly God's except the Spirit of God,"[40] who is so foolish as to say that what is certainly needed for our instruction is hidden from the knowledge of the Spirit? If this were true, the Spirit should be thanking us since it was because of us that he learned what he did not know. But since those who hear something

from someone who himself has learned it from another speaking to him—so that both, then, equally know the same thing—just like the one about whom it is said, *for he will not speak on his own,* that is, "He says nothing foreign or contrary to the Father"—this is why he adds, *whatever he hears,* saying this in a material way according to his custom. In other words, "The Spirit speaks what he knows together with me and my Father."

Jesus signifies the perfect equality of knowledge that the Spirit has by using the phrase "he hears," just as he did when he said about himself, "What I speak, therefore, I speak just as the Father has told me,"[41] by which he meant, "I teach what I know to be pleasing and agreeable to the Father." He said this to the Jews in order to indicate that he was not teaching anything foreign to the Father and that they were involving the Father in this argument in vain. And so, when he talks about the Spirit, he means that the Spirit says nothing foreign or contrary to the will of the Father, but only what is agreeable and pleasing to him.

Also, by adding one further argument, *he will declare to you the things that are to come,* he provided no small proof of the Spirit's power in communicating to people the foreknowledge of the things to come.

But the strongest argument, greater than any previous one, comes at the end when he says, [16:14] *He will glorify me, because he will take what is mine and declare it to you.* I think it is inappropriate for us to report in detail everything the heretics say in diminishing the person of the Spirit when they foolishly speculate about this statement.[42] Let us instead try to elucidate the meaning of this verse with the help of God. He does not say the Spirit will take "from me" but that he will take *what is mine.*

It is necessary for us to investigate what is indicated by this phrase "his own," from which

[40]1 Cor 2:10-11. [41]Jn 12:50. [42]Again Theodore refers to the Arians, who assigned a subordinate position to the Holy Spirit as well as to the Son.

the Spirit will take and which he will declare to them. Certainly he meant the following: "Christ-in-the-flesh, when he was not yet in his nature so that he was united with God the Word, necessarily needed the mediation of the gift of the Spirit. And after receiving every perfect grace, which he received thanks to his anointing, he lived a life of great integrity in a way that is not possible for human nature. Therefore, the assumed man also received a share in that which is the principle of all goodness on behalf of all humanity because we will participate in all the things that happened to him—in resurrection, in the ascension into heaven and in the kingdom and glory. "If we suffer with him, we will also be glorified with him."[43] And, "If we endure, we will also reign with him."[44] It follows, then, that we will also receive the grace of the Spirit so that we may be regenerated by its power by symbolically fulfilling through baptism the event of the death and resurrection of Christ. "Do you not know that all of us who have been baptized into Christ Jesus were baptized into his death? Therefore we have been buried with him by baptism into death, so that just as Christ was raised from the dead by the glory of the Father, so we too might walk in newness of life."[45] Thus, this is what we too have to look forward to in the future. Therefore, the congregation of the faithful is also called the body of Christ, and each one of us is a member of his, and he is the head of us all because through the power of the Spirit we will receive, as it were, a natural conjunction with him, as the apostle also says, "For in the one Spirit we were all baptized into one body."[46]

Therefore our Lord, intending to highlight the Spirit's power, says, *He will glorify me, because he will take what is mine and declare it to you.* In other words, "He will reveal my glory to everyone." Just as when he says to the Father, "I glorified you on earth," he means, "I revealed

your glory before everyone," so also here he said that the Spirit *will glorify me;* that is, "He will reveal my glory, what it is and how great it is." "All of the grace of the Spirit," he says, "is with me because I am joined together with God the Word, and I received true sonship. From the grace that is in me and with me a small portion will come upon you so that you also may be called sons of God, even though you are quite far removed from the honor that I have as the Son. When this portion [of grace], through the mediation of the Spirit, accomplishes all these things such as performing miracles, healing, driving out demons, foretelling the future and revealing what is hidden, then my greatness will clearly be made known. If indeed the portion that is in you is so powerful and capable of enrapturing everyone in their admiration, just think of the glory that is mine."

Then, he demonstrates the difference between them and him, saying, [16:15] *All that the Father has is mine.* "Indeed I also received universal dominion," he says. And we believe that it is so since he has a share in everything that belongs to God the Word because of his conjunction with him. And this conjunction was accomplished through the gift of the Spirit. Therefore he attributed the cause of his universal dominion to the Spirit.

And he explains what he means by this. *This is why I said that he will take what is mine and declare it to you.* "In fact," he says, "every grace has been given to me so that it might be proven that I am the Lord of all. This, however, cannot happen in your case since you can only share a small portion, which is in no way equal to mine. Otherwise, you too might be called "lords" like me. Therefore this is why I did not say "from me" but *what is mine,* because you will not receive all of the grace that is in its entirety in me. As it is, you will receive only a portion that is small enough to be suitable for you."

[43]Rom 8:17. [44]2 Tim 2:12. [45]Rom 6:3-4. [46]1 Cor 12:13.

He demonstrates the power of the Spirit and its power through everything he says here, because it was through the Spirit that he was established in his dignity and that great things would happen to his disciples and, similarly, because the Spirit's advent was extremely helpful in strengthening his followers and confounding his enemies. He also spoke these words in order to show that his passion would greatly benefit them, as would those things that would happen later. Without these, they would not have received grace. And if they did not receive grace, they would be deprived of all these blessings. For, consoling them with the words mentioned above so that they might not be grieved by his passion, he said, "If I do not go away, the Paraclete will not come to you." Then, in order to show how beneficial and excellent the advent of the Spirit was, he spoke the words we are now explaining so that he might confirm what he had said in a number of ways. After telling them this and demonstrating that his departure was beneficial to them, he turned back to the object of his speech, saying:

[16:16] *A little while, and you will no longer see me, and again a little while, and you will see me,* [16:17] *because I am going to the Father.* The words, *because I am going to the Father,* are not the cause of what he said previously. They have their own meaning. In fact, there are really three separate statements in what he said. The first is: *A little while, and you will no longer see me;* the second is: *and again a little while, and you will see me;* and the third is: *I am going to the Father.* By returning to the subject of his discourse after providing the evidence [for what he said], he intends now to provide a summary: "Since you are about to receive such great grace, do not be grieved if I go. But know this: *A little while, and you will no longer see me*—because he is about to die and be buried; *and again a little while, and you will see me*—because he will be easily delivered from death. Then you will also see me ascend-

ing *to the Father,* but you can rejoice even now because of all these things."

The disciples were amazed at these words that were spoken before the event, obviously not understanding what he was saying because they still did not comprehend any of them—not the phrase "a little while and they will not see him," or the phrase, "and again a little while and they will see him," or the phrase, *because I am going to the Father.* And the Evangelist alludes to this, saying, [16:19] *Jesus knew that they wanted to ask him, so he said to them, "Are you discussing among yourselves what I meant when I said, 'A little while, and you will no longer see me, and again a little while, and you will see me'"?* And yet, he does not explain his enigmatic speech in what he says here, thinking that the time for an explanation had not come yet. Instead, he would let them gain understanding afterward from the events themselves. And so he tells them what he knows will be a comfort for them because they were saddened by his passion.

[16:20] *Amen, Amen, I tell you, you will weep and mourn, but the world will rejoice; you will have pain, but your pain will turn into joy.* "I know," he says, "that my passion will provide great joy to my enemies and mourning to you. But know that great joy will also come to you from this sadness, when you enjoy the blessings that derive from this suffering." But since it seemed impossible that joy might come from sadness, he wanted to convince them by making a comparison with what happens to women, "Just as a woman gives birth in great pain, but when she has actually delivered her child and has been relieved from the contractions and has forgotten her pain, she rejoices because from that pain an amazing, wonderful life has come into the world—so also the time of my passion and death will be as though you are in labor. But when you see me rise from the dead and see that I have come out of the tomb as if a new man was born to immortality from these pains, then you will experience an immense joy because you hope to participate in this as well, and your joy will never be taken away from you again. I cannot die again, nor can your participation with me be taken away from you." [16:23] *On that day you will ask nothing of me.* He means, "You will have no need to make a request. Indeed, you will have participation in every blessing through the gift itself of the Spirit." But he also intends to say this in a figurative way as he has done with other statements. However, just in case they might have the idea there was already no need to make requests, he says, *Amen, Amen, I tell you, if you ask anything of the Father in my name, he will give it to you.* But the words, *you will ask nothing,* seem contradictory to the words, *if you ask anything.* With the first he forbids them to ask; with the second he persuades them to ask. However, as I said, like many other things these statements too are said figuratively. What he in fact means is, "When I ascend into heaven and you receive the grace of the Spirit, you will possess such an abundant treasure of gifts that you will have no need for prayer in this respect." Indeed they performed more miracles through the grace they had received than through prayers.

[16:24] *Until now you have not asked for anything in my name.* Actually, up to this point they had not considered asking him through prayer. *Ask and you will receive, so that your joy may be complete.* "From this time on," he says, "ask constantly, and you will receive, and you will rejoice as well because of the gifts granted to you."

[16:25] *I have said these things to you in figures of speech.* Here he openly declares, as we have said many times, that he is speaking to them figuratively. Then he adds, *The hour is coming when I will no longer speak to you in figures of speech, but will tell you plainly of the Father.* He indicates the time of the descent of the Spirit from which they will receive a true understanding of the Father and the Son, after the outpouring of the Spirit's grace. He told them they would receive a clear understanding concerning the Father because they would know that the Father had begotten the Son from his substance, since they did not yet know nor could they understand him when he referred to him as "my Father." They thought that he, just like any other person, called God his Father because of God's providential care for him.

Therefore, at this point in the order of the argument he appropriately adds, [16:26] *On that day you will ask in my name.* Those who understood this would necessarily ask of the Son what they were asking of the Father. *I do not say to you that I will ask the Father on your behalf.* [Above he says, "And I will ask the Father,][47] and he will give you another Paraclete"; [here he says, *I do not say to you that I will ask the Father on your behalf.* These words certainly seem to be contradictory].[48] Actually in that earlier statement, he was discussing his ascension into heaven which would be followed by the descent of the Spirit. Therefore it was appropriate for him there to say, "I will ask," as was suitable to the man; and it should be clear to anyone that he himself [in his humanity] ought not to have asked. For how could he have known what was to be given to them, and, for that matter, how could he have promised his disciples something that he himself could [only] obtain by petition? But [in that previous instance] he refers to his petition as the cause of the gift. Here when he says, *I will not ask,* they would clearly recognize that he was referring to the majesty of the Godhead, indicating that he will not need to ask on their behalf since he himself can grant petitions just

---

[47]The words in square brackets are missing from the Syriac text and are integrated from the Greek fragment: PG 66:780B-C; Devreesse, *Essai sur Théodore de Mopsueste,* p. 402 (fr. 132); Theodore of Mopsuestia, *Commentary on John* (Kalantzis), pp. 128-29. [48]The words in square brackets are missing from the Syriac text and are integrated from the Greek fragment.

like the Father does. He said this openly, as was suitable to his divine nature. But in order that he might not appear to the weak minds of his disciples as someone who was looking for glory, he added, [16:27] *for the Father himself loves you.* "Because of your love for me, the Father gives you everything." With the words, *I will not ask,* he alluded to his divine nature; with the words, "the Father will give you," he also removed any suspicion of pride. And, with regard to himself, he suggested that he is also a participant in the gift. In fact, if he does not ask at all, even though he has great care for them, it is evident that he also gives together with the Father.

[16:28] *I came from the Father and have come into the world; again I am leaving the world and am going to the Father.* The words, *I came from the Father,* only mean that he himself[49] was in the man. When he said, *I came from the Father,* he was using the phrase in the same way as when he referred to his conjunction [with the Father] when he said, *I am going to the Father,* since people believed that he was only a man without any share in the nature of the Father. However, there was no way for him to be separated from this conjunction [with the Father]. This is why he said, *I am going,* with reference to the present event while alluding to the future conjunction [with the Father]. But the action alluded to in the phrase, *I came from the Father,* did not happen in this way. How could he have been separated from his communion with the Father? Rather, he said this in deference to the human opinion about him which only saw that he appeared to be a man. And it was only right that they would think this since a human being cannot have any natural communion with the Father. Therefore this is the mixture[50] of both God the Word and the man whom he assumed, as in the phrase, "No one has ascended into heaven,"[51] as we have shown

in our commentary with the help of God.

Therefore the phrase, *I came from the Father,* as I have said, can certainly be understood as referring to the Godhead and not as referring to a separation. It clearly does not, however, refer to the assumed man. The phrase, *I am leaving and going,* in turn, has no reference at all to the Godhead, nor is it used in the sense of a migration or a conjunction. This could never be allowed. But it could be said about the man. Thus, both phrases cannot be attributed at the same time to one of those natures; indeed, attributing both of them either to God the Word or to the man would be inappropriate. According to the meaning explained by us—and no one may propose a clearer and more suitable meaning to the context—the first appears to suit the Godhead, while the second appears to suit the assumed man, because of the joining of the natures through which they both reached a certain unity. What he says sounds like this: "I was in the man and was considered to be a man by those who did not know me. Through him I did everything for the salvation of the human race, and I assumed him so that I might join him to the Father."

The disciples thought they correctly understood what he was saying, which is why they said, [16:29] *Yes, now you are speaking plainly, not in any figure of speech!* [16:30] *Now we know that you know all things, and do not need to have anyone question you; by this we believe that you came from God.* They thought they knew and understood all these things so that they could now answer him because his words were no longer parables to them.

What does the Lord answer? [16:31] *Do you now believe?* [16:32] *The hour is coming, indeed it has come, when you will be scattered, each one to his home, and you will leave me alone. Yet I am not alone because the Father is with me.*

---

[49]That is, God the Word. [50]Even though Theodore speaks here of a mixture of God the Word and the man, he does not recede from his dualistic Christology of the "two natures." See also translator's introduction, esp. quotation from Norris, p. xxvi. [51]Jn 3:13.

He wanted in some small way to reprove their weakness. He did not openly say that they had not understood his words because this was not the time to explain and interpret what he had said. And it was useless to reproach them when they would not have understood anything more even after his rebuke. But he announced their weakness ahead of time, by noting that they vainly boasted about their faith, which they would soon abandon, which is exactly what happened.

He also added, indicating the reason of his prediction, [16:33] *I have said this to you, so that in me you may have peace.* "I predicted your future error," he says, "so that, when it happens, you might admire the power of the predictor and take care not to err again, because you will deny me, your Lord. However," he continues, "there will be a great persecution." *In the world you face persecution. But take courage; I have conquered the world!* Even though those who persecute you are powerful, rejoice and be confident: I will conquer your oppressors. Since I will live beyond the death that they inflicted upon me hoping to destroy me, believe that you too will participate in the resurrection because you also participated with me in my suffering. Do not get upset over the things they do; rather, rejoice for what you will be granted later."

This is what the Lord said to his disciples, thinking that it would be beneficial for their instruction. And through his words he comforted them by telling them of the benefits that outweighed the tribulations they would experience, so that they would not grieve when they heard about his suffering. He also told them other things, some of which would happen to him, others—quite glorious—that would happen to them too. But since the disciples were still weak before his passion, they did not understand some of his words, as our Lord mentioned to them. There were also other things they were just not ready to hear. This is why he told them many things in parables.

At this point, he turns his speech from the disciples to the Father, speaking in the form of a prayer, mentioning what would be given to him and what to them. Even though, when he spoke then, they could hardly have believed many of the things he was saying, nevertheless, since he offered this request in a prayer, they thought that any doubt on their part would be inadvisable. They knew there was nothing— not even the greatest thing imaginable—that the Father could not give if he wanted to. The force of the commentary will clearly show this, that is, that there is no real prayer here. It was simply the form of a prayer. He also spoke these words of prayer as parables too. If one wants to judge them simply in a literal sense, he will find that there is no reason for many of these prayers to have been spoken, especially when they appear to have no logical connection between them.

Therefore the Evangelist says, [17:1] *After Jesus had spoken these words, he looked up to heaven and said, "Father, the hour has come; glorify your Son so that the Son may glorify you, [17:2] since you have given him authority over all flesh."* Many, far from understanding the meaning of these words, upset their logical sequence by not reading them in the right order. They take these words outside the order in which they should be read and refer them to other contexts. For instance, some have connected the words, *since you have given him authority over all flesh,* to those following. But in this context they fit better with those which precede, as they have been quoted by us. Great glory was most certainly conferred by God after the suffering of the assumed man when he was resurrected, when he ascended into heaven and when because of his conjunction with God the Word he gained universal dominion. This is also why he is to be worshiped by all, as the apostle said, "Therefore God also highly exalted him and gave him the name that is above every name, so that at the name of Jesus every knee should bend, in heaven and on earth and under the earth."[52] But when our Lord actually said this, it was too much for the disciples to believe since their human weakness could not be convinced to accept what he said in light of the intense humiliation that was apparent [before their very eyes]. Thus desiring to make this known to them in the form of a prayer, he says, "Since the time is near, glorify your Son, just as you gave him authority over all flesh, so that your Son may also glorify you." Indeed this is the logical order, so that the words, *so that the Son may glorify you*, may be read after all the other words.

Therefore he said: "As you have given him such an honor that he might receive universal dominion"—although in reality he received this after the fact even though, with regard to the honor, it was due to him already as the one chosen by God—as, therefore, he says, "you gave me this, so now glorify me." In other words, "In a way appropriate to the honor of which you made me worthy, reveal me before everyone at the time of my passion so that through the events which will happen on the cross everyone will know how great my honor really is and recognize that I did not deserve to suffer, but that I died willingly for the manifold benefit of others." Thus the phrase, *glorify [me]* does not mean "give me glory," but, "reveal my glory that was given to me by you." Having the same meaning in mind, he added, *so that the Son may glorify you*; that is, "by those things you also will appear to be great and glorious through me. The more my works appear to be admirable, the more your dignity becomes known."

However, he does not say the words, *so that your Son may glorify you* in a causal way. The Father, in fact, did not glorify [the Son] for the purpose of being glorified by him [in return]. Rather, he says this because this is what would logically follow, according to the custom of divine Scripture, as for instance when it says,

"For this reason the Father loves me, because I lay down my life in order to take it up again."[53] [The Father] did not love him because he was about to lay down his life. Rather, [the Son] was speaking about something that necessarily followed from [the Father's love]. This is also the meaning of the verse following. He adds, *to give eternal life to all whom you have given him*. Also here he does not indicate the cause but what necessarily follows. Indeed this means that he has received universal authority in order to give eternal life to those who believe in him. He declares how he will give eternal life by adding, [17:3] *This is eternal life, that they may know you, the only true God, and Jesus Christ whom you have sent*. "This is how," he says, "eternal life will be given to them: when they fully know the divine nature, without wandering here and there, and without indicating by this name beings that are not gods because they will acknowledge me as the one who has done everything in this world, according to your command, for their salvation." They certainly must know him fully and rightly honor him for everything he has done.

At that time there were two doctrines among the people: paganism and Judaism. Christ introduced a third doctrine, the Christian doctrine, which is the true one, defined concisely in these words [of John 17:3]. Indeed Christian doctrine is opposed to paganism in every respect. If it is compared to Judaism, it refutes it too as something quite distant from true knowledge. Paganism, for its part, openly preaches about many gods, a concept Christianity absolutely opposes. Judaism, although it appears to have an understanding of the divine nature, nevertheless is not perfect in that understanding. The Jews knew God simply, but they understood nothing more than this because they did not know the nature of the Father, who bore the Son in an ineffable mystery, nor did they know the person of the Son, who

---

[52]Phil 2:9-10. [53]Jn 10:17.

was in the beginning with the Father. They also were confused about the Spirit. They also did not yet know that a man had been assumed and joined together with the divine nature.

Thus, briefly expressing all the doctrine of the truth that distinguishes us from paganism and Judaism, Jesus desired to teach us, after we knew and understood this doctrine, to obtain eternal life through him. Since he had received universal authority, he prepared immortality for us. The order itself of the sentences and the obvious meaning of the words is sufficient to unmask the foolishness of the heretics.[54] Now let us say this, however: obviously the words, *the only true God*, are not spoken about the Father as if they were said in opposition to the Son. Also, the words, *and Jesus Christ whom you have sent*, surely do not refer to the nature of the Only Begotten. In fact, by saying, *whom you have sent*, he clearly reveals what he means. This is not the time to express in our discussion the words that should be said in reply to their[55] objections. Our accurate interpretation is sufficient to answer their objections, together with what we have said before. Even though we have said this with few words, it is quite true and credible for the wise.

After he had said these things and introduced them to what he was saying, he continued by further expounding on the phrase "glorify your Son," by saying, [17:4] *I glorified you on earth by finishing the work that you gave me to do.* "I have accomplished what I was supposed to do," he says. "I have revealed your glory to everyone on the face of the earth and have perfectly fulfilled the task given to me for the salvation of all." What follows? [17:5] *So now, Father, glorify me in your own presence with the glory that I had in your presence before the world existed.* "Therefore," he says, "since I accomplished what I was supposed to do—that is, what was necessary at this time and especially at the time of my passion—reveal now

who I am before everyone, so that when they observe my suffering they may not dwell only on what is apparent, since they are incapable of conceiving anything higher about me. Reveal me the way I am." How? "By revealing before them that glory and nature that I had before the world existed. And, just as I revealed your invisible glory before everyone, this is how you should reveal me, because people still do not know who I am." The dignity of the assumed man was so great that God dwelled in him, and we worship him because we believe this to be the case. On the other hand, who is foolish enough to worship the man separately? Therefore, after he had said, "Since I have accomplished everything, now I must be revealed," he appropriately added here as well, "Do not reveal to them the one they can see—indeed they knew who this was and considered him vile—but reveal where I actually am from." And now all those things were about to happen, as our Lord himself had predicted many times. The reason these things were said is the same that we have expounded above; that is, [the Lord] spoke in the form of a prayer about those things which would happen to him and the disciples.

After mentioning these things about his glory, he turns his speech to the disciples by also announcing what will happen to them. He teaches them what they must know, both in order to confirm their faith and in order that they might remain firm amid the tribulations which were about to befall them. He begins with the words that will support their faith, saying, [17:6] *I have made your name known to those whom you gave me from the world. They were yours, and you gave them to me, and they kept your word.* All of these words seem like parables, especially those he says here. What he means is this: "I made your name known to humanity and hid from no one what I had to say about you. However, not everyone came to believe in the same way. I wanted everyone to know of my love; your choice, in turn, distinguished who was yours. Out of all those in the entire world, those who are really yours and who conform their will to yours are the ones who believed my words and kept them diligently." He says, *those whom you gave me from the world*—that is, "out of the entire world, those who are really yours were given to me by you"—in order to signify that "those who are in a close relationship with you are the ones who are my disciples."

What he says here serves to strengthen the disciples in their faith since these words demonstrate that whoever is close to Christ cannot be a stranger to the Father: *They were yours, and you gave them to me.* Those *who are from the world* serves also as a reference to the Jews. Further, when he says, "Everything that the Father gives me will come to me, and anyone who comes to me I will never drive away,"[56] he means that "those who are close to the Father believe my words too, and I receive them as mine." These words were intended as a reproach to the Jews who did not believe and who vainly boasted of their close relationship with the Father, but these words were also quite appropriate for strengthening his disciples.

He goes on to add the following: [17:7] *Now I know*[57] *that everything you have given me is from you;* [17:8] *for the words that you gave to me I have given to them, and they have received them and know in truth that I came from you; and they have believed that you sent me.* If this speech is interpreted literally, it is evident that it is not true either. He does not, in fact, come to know here for the first time that his [followers] are from the Father and were given to him by the Father; nor is this the reason for his realizing that "they believed." Rather, just as God said to Abraham: "Now I know that you

fear God";[58] that is, "You gave great evidence of your devotion to me," so here also, if we take the words in their logical sequence as referring to the preceding sentence, he means, "The fact that they believe the words that I say are yours is proof that those who believe in me are in a close relationship with you." This is what he meant when he said, *for the words that you gave to me I have given to them.* "Thus, they also received me as one who came into the world according to your will and as one pleasing to you. I preach to them, and thus, through the faith that they have in me, you are honored too." It was only appropriate, then, that he saw all these things as proving that those who believed in him were also in a close relationship to the Father.

[17:9] *I am asking on their behalf; I am not asking on behalf of the world, but on behalf of those whom you gave me, because they are yours.* [17:10] *All mine are yours, and yours are mine; and I have been glorified in them.* So far, he has spoken of those things which were intended to confirm their faith. From this point forward he begins to speak by way of exhortation about those events that will happen to them, thus enabling them to easily withstand their tribulations. What then? This speech does not concern everyone, but only believers. Indeed, the words, *on behalf of those whom you gave me,* are a reference to believers. "Those who are yours are also mine, because of [our] indivisible harmony and because of [their] participation in divinity. This is also why I, in my conjunction with God the Word, received them and was glorified among all people." What is it, then, that you are asking now that you did not ask before? [17:11] *And now I am no longer in the world, but they are in the world, and I am coming to you.* "Since I am leaving this world," he says, "and they still remain in the afflictions of this world and need much assistance—what

---

[56]Jn 6:37. [57]This is the reading in the Syriac text and the Peshitta, as well as that followed by Sinaiticus. The majority of the Greek New Testament textual witnesses read, "Now they know." [58]Gen 22:12.

is it that you are asking?" *Holy Father, protect them in your name that you have given me, so that they may be one, as we are one.* This is what he says, and it is necessary that we explain this speech in detail.

After the first human being was created by God, he was condemned to death because of his sin, together with all those who were born from him—those who received their existence from the portion, as one might say, of the nature [they shared] with the first human beings. Thus, because human beings are still able to give birth, for this very reason they receive a natural participation with the first human beings. And since human beings have a common nature, they also thus contracted the death imposed upon that nature. When our Lord wanted to put an end to that death and make humanity imperishable and worthy of great honor, he assumed one man as the principle of all in which God the Word dwelled. He caused him to perform and endure all the things that happen to human beings while living a life of the utmost integrity. At the end of his life he also accepted that end through the coming of death. But after he rose from the dead, he was born into another life instead of the previous one as a new imperishable man. And after receiving the entire gift of the Spirit, he easily did all the things that were required in this world for our salvation. And since he received immortality after his resurrection, he was made Lord of all in his conjunction with God the Word.

Since we also will participate in his resurrection, just as our Lord wants us to, it was necessary that those who had received through natural birth their participation in Adam—and thus expected the sentence of death—would be born after death through resurrection to a new birth like that of the Lord so that they also might take part in eternal life. Therefore what happened? Since Christ-in-

the-flesh obtained the resurrection through the Spirit, we also necessarily will receive the same dispensation from the Spirit. And the apostle teaches this openly by saying, "If the Spirit of him who raised Jesus from the dead dwells in you, he who raised Christ from the dead will give life to your mortal bodies also through his Spirit that dwells in you."[59] In fact, he would not have raised him in resurrection in the name of the Spirit if this had no purpose at all for the resurrection of our Savior. And he demonstrates this most significantly not by saying "the Spirit of God," but "the Spirit of him who raised Jesus." Just as previously [the Spirit] has shown his power, so here it remains consistent in raising him.

Thus we are regenerated through baptism, in which we fulfill a type of the death and resurrection of our Lord. This is what the apostle had said and what we have frequently shown. And we do believe that this can only happen to us again through the power of the Spirit, according to the word of the Lord. Therefore, just as the first human beings were born from the small portion received by means of Adam (and the same thing happened to those who were born later), so from the fullness of the gift of the Spirit—received by the apostles in a smaller portion from Christ-in-the-flesh, whose anointing was, in fact, just such a gift and is something that is always with him—in the same way, all true believers receive grace through these [apostles], and thanks to the service of priests throughout the centuries. And through [this grace], they obtain a sort of natural conjunction with Christ. Just as indeed that certain natural small portion [we spoke about previously] through the inscrutable wisdom of the omnipotent Creator produces a likeness of its nature, so also this portion of spiritual grace brings about a participation in honor and glory. Therefore, just as he [Adam] is one, and we all are called a single man

---

[59]Rom 8:11.

[Adam] because each of us is like a member of the whole, in the same way those who were born in Christ are called his body, and each of them is a member of his, even as Christ is the head of us all. If these same concepts were already spoken about elsewhere in our commentary on the Evangelist, we must not think that they are superfluous here. Anytime we find words like this that cannot be explained in a few sentences, we must examine them completely, especially when the figurative style of the words offers the heretics an occasion to corrupt the truth.

Thus God the Word is naturally united with the Father. Through his conjunction with him,[60] the assumed man also obtained conjunction with the Father. And we, in a similar way, by virtue of the natural conjunction we have with Christ-in-the-flesh, insofar as is possible, also receive spiritual participation with him and are his body, and each of us is a member of his body. Therefore we hope to rise again like him afterward and be reborn into eternal life. Thus, by reaching God the Word through him, we necessarily receive friendship with the Father. This is why he said, [17:11] *Holy Father, protect them in your name that you have given me, so that they may be one, as we are one.* In other words, "As you joined me with God the Father through the Spirit, and made me worthy of sonship so that I might call you my Father, so also, after conferring the grace of the Spirit, make them your children so that, like me, they also may be one and may have the same union with you and faithfully call you Father." Paul spoke in a similar manner when he said, "[You have received] a spirit of adoption, in which we cry, 'Abba, Father.'"[61] It is evident that in the Spirit we are worthy of adoption as children and to call God our Father. *In your name that you have given me,* in this same name preserve them too, and give them the grace of the Spirit so that they also,

like me, may call you Father, after being made one through spiritual regeneration. He therefore says, *in your name,* that is, [in the name] of the Father whom they will also invoke when they are endowed through the Spirit with adoptive sonship.

At this point he begins to exhort them to endure tribulations with courage by saying, [17:12] *While I was with them, I protected them in your name that you have given me.* This is not because they had already received the Spirit of adoptive sonship. Indeed, how could they when our Lord himself taught them to wait for the promised Spirit that they heard about, according to what Luke relates?[62] Rather, he said this in the form of prayer: "While I was with them, I made sure that they would not depart from the fear of God, so that they might be able through friendship with you to have a share in what I was asking you to give them, that is, adoption as children."

And since he had said, *I protected them,* he then added, *that you have given me. I guarded them, and not one of them was lost, except the one destined to be lost, so that the Scripture might be fulfilled.* "In addition," he said "all of them remained in your love and none of them erred, except the one who it was known would be lost even before he was born." After introducing the destruction of Judas into his speech, he connected what he was saying about him to his exhortation so that they might endure easily the tribulations that were about to be inflicted upon them by their enemies.

The words, *While I was with them, I protected them,* are contrasted with what in logical sequence he says next, [17:13] *But now I am coming to you, and I speak these things in the world so that they may have my joy made complete in themselves.* [17:14] *I have given them your word, and the world has hated them because they do not belong to the world, just as I do not belong.* [17:15] *I am not asking you to take them*

---

[60]That is, through the assumed man's conjunction with God the Word. [61]Rom 8:15. [62]See Acts 1:4.

out of the world, but I ask you to protect them from the evil one. Just as in the form of a prayer he had previously said what would happen to him and his disciples, so again, in the form of prayer, he consoled them concerning their tribulations by teaching them not to lose courage in the face of the events that were about to unfold against them. Therefore he says, "Since I am about to depart from this world, I want them to rejoice in me as they hear of the great honor that awaits me, so that they may not lose their courage in the tribulations that they will face when they preach about me, since they are hated by the world. This is why," he says, "I do not ask that they may be taken out of the world but that they may be protected from its evils." He again spoke about these things that might happen to them in the form of a prayer which, in fact, did happen to them through the Spirit when they rejoiced while suffering for him—those who had previously abandoned their teacher under the slightest pretext.

After exhorting them in this way, he again instructs them about what will happen to them. [17:16] They do not belong to the world, just as I do not belong to the world. He alludes here to their regeneration since after their regeneration they will no longer be called the body of Adam or his members but the body of Christ. This is why they must focus their attention on heavenly things, as the blessed Paul said as well, "Our way of life is in heaven."[63]

He declares how they will no longer be of this world, saying, [17:17] Sanctify them in your truth. "This will happen, he says, when they receive true holiness," but he meant their participation in the Spirit. The words, in your truth, mean, "truly and accurately." This is the usual expression of Holy Scripture, and its use is frequent in the blessed David, as for instance when he says, "Your mercy and your truth always help,"[64] meaning, "Your true mercy." Then he adds, your word is truth; that

is, "They will obtain this true holiness through the Spirit, as you willed and asked." He calls "his word" the will and command of God, as in the verse, "By the word of the Lord the heavens were made,"[65] that is, "by his will and command."

When this happens to them, they will indeed be apart from this world and will be thinking about having another mother—the heavenly Jerusalem. And he says what the result of this will be: [17:18] As you have sent me into the world, so I have sent them into the world. "The participation in the Spirit will not only give them the power to be freed from evil but will make them so strong that they may walk throughout the world and proclaim the message about the fear of God just as I also made such proclamation."

[17:19] And for their sakes I sanctify myself, so that they also may be sanctified in the truth. "Therefore," he says, "I allowed myself to undergo suffering so that when they acquire these things through me, they might gain true holiness, that is, the grace of the Spirit. And they will preach the truth, believing in the hope of the resurrection and expecting the delights of the heavenly kingdom." Since all these things were given to them by the Holy Spirit, and our Lord through his passion and resurrection prepared the grace of the Spirit for them, it was only right that he said, for their sakes I sanctify myself, so that they also may be sanctified in the truth. Through the words, I sanctify myself, he hints at his passion. But one who comes to read this book must know that these words, reported in the form of a prayer, are a prophecy of what will happen to the disciples. One should not consider their form or the different times [at which they were spoken] or their appearance as prayers in what they say; rather, one understands them as words of prophecy about future events.

Therefore, after our Lord had spoken, in

[63]See Phil 3:20.   [64]Ps 40:11; 94:18.   [65]Ps 33:6.

the hearing of his disciples, about what would happen to believers, he added something further so that the disciples might not think that these things were only going to happen to them: [17:20] *I ask not only on behalf of these, but also on behalf of those who will believe in me through their word.* "I do not want these things to happen only to them, but to all those who will believe in me through them." What then does he want to happen? [17:21] *That they may all be one. As you, Father, are in me and I am in you, may they also be one in us, so that the world may believe that you have sent me.* Just as those who come into this life and are human beings constitute a single whole under the aspect of nature, so also those too, who after death through resurrection are born again into another world, are a single whole in [spiritual] nature since they have been changed into something that is beyond perishable nature. They no longer consider Adam as the head and beginning of their existence but Christ-in-the-flesh, the one who was made for them the beginning of that [new] life.

Baptism is the symbol of these things, that is, of the death and resurrection of our Lord. We are indeed buried together with him as in a symbol of his death, as the apostle also said,[66] and we rise with him by ascending from here. Baptism is also appropriately and with good reason called a birth because in this symbolic action performed upon us we immediately are born into a life that is eternal and imperishable through resurrection. Thus, we are all referred to as a single body of Christ, and the head of us all is Christ. Through him we receive our affinity with God the Word and thus are joined to the Father. And the blessed apostle demonstrates this clearly when he says, "For just as the body is one and has many members, and all the members of the body, though many, are one body, so it is with Christ."[67] Here he calls the church and the congregation of the

faithful "the body made of many members," which is indicated by the name of Christ. Just as, indeed, "man" is called Adam, and each and every one of us is connected in this name, so also those who are like the body of Christ through spiritual birth are appropriately designated by the term *body*. This is also why the apostle says, in explaining and demonstrating who is designated by the name of Christ, "For in the one spirit we were all baptized into one body."[68] Therefore he says, "Allow everyone to receive conjunction with us. Through the things that happen among believers, everyone will know that I came according to your will, because the great blessings that will happen to them will clearly show that I did not come without you, as the Jews insinuate."

[17:22] *The glory that you have given me I have given them.* This evidently proves that these words are not some kind of prayer to obtain gifts but are a prophecy about future events related in the form of a prayer. If he was asking in order that something might be given, how could he have said with authority, *The glory that you have given me I have given them?* And he clearly shows that he does not mean that he gave anything more than this when he adds, *so that they may be one, as we are one,* [17:23] *I in them and you in me, that they may become completely one, so that the world may know that you have sent me and have loved them even as you have loved me.* This is clearly a repetition of what he had already said above. There, in fact, he speaks as if he is still asking for something to be given to them; here, on the other hand, he speaks as if he has already given it to them. How does he ask and, at the same time, say that he has already given? If this is true, what was said before appears to be superfluous. Yet, if he were truly asking out of necessity, there would be pride evidenced in this other formula, unless, as we have said, a form of prayer was being used out of deference

---

[66]See Rom 6:4. [67]1 Cor 12:12. [68]1 Cor 12:13.

to the weakness of his audience. The words, *so that the world may know that you have sent me and have loved them even as you have loved me*, mean the same thing he had said above. In other words the gifts to be given to them will show that I did not come without you and will prove that they are companions with me in the same love [you have] for me, having received the gift of adoptive sonship.

After these words that he had taught them about spiritual birth through baptism, and after revealing their conjunction with him, he spoke, still utilizing the same form of prayer, about other things that would happen to them. [17:24] *Father, I desire that those also whom you have given me may be with me where I am, to see my glory that you have given me because you loved me before the foundation of the world.* "Those," he says, "who have been regenerated in baptism through faith, having received conjunction with me, are those I want to be with me always and to enjoy the pleasures of heaven with me as they see how admirable my honor is and as they become convinced, through the great privileges conceded to me, that you have not only recently had in mind all this about me. Indeed, long before the creation of the universe, in your inscrutable knowledge, you knew what I would be. You loved me already then in your foreknowledge and established me as lord over all these blessings. And this will also happen to the righteous so that they may enter heaven with Christ, as the apostle himself said, 'We will be caught up in the clouds to meet the Lord in the air; and so we will be with the Lord forever.'"[69]

After he had spoken about what would happen to those who believed in him, he made known in righteousness that these things are happening to them rather than to other human beings, [17:25] *Righteous Father, the world does not know you, but I know you; and these know that you have sent me.* [17:26] *I made your name*

known to them, and I will make it known, so that the love with which you have loved me may be in them, and I in them. "For it is only by right and by merit," he says, "that I have come to be in those who are good more than in other human beings, and it is only right that they should be companions with me because, while no one else knew you or wanted to know you, I knew you, and they did too because they believed what I said and received what I revealed about you. Therefore it is only right for me to ask that the love with which you love me may embrace them as well." And what comes next? *I will be in them.* He repeats the same idea he had said above. After they have been endowed with the grace of the Spirit and made participants in sonship by adoption, and in this way judged worthy of conjunction with him, our Lord necessarily is seen now to be the head of his body.

This is how our Lord concluded his speech to his disciples. He includes his passion as the fulfillment of his words. Therefore the Evangelist continues [his narrative] by saying, [18:1] *After Jesus had spoken these words, he went out with his disciples across the Kidron valley to a place where there was a garden.*

End of the Sixth Book.

Book Seven (John 18:1–21:25)

[18:1] *After Jesus had spoken these words, he went out with his disciples across the Kidron valley to a place where there was a garden, which he and his disciples entered.* This also shows, as has been shown already many times before, that he was aware of his passion and thought that his time had come. He was so far removed from escaping his trials that he even delivered himself into the hands of those who wanted to arrest him. Then [the Evangelist] adds, [18:2] *Now Judas who betrayed him, also knew the place, because Jesus often met there with his disciples.* Therefore he came to his custom-

[69]1 Thess 4:17.

ary place, even though he could have gone to some other place. He was demonstrating that he was not avoiding his passion; rather, on the contrary, he actually delivered himself to those who arrested him. And Judas came after him, by leading high priests and Pharisees, guards, and a great crowd with stones and weapons to the place. They also carried lanterns because of the darkness, in order to see him, and weapons, because they intended to use them against anyone who would oppose them to defend Jesus.

[18:4] *Then Jesus, knowing all that was to happen to him, came forward and asked them, "Whom are you seeking?"* [18:5] *They answered, "Jesus of Nazareth." Jesus replied, "I am he." Judas who betrayed him, was standing with them.* [18:6] *When Jesus said to them, "I am he," they stepped back and fell to the ground.* Here too the Evangelist shows that Jesus voluntarily did not escape his passion. Instead he came out to meet those who arrested him, although he knew well that his suffering was near. After he had asked them who they were looking for and they had answered, *Jesus of Nazareth*, and he had said to them, *I am he*, they fell backward. Our Lord did this in order to show before everyone that he could destroy them easily if he wanted. But he willingly accepted suffering for the benefit of all of humanity. He who threw everyone to the ground with just a word could even more easily destroy them all by making use of his power. The Evangelist quite appropriately alludes to the fact that Judas was also among them, therefore displaying the hardness of his will because he did not change his mind even though he saw what happened.

Our Lord then questioned them again. And when they told him again whom they where looking for, he answered them but did not permit the same thing to happen that had happened previously. Indeed once was enough

in order to demonstrate his power. He was doing what was necessary in order to accomplish our salvation. After he said, [18:8] *I am he*, he added, *If you are looking for me, let these men go.* [18:9] *This was to fulfill the word that he had spoken, "I did not lose a single one of those whom you gave me."* His disciples are not saved in order to fulfill what he said; rather, he made this prediction because he knew what was going to happen. But here the Scripture follows its usual style, by expressing in this manner what would happen.

[18:10] *Then Simon Peter, who had a sword,* was overcome with fierce rage because of his love [for Jesus], and drew his sword and cut the ear of the high priest's slave whose name was Malchus, as the Evangelist reports. What did our Lord say to Simon? [18:11] *Put your sword back into its sheath. Am I not to drink the cup that the Father has given me?* "This [sword] is not necessary, he says. I must undergo suffering because the Father desires this for the redemption of the entire human race." Therefore the words, *Am I not to drink the cup*, must [not] be read interrogatively;[1] that is, they should be read instead as, "It is necessary that I drink [the cup]."

Luke accurately reports that our Lord restored the ear of the servant and healed him,[2] so that he might reveal his power by healing the sick and, through all these events, might show that he wanted to suffer voluntarily and without harming anyone. We must not be surprised if this detail is not included by [John] the Evangelist, for people do not always relate in the same manner everything that happens. Some, in fact, do report everything without omitting a single detail; others, however, omit those details that are not useful to the purpose of their narrative. This is an example of the lack of agreement of the narratives of the Evangelists who, while writing their books, did

---

Book Seven [1]The Syriac text and Latin translation both call for the words to be read interrogatively, but this makes no sense in Theodore's argument, where he is obviously making a declarative statement. [2]See Lk 22:51.

not meet together or exchange their opinions. Instead, each of them wrote the development of the facts on his own, as seemed most appropriate. And it must be noted again, as we have said many times, that the blessed John took care to report especially those details that had been omitted by the others, while only hinting at those things which had been reported already by his companions at those times when either the development of the narrative or something else worthy of notice led him to proceed in this way.

After he had demonstrated his power through these events, our Lord voluntarily surrendered and was bound. First they took him to Annas, who was the father-in-law of Caiaphas, the high priest. His disciples Simon Peter and John, who wrote this Gospel, followed him. John, who was known to the high priest, went into the courtyard unafraid. Simon, on the other hand, stayed alone outside the gate, because he had no friend through whose agency he might go in confidently. When John saw that Simon did not get in, he went out and told the woman guarding the gate to let him in. She no doubt let him in due to [John's] familiarity with the high priest. Once Simon had entered, the woman asked him whether he was one of Jesus' disciples. But he denied it. There were some slaves and guards who were standing around and warming themselves at a fire they had made because it was cold. Simon also was standing there with them after he had entered, and he too was warming himself. Those who were around the fire asked him whether he was a disciple of Jesus. When he again offered a denial, one of the slaves, a relative of the man whose ear he had cut off, said that he had seen him in the garden with [Jesus]. But he again offered another denial. After this the rooster crowed, in accordance with the word of our Lord, convicting Peter's arrogance and proving the truth of our Lord's prediction.[3]

Nevertheless, however, the Evangelist does not develop his story according to the order that we have just followed. Rather, after mentioning that the slaves and the guards had made a fire and were warming themselves because of the cold, while Simon was standing there with them, he preferred to relate first something that actually had happened later, turning his attention to the questions that the high priest asked our Savior when they introduced him to be judged before him. He narrates, [18:19] *Then the high priest questioned Jesus about his disciples and about his teaching;* that is, he asked him what he had taught his disciples. And our Lord briefly replied, [18:20] *I have spoken openly to the world; I have always taught in synagogues and in the temple, where all the Jews come together. I have said nothing in secret.* [18:21] *Why do you ask me? Ask those who heard what I said to them; they know what I said.* He answered in such a way in order to provide them with no pretext for thinking that they had a good reason for punishing him. He said, "If I had not made my teaching public, it would be necessary at this point to make an accurate investigation. But since I openly preached before all the people on many occasions while all the Jews were present, thus providing any number of witnesses to what I said, question them now, those who would have no reason to lie in order to defend me." And as he had said these words, one of the guards struck him with his hand, as if he had answered the high priest presumptuously. And our Lord humbly answered by saying, [18:23] *If I have spoken wrongly, testify to the wrong. But if I have spoken rightly, why do you strike me?* "Why," he says, "do you blame the form of my reply without considering its content? If I said anything false, prove it; but if what I said is true, why do you hit me?"

After this, the Evangelist says, Annas sent the Lord, still bound, to Caiaphas. Having

---

[3]See Jn 13:38.

thus interjected into his narrative the high priest's words and Jesus' reply in answer to him, [John] now returns to the previous situation, mentioning that Simon was questioned by those who were standing with him by the fire, and that he then offered his denial, according to the order in which we reported these details above. But [John] did not do this without a reason, but in order to develop his narrative according to the sequence in which the events happened. Evidently, while Simon and those who were with him were still standing by the fire, the questioning of our Lord took place inside before the high priest. When the questioning was coming to a close, or was already over and the Lord had already been ordered to go to Caiaphas, Simon was then questioned by those who were with him by the fire, and he offered his denial. The threefold denial and the crowing of the rooster occurred while Jesus, still bound in chains, was leaving. The blessed Luke adds the following to these details: "The Lord turned and looked at Peter. Then Peter remembered the word of the Lord and how he had said to him, 'Before the rooster crows today, you will deny me three times.'"[4] It is evident that the Lord did not look at him while he was inside before the tribunal but when they were taking him away.

The Evangelist adds further details: [18:28] *Then they took Jesus from Caiaphas to Pilate's headquarters. It was early in the morning.* Notice, he does not mention what happened in the presence of Caiaphas, nor does he report on whether Caiaphas questioned him or not. He only says that he was taken from Annas to Caiaphas and now from Caiaphas to the praetorium. He had no desire to relate all the other things that had been already reported by the other [Evangelists]. He reported the episode of Annas and his questioning with the reply of our Lord because it had been omitted by the others.

It is necessary that we draw attention to this: the different Evangelists had different ways of reporting the words that were said before Caiaphas and then before the high priest, some saying this, others saying that, as each of them heard or remembered them. Indeed almost all of the disciples of our Lord ran away when the Jews arrested him. And this is, in my opinion, a sign of the sincerity of their narrative, because they differ not only in the words but in the places as well. For each of them to say just what they wrote was sufficient, even though there were many things that our Lord did and that were done by others to him.

The [Jews] themselves did not want to enter the praetorium lest they be considered impure before celebrating the Passover. Therefore Pilate came out to them and asked what their accusation was against [Jesus]. They, however, said nothing about the reason for their accusation; rather, taking on an air of authority, they dismissively asserted their reason for arresting him by saying, [18:30] *If this man were not a criminal, we would not have handed him over to you.* Therefore Pilate replied in kind. In fact, he said to them, [18:31] *Take him yourselves and judge him according to your law.* "Since you arrogate to yourselves the right to judge, then conduct your own trial as you wish. But if you want me to judge this man, then you should describe to me the case as well." What did the Jews say? *We are not permitted to put anyone to death.* They said this because of the Passover, as if, by handing him over to be killed, they would not be the ones killing him. The Evangelist added, [18:32] *This was to fulfill what Jesus had said when he indicated the kind of death he was to die,* meaning, "His passion had to be fulfilled according to what he had predicted insofar as he was certainly to be handed over by them to the Gentiles."

After the Jews had said this, Pilate again entered and called Jesus and said to him,

---

[4]Lk 22:61.

[18:33] *Are you the King of the Jews?* The Jews, in fact, had accused him of wanting to overturn the law of the Romans and of endeavoring to give the kingdom back to the Jews, in order that they might excite in Pilate the anger of a judge. What, therefore, did the Lord answer? [18:34] *Do you ask this on your own, or did others tell you about me?* Pilate alone had introduced and interrogated him, and evidently did this as a favor to the Jews. The laws, in fact, require accusers to be present so that when they put forward their accusation they do so with appropriate caution, and the judges, in turn, listen justly and equitably and then pronounce sentence against the accusers if they appear to be perjurers after examination and inquiry. Therefore our Lord suggests to Pilate that he is not conducting things according to due process. He asks, "Are you accusing me, or did you hear this from others? Indeed, since there is no one else, I do not know who has accused me."

These words affected Pilate: [18:35] *I am not a Jew,* he said. "Your fellow citizens have handed you over to me. What did you do? Speak." To this our Lord briefly replied by saying, [18:36] *My kingdom is not from this world. If my kingdom was from this world, my followers would be fighting to keep me from being handed over to the Jews. But as it is, my kingdom is not from here.* "If," he says, "you ask me whether I want to seize the kingdom of the Jews, then know that I am a king. But mine is not an earthly kingdom, otherwise my soldiers would fight for me to protect me from my enemies. But now, since I have been handed over without a fight and have left myself defenseless against those who wanted to arrest me, it is obvious that my kingdom is of a different nature, one in which I will most surely be the victor when I come into it."

To this Pilate replied, [18:37] *So you are a king?* Although our Lord had not clearly said this just yet, [Pilate] nevertheless understood that this was exactly what he meant by his

words. *Jesus answered, "You say that I am a king."* "Even though I have dignity worthy of a king," he says, "I have avoided saying this openly since I want to spare myself any suspicion of pride." Having clearly revealed the reason why he has avoided speaking publicly about his dignity, he says, *For this I was born, and for this I came into the world, to testify to the truth. Everyone who belongs to the truth listens to my voice.* "I stop short of an open declaration, but I do not hide the truth. My mission is to speak everything openly. However, since not everyone listens to the truth or believes what is said, it is evident that I must not speak openly when it is not required to do so in order not to give any suspicion of pride, as if I were making a vain boast of a dignity that I did not possess."

After hearing this, Pilate said to him, [18:38] *What is truth?* He does not ask in order to learn but because he is in doubt about what has been said. And this is confirmed by the fact that, immediately after he said this, he went out again to the Jews and said to them, "I do not find that he deserves death; but since this is the time when one of those condemned is usually freed according to your request, I will free this one, if you want." But they all shouted, [18:40] *Not this man, but Barabbas!*—a bandit who was in prison for murder.

[19:1] *Then Pilate took Jesus and had him flogged.* Since the high priests accused him of wanting to conspire against Roman law and be king over the Jews, the soldiers mocked him because there was no use in him wanting something so out of his reach. [19:2] *They wove a crown of thorns and put it on his head, and dressed him in a purple robe.* And as they struck him on the face, they said, [19:3] *Hail, King of the Jews!* After this Pilate went out again to the Jews and said to them, [19:4] *Look, I am bringing him out to you to let you know that I find no case against him.* So Jesus came out wearing the crown of thorns on his head and the purple robe in which the soldiers had dressed him. When Pilate showed him to them, the high priests and the guards shouted, [19:6] *Crucify him!* Then Pilate told them to take him and crucify him wherever they wanted. He thought that the burden [of his conscience] would be lighter if he handed Jesus over to them for them to do as they wanted rather than if he had to condemn him without a proven sentence. But the Jews alleged against this their own law, saying, "He deserves death because he had the audacity to say that he was the Son of God."

When Pilate heard this, he was even more afraid because of what they had said. He certainly had heard about the miracles accomplished by Jesus. So he entered the praetorium again and asked him where he was from. He hoped in this way to come to know whether he was really the Son of God. But since our Lord, with good reason, did not answer him because of the foolishness of the question, Pilate, in an attempt to confuse the issue, said, "Answer me. I have the power either to release you or not to do so." What then did the Lord reply? [19:11] *You would have no power over me unless it had been given you from above; therefore the one who handed me over to you is guilty of a greater sin.* "You are mistaken," he says. "It is not because of your power that I suffer. And God would not have tolerated the things that have been done to me unless he knew this was for everyone's benefit. You should know that a greater punishment than yours is to be inflicted upon those who handed me over to you because they committed a greater sin since they are the cause of all of this." Pilate wanted to release him because of these words of Jesus and perhaps even because he had realized that his own words were just. But the Jews said, [19:12] *If you release this man, you are no friend of Caesar. Everyone who claims to be a king sets himself against Caesar.* In other words, "He rebelled against the rule of Rome and is seek-

ing to divide and conquer. If you allow him to live, you concede life to an adversary of the emperor." After hearing this Pilate was afraid, so he brought Jesus outside, and sat at the tribunal. [19:14] *It was the Day of Preparation,* that is, the sixth festival day of the week, and it was about noon.[5]

For those who think that the words of the Evangelists are in contradiction, since some say it was nine in the morning,[6] others noon, it is necessary that we say something in this regard. Matthew[7] and Luke,[8] similar to John, say that there was darkness at about noon. Indeed Pilate went out immediately and sat at the tribunal and handed Jesus over to be crucified, and after he was nailed to the cross, the darkness began to spread, as the Evangelists said. There are many reasons why it is not surprising that Mark[9] mentions that it was nine in the morning. First of all, Mark was not present. Secondly, he was not a disciple of our Lord, but learned these facts from Peter or some other apostle. And finally, everyone has different opinions about times and hours, and the doubt about the hours does not affect in any way the reported facts. In addition we especially must notice that Mark did not say that it was nine about any specific and well-known fact. Rather, by relating in a simple way and in general the things that happened, it was appropriate for him to say that the events took place at nine, thus designating the entire length of time in which these events occurred. Then he added, "They crucified him."[10] Therefore the sentence, "it was nine in the morning,"[11] refers to the account of all those events that occurred in the meantime, while the phrase, "they crucified him," then, is added in order to that which precedes it.

Thus Pilate, mocking the Jews, said, *Here is your King!* [19:15] *They cried out, "Crucify him!"* But Pilate, reproaching them because they acted unjustly and at the same time

---

[5]That is, the sixth hour. [6]That is, the third hour. [7]See Mt 27:45. [8]See Lk 23:44. [9]Mk 15:25. [10]Mk 15:25. [11]Mk 15:25.

despising them, said, *Shall I crucify your King?* *The chief priests answered, "We have no king but Caesar,"* in order to frustrate him and force him to kill Jesus against his will. After these words he handed him over to them to be crucified.

We certainly must know this. On the day of the Passover in which they denied our Lord and declared that the emperor was their king—on that same day, as Josephus writes in his historical work on the fall of Jerusalem,[12] the war of the Romans commenced against them. All the Jews who had gathered in Jerusalem—as if in a prison—suffered many afflictions there. Many of them starved to death; many were killed by the sword or in ambushes; nearly all of them were killed through various punishments.

So Pilate, even though he did not want to hand our Lord over to the Jews because, after considering the facts, he had not found him deserving of any punishment, in the end he nevertheless had to comply with the requests of those who through intimidation asked for him. Therefore he handed him over, and they took him and led him to be crucified.

The Evangelist faithfully records, [19:16] *So they took Jesus;* [19:17] *and carrying the cross by himself, he went out to what is called the place of the Skull, which in Hebrew is called Golgotha.* [19:18] *There they crucified him.*

Some think here too the words of the Evangelists do not agree with one another, because John said, *carrying the cross by himself, he went out,* while others wrote, "They seized Simon of Cyrene to carry his cross."[13] Rather, both of these things happened. Indeed when Pilate condemned him and handed him over to them to be crucified, they laid a cross on him and took him out of the tribunal. Then, while they were proceeding to Calvary where he would be crucified, they met Simon and laid the cross on him. The others Evangelists no doubt meant to say this, but John, being focused here only on

his own purpose, related only that which was missing in the others. And in order not to extend our book by repeating in detail what has been said already by others, I only place here, in confirmation of my hypothesis, the words of Luke, "As they led him away, they seized a man, Simon of Cyrene who was coming from the country, and they laid the cross on him, and made him carry it behind Jesus."[14] Therefore John said, *Carrying the cross by himself, he went out,* while Luke, on the other hand, said, "While they led him away, they laid his cross on Simon of Cyrene, who was coming from the country." It is evident that this event [in Luke] happened later while they were going along the way, whereas this event [in John] happened immediately after he was condemned to death when he went out of the tribunal.

They crucified with him two bandits, one on his right and one on his left. Pilate, again intending to mock the Jews, wrote an inscription and affixed it to the cross. Since he wanted to make known why Jesus had been crucified, he ordered that it be written, [19:19] *King of the Jews,* in Latin, Greek and Hebrew, so that all those reading might deride them even more. Since the high priests understood he was mocking them, they asked him not to write simply *King of the Jews,* but also that he had defined himself so. Pilate, however, did not accept their proposal and left the inscription as it had been written.

Thus, after crucifying our Lord, the soldiers who were there as sentinels divided his garments into four parts, and each of them received his part according to his number. But they did not want to divide the tunic. They said, "let us cast lots for it so that the winner may take it." They avoided tearing it because it was not sewn together but woven in one piece. At that time many did not only make garments sewn together according to our use but also wove clothes in the shape of hoods and then

---

[12]See Josephus *Jewish Wars* 5.3.1. [13]Mt 27:32; Mk 15:21; Lk 23:26. [14]Lk 23:26.

joined them together at the shoulders and used them as tunics. This is still how they make the garments of the soldiers. [19:23] *The tunic was seamless, woven in one piece from the top;* that is, it was not connected with seams but was woven together like our modern tunics [for soldiers]. To this the Evangelist added, [19:24] *This was to fulfill what the Scripture says, "They divided my clothes among themselves, and for my clothing they cast lots."*[15] And this is what the soldiers did.

[19:25] *Meanwhile, standing near the cross of Jesus were his mother, and his mother's sister, and another Mary.* And John was there as well. While Jesus was on the cross and saw them standing there, that is, his mother and John, he said to her, [19:26] *Here is your son,* and to him, [19:27] *Here is your mother,* showing with these words his great love for him and that he considered John as his other self since Jesus wanted him to take his place with his mother. And so John, moved by these words, immediately received her, and she remained with him. It would seem that the Lord loved John for many reasons and with good cause; indeed, he alone among all the disciples remained with him after these tribulations.

[19:28] *After this, when Jesus knew that all was now finished, he said (in order to fulfill the scripture), "I am thirsty."* [19:29] *A jar full of sour wine was standing there. So they put a sponge full of the wine on a branch of hyssop and held it to his mouth.* [19:30] *When Jesus had received the wine, he said, "It is finished." Then he bowed his head and gave up his spirit.* The Evangelist wanted to indicate through this that Jesus suffered in order to accomplish our salvation, not out of necessity. Therefore, since he knew that something was missing for the complete fulfillment of the words of the prophets,[16] he asked for a drink of water. And when they gave him sour wine, he bowed his head and gave up his spirit so that it might ap-

pear that this also happened when he wanted it to happen. Again, the Jews were careful to make sure that bodies did not remain affixed to crosses without burial in order that they might not appear to violate this day of solemnity. Therefore, they asked Pilate to break their legs, as if they were performing an act of mercy. Indeed, they could not bury them before they were dead. And since it was possible that they might remain alive on the cross for some time, they wanted to break their legs—with an order from the judge to do so—so that they might die more quickly, and then they could bury their bodies before evening. After receiving this order from the judge, the soldiers broke the legs of the two bandits. When they reached Jesus and saw that he was dead already—indeed he had no desire to be subject to the law of nature but gave up his spirit by acting according to his will—they left him alone. Therefore, since breaking his legs seemed to be useless, one of the soldiers who had been entrusted with this task, wanting to ascertain whether he was dead, struck his side with a spear, and at once blood and water came out—water, which was the sign of regeneration (through baptism), and blood, which was the sign of the mystery of the Eucharist.

And the Evangelist adds, [19:35] *He who saw this has testified so that you also may believe. His testimony is true, and he knows that he tells the truth.* He alludes to himself because he always talks about himself without mentioning his own name. From this it is clear that John was present at these events. It seems also that he wants to suggest that the emission of blood and water did not occur so that everyone might see it, but that it remained invisible to many. Indeed he points this out by saying, *He who saw this has testified,* meaning that only he saw and testified to this event. But he was worthy of credibility regarding this event, even though he said that he alone saw and testified. There-

---

[15]Ps 22:18. [16]See Ps 22:15; 69:21.

fore he also recalls the words of the Scripture. Indeed these events happened just as they had been written. This then is how the death of our Lord occurred.

A certain man, named Joseph of Arimathea, who was a disciple of Jesus—because of his fear of the Jews he was not known to many— came and asked Pilate to let him take away the body of Jesus in order to bury it. After ordering him to do so, Nicodemus, who had come to Jesus by night, also came and brought in abundance all that was necessary for the burial and took care that all the procedures due the dead were met, by wrapping the body in linen cloths with many spices and then burying him with great honor, in accordance with the law of the Jews.

It happened, according to the will of God, that there was a garden in the place where he had been crucified. And in the garden there was a new tomb in which no one had ever been placed. This helped to quiet any doubt about the resurrection of our Lord that might arise. Indeed, since he alone had been placed in this tomb and they could not find him later on when they were looking for him, it is evident that he and no one else rose. They placed him there because of the nearness of the tomb and because of the [solemnity of the] day. They were not allowed on that sacred day to carry a dead body in the middle of a crowd nor to move it to another place.

[Chapter 20] Up to this point [the Evangelist] has related what happened in the course of his burial. From this point forward he begins to narrate his resurrection.

He does not say anything about the resurrection itself, that is, how it happened. None of the other [Evangelists] seems to have tried to give an account about it either. They thought, indeed, that they were unqualified to talk about something so superior to the human mind. They do all record how the resurrection

appeared to them and how, after they were convinced that it had indeed occurred, they declared so publicly. They also mention how they willingly consented to suffer for announcing it. But since his resurrection was only revealed by the fact that the women went [to the tomb] on the third day to fulfill the usual ritual for the dead—and thus they [first] came to know of his resurrection—all the [Evangelists] in a similar way turn to the story of the women after the burial.

It seems to those who dissent [from the orthodox faith] that here too the words of the Evangelists do not agree with one another. On the contrary it seems to me that on the basis of their accounts their words are perfectly consistent. It is now necessary that we report one by one the words which the four Evangelists report about the resurrection.

John says, [20:1] *Early on the first day of the week, while it was dark, Mary Magdalene came to the tomb.* Matthew: "On the evening of the sabbath, as the first day of the week was dawning, Mary Magdalene and the other Mary went to see the tomb."[17] Luke: "But on the first day of the week, at early dawn, they came to the tomb, taking the spices that they had prepared. They found the stone rolled away from the tomb, but when they went in, they did not find the body."[18] Mark: "And very early on the first day of the week, when the sun had risen, they went to the tomb. They had been saying to one another, 'Who will roll away the stone for us from the entrance to the tomb?' When they looked up, they saw that the stone, which was very large, had already been rolled back."[19]

This is the tradition of the four Evangelists about the resurrection. I do not know what those who want to censure their words as inconsistent exactly mean. If the opinion of them all about the resurrection had not been the same, if they had not written that it was the same day when it happened, or if they had

[17]Mt 28:1. [18]Lk 24:1-3. [19]Mk 16:2-4.

not unanimously said that it was the women who first came to the tomb in order to honor the dead, perhaps such a vain and foolish reproof would be tolerable. But since in all these details [the Evangelists] demonstrate perfect harmony—they all declare the resurrection, and indicate the same day and assert that the women came first to the tomb—I really do not know why they want to argue about minor details. In my opinion, nothing else is needed to confirm the truth of their words than the fact that in the necessary details they demonstrate overwhelming harmony. In the small details, and in those things which they considered not to be important from their human point of view, it can be found that their words are not unanimous with regard to moments and hours. If they had really wanted to deceive, they would have had the same consistency in all their words. Nothing, in fact, prevented those who wanted to deceive from agreeing among themselves, so that they might maintain perfect agreement in their narratives. But since they wanted to relate the facts, and each of them wrote on his own, it is inevitable that there would be some difference in minor details. And there are any number of reasons why this happened to them: first of all because not all of them were among the disciples who lived with our Lord; Luke and Mark were not in the group of those who always accompanied him; second, not even the others were present for those events that happened toward the end since they ran away in the turmoil of those [dramatic] events. Therefore also in those details where the slanderers find discrepancies, I find perfect consistency. And I want to show this by examining these words carefully, even though they may appear, at first sight, to have discrepancies.

Thus, the resurrection of the Lord occurred on the first day of the week at night. This is evident not only from the fact that

we everywhere celebrate this commemoration by unanimous consent and eagerly gather together at daybreak as if that was the time that our Savior rose and just as appropriately dismiss the assembly in the church at the same hour[20]—but it is also evident from the books of the Evangelists who unanimously wrote that this was indeed the day.

In fact, John says, *Early . . . while it was dark*. The word *early* is not referred here to the morning. In fact, he does not say, "While it was *still* dark," which should have been said with regard to the morning. But he wrote, "while it was dark," that is, on the next day when the night began, designating with the term *early* the entire day, so that he might indicate the day after the sabbath. The Holy Scripture usually indicates both day and night with the word *day*, because the sun, after its course throughout the night and the day, brings about the beginning of the next day by returning to its place in the west. And this is confirmed by Moses, who says, "And there was evening and there was morning, the first day."[21] This is also how he speaks about the second day and the third day and all the others. Therefore it is evident from this that he calls *day* both the daytime and the nighttime. And this is correct, because the sun in its perpetual course illuminates wherever it is, so that there is always daytime somewhere because the sun is always shining. Among us, however, its times differ. We think that it is *daytime* now when the sun appears to us, whereas we call the time when the sun is far away from us *nighttime*. John says, *Early on the first day of the week*, indicating the next day. In other words, he says, *on the first day of the week*, when it was dark, meaning, "When the night began, the women came, in order to perform the honor due according to custom."

And what Matthew said agrees with this: "On the evening of the sabbath, as the first day

---

[20]Theodore is referring to the common practice of the Easter vigil, which was already in use at his time. [21]Gen 1:5.

of the week was dawning."[22] Here he refers to *evening* not as the time in which the day ends and the night begins, as we usually say, but he evidently designates the night in the same way as Moses did when he said, "And there was evening and there was morning."[23] Moses was not indicating the beginning of the day when he used the term *morning*, nor was he indicating the beginning of the night by the term *evening*. Rather, he calls the [entire] day *morning*, and the [entire] night *evening*. And thus Matthew too refers to the night as *evening*. Therefore he said, "On the evening of the sabbath," that is, on the evening after the sabbath, in order to indicate the night; he then clarifies about which night of the sabbath he is talking, whether he is talking about the night preceding the sabbath or that following the sabbath which is part of the first day of the week. He does so by adding, *as the first day of the week was dawning*, that is, the [time when it is still] night in which the first day of the week begins. Who does not see that this is consistent with the words of Luke, who said, "But on the first day of the week, at early dawn, they came to the tomb"?[24] It seems to the slanderers who endeavor to maliciously insist on their objection that the text of Mark[25] reveals a discrepancy; even though he too talks about the same day and also relates the same facts in the same way. And he certainly does not speak of the resurrection in a different way.

Concerning the discrepancy of the hours, who could ignore the fact that this happens frequently, with one person calling it the third hour, another the fourth hour, and another even something more different, but all referring to the same hour? Indeed it is hard enough to discern accurately the hours of the night when the hours of the day are not even recognized that easily if the sun is hidden by thick clouds. We may also say this to the slanderers. If the words of Mark appear to differ [from the rest], they must consider that the harmony of the other three is sound, and even more so because two of them were in the number of those who followed [Jesus]. Mark, on the other hand, as they say, was a disciple of Simon and did not follow Christ. Those who reprove his discrepancy in this passage should admire his harmony in other passages. But I do not want to say [these things] against them lest they may think that I am forced to take refuge in these words because I have no other argument. Instead I will show that the words of Mark contain no contradiction and are consistent with the words [of the other Evangelists], if one would like to examine them in a logical manner and with human reasoning.

For the sake of clarity, it is necessary that we first report the train of events according to the order of the Evangelist John. Then we will demonstrate how the supposed discrepancy in the words of Mark is in perfect harmony. Also this must be known: the other Evangelists briefly related the many varied things that happened in the course of the resurrection and by which the faith in the resurrection was confirmed in the first place. They also were not careful in indicating the order in which these events actually happened. Since this is quite useful for those who want to know how these single events happened, John eagerly took care to do what had been neglected by the others, that is, to relate in a logical order the things that happened. And for this reason the following must be noticed as well. While the others say that many women came [to the tomb], John only mentions Mary, because the succession of the events brought him to do so. Indeed when the other women did not find the body placed in the tomb, they returned home one by one. Mary, however, because of her great sorrow, did not want to go back and rest like they did. Instead she went to inform the disciples that the body was not in the tomb anymore, with

[22]Mt 28:1. [23]Gen 1:5. [24]Lk 24:1. [25]Mk 16:2.

the hope that their devotion would help them find the body. She thought that somebody had removed the body from that place. This is clear from her words to the apostles. Therefore she went back to the tomb with them, and after they left, she did not want to leave the tomb. Thus she deserved to see our now-risen Lord before anyone else. The Evangelist was thus obliged to give this account by the order of the events themselves. He had no thought to write in his book that other women first came with her and then left her and went back home. His purpose was this: first to report in good order what happened, then to show the love that Mary proved by her actions. There was no intent at all to accuse the other women. It is extremely easy for anyone who wants to do so to know from many other episodes that Mary had great love for our Lord. The Evangelist took extreme care in showing this. For just as he always accuses the unbelievers—this, again, is something we recall and have already mentioned from the beginning—and therefore narrates everything without omitting any of those details, thus leaving the adversaries with no excuses; so he also wants to honor publicly those who not only believed but also demonstrated their faith with great love. But let us come to what we promised, and let us speak of the order of the events that also this Evangelist observed in his narrative, and let us show the harmony of the words of Mark with those of his colleagues.

[John] says, "Mary Magdalene came by night, in order to fulfill for him the service which was usually reserved for the dead. She saw that the stone was not placed against the tomb but did not look or go inside." This is the account of the Evangelist. She was in a hurry and, being overwhelmed, ran to the disciples. And when she found Simon, and John, who wrote these words, she said to them, "They took away our Lord's body and moved it somewhere else." After hearing this, the disciples immediately took off running, wanting to see what had happened. While they were running together, John overtook Peter but did not go into [the tomb]. After looking around, he saw the linen wrappings lying there. Then Simon came, and when he went into the tomb he saw that all the linen wrappings were lying in a single place, while the shroud that had been on his head was in another place. It was providential that our Lord did this, for by doing so the disciples would not think that a theft had been committed. Indeed no one would have stolen only the body and left the linen wrappings in the tomb. Even though resurrection was then absolutely incredible for a human mind, however, they were forced to think of it, and even to believe it. In order that they might not think that the linen cloths had been left by the thieves in their haste, he placed them in an orderly arrangement, leaving in one place only the shroud that had been on his head and that he had received first, and in another place the rest of the linen wrappings. In this way they would understand, through all these things, that the one who had been nailed to the cross and had died according to the weakness of nature had now resurrected in an amazing way through inscrutable, divine power, beyond any human expectation, and had received a better life in an imperishable body and an immutable soul. He laid the linen cloths in their proper places and left them as signs of his resurrection, which he had predicted many times also before his passion. In addition, he proved then that he did not need a human garment because he had assumed forever the sublime and admirable garment of immortality. After Peter, John also went in, and both saw the same sight. He adds, [20:9] *for as yet they did not understand the Scripture, that he must rise from the tomb.* This clearly shows that the disciples had a weak knowledge of Christ before the resurrection, which later they were gradually able to receive in its perfection.

Then the disciples went back home. But Mary, guided by her usual love for our Lord, stayed by the tomb and wept because she had not found the body buried there. While she was weeping, as usually happens to one who has a deep love, she kept looking, in her astonishment, at the place where the body of the Lord had been placed. While she took another look at the tomb—indeed she could not get enough of that sight—she saw two angels in white, one sitting at the head and the other at the feet [of the place where the body had been lying]. And they said to her, [20:13] *Why are you weeping?* She answered: *They have taken away the body of my Lord, and I do not know where they have laid him.* [20:14] *When she had said this, she turned around*—and this happened through a special dispensation of grace—*and saw Jesus standing there, but she did not know that it was Jesus.* And our Lord acted this way so that, by seeing suddenly and beyond all hope he who was still considered to be dead, she might not be overwhelmed with emotion and think that he was a demonic apparition. He wanted her first to speak to him gradually as to a man. Then, after she had realized that she was speaking to a real man, she might finally understand who he was and at the same time might believe and admire the greatness of what had happened.

He then asked, [20:15] *Why are you weeping?* But she, thinking that he was the gardener—the proximity of the garden was the reason why she thought so—began to ask, "Did you carry him away? Tell me where you laid him, and I will gladly take him." Then, since the Lord wanted to reveal himself to her, he called her by name with a smooth, sweet voice, and by pronouncing her name he made himself known. And once she recognized him, with great joy she called him *teacher.* And when she wanted to embrace his feet, he did not permit it but told her, [20:17] *Do not hold on to me, because I have not yet ascended to the Father. But go to my brothers and say to them, "I*

am ascending to my Father and your Father, to my God and your God." It is the custom of our Lord that, while his providence is preparing one thing, he seems to do something else than his words would seem to indicate. This is how he acted, for instance, with the woman who suffered from hemorrhages.[26] He asked, "Who touched me?"[27] even though he certainly knew who had done so. He, however, seemed to ask as if he did not know so that the woman who had touched him might be afraid and reveal the miracle and show her faith through which, since it was adequate, she had received her healing. He acted in a similar way toward the fig tree.[28] It seems that he caused it to wither in his anger. In truth, however, he caused it to wither in order to show his power. And if one makes an inquiry, he will find the same in many other episodes. But our duty is not to gather testimonies: two of them are sufficient to prove what we have said.

And here it is so as well. He first showed himself to the woman after his resurrection when he was about to ascend into heaven. But by this time, he wanted to teach the disciples that they should believe in the resurrection not only because their sight testified to the reality of the facts but also in order that they might know that he was not going to remain on earth after his resurrection but would ascend into heaven to receive great glory with his Father. And so, when he says what he does to the woman, while it seems that he forbids her to touch him as if she were no longer supposed to come into contact with his body in the same way but rather from a distance, since he was now provided with a different and much more powerful body, the real meaning of what he was saying was that he was trying to teach his disciples about his resurrection and, at the same time, about his ascension. It is clear that he certainly did not prevent the woman from coming into contact with him because later

---

[26]See Lk 8:43. [27]Lk 8:45. [28]See Mt 21:19-20; Mk 11:13-14, 20-21.

he showed himself again to the disciples who were in doubt and ordered them to touch the wounds on his body where the nails had been. And we cannot say that she was prevented because she was a woman. Indeed he allowed her to touch his feet many times. If she could not touch him because she was a woman, he would have forbidden her to do so even before. If he had forbidden the woman because his body had been transformed into a better state, he would not have allowed the disciples to confirm with their touch their faith in his resurrection. And then, if she also, by any chance, had doubted like they did, would he not have allowed her to confirm her faith through touching him? If someone says that he did not care about the faith of this woman or her unbelief, this is quite foolish. But since he had allowed her to come to him then, is it possible that the reward that he gave her for her faith was the privation of any contact with him? And does this not look rather spiteful, especially to educated people? Rather, he revealed two things by what he said: first, that his body after the resurrection was in a stronger and more excellent condition than before and therefore should not be exposed to any human contact; second, that he would be assumed into heaven to be joined forever in honor with the Father.

No one is so demented as to assert that the words, to my Father and your Father, to my God and your God, are meant to convey anything other than the temple of God the Word; that is, they refer to the man assumed for our salvation, who died and resurrected and would ascend into heaven, and called God his Father along with his disciples, and deserved the grace of adoption. He also calls God his God because it was from him that he obtained his existence with other human beings. Therefore, because of his common nature [with humanity] he says, my Father and your Father, and,

my God and your God. He separated his person from other human beings, however, by indicating that he had received a more excellent grace[29] through which he is joined together with God the Word like a real son and must be honored by all men. After hearing this, Mary came to announce to the disciples that she had seen the Lord and to report the words spoken to her. This is the succession of events in the narrative of this Evangelist.

Now we must compare the narrative of Mark with these words so that the apparent dissonance of his account may turn out to be a harmony. He says, "And very early on the first day of the week, when the sun had risen, they went to the tomb. They had been saying to one another, 'Who will roll away the stone for us from the entrance to the tomb?' When they looked up, they saw that the stone, which was very large, had already been rolled back. As they entered the tomb, they saw a young man, dressed in a white robe, sitting on the right side; and they were alarmed. But he said to them, 'Do not be alarmed,'" and so forth.[30] First of all it is clear that the term early does not agree with the phrase when the sun had risen. We refer to "early [morning]" as the time in which the day has not yet begun completely. Therefore it is clear that the phrase, when the sun had risen, refers to the words that follow this phrase. He says that they came early and then demonstrates that all the other events occurred when the sun had risen, without mentioning what had happened in the meantime, namely, that the women had gone to Simon and John along with everything else the Evangelist John appears to relate in good order. While they went and came back, and Mary stayed there weeping, the sun must have risen and the day begun. Therefore [Mark] made no error because he posited two occasions: one when the women came alone, and another when the others came. Someone like Mark,

---

[29]A further instance of Theodore's typical Christology: see translator's introduction, esp. quotation from Norris, p. xxvi.   [30]Mk 16:2-6.

who had no concern to describe events sequentially—relating them in brief instead—could not accurately indicate the [precise] moment in which any single event occurred.

Therefore I ask this, Can those who endeavor to demonstrate that these words are in contrast with one another really assert that the words of the Evangelists are just a game and that no one actually rose from the dead, and that the women did not go nor did they see anything, and that the accounts that they wrote are not true but just fables and vile nonsense composed by these writers to deceive people? But how, then, could they clearly speak not only about the resurrection but also about the day itself in which the mystery of the resurrection occurred? Perhaps they will answer, "Because they arranged and agreed among themselves to report these events deceitfully." But how then is it that they do not seem to be unanimous about any single detail? This is what should have happened if they all had decided to lie together, fearing that their inconsistency might betray their fraud. The more they knew they were being deceitful, the more they would have ensured that their fraud might not be detected through any difference in their words. And I pass over this [argument]: "It is impossible that those who falsely arranged these things would have been trusted by their audience. If indeed they were speaking the truth, no one would have ever believed their true account about the resurrection unless they had given their audience clear signs that would confirm their words. If they are consistent with regard to the facts, to the day and the time, and only differ in the ordering of the story insofar as one says this and that, another adds certain other details, another adds other details—and this happened especially among those who were not careful about relating the facts in order—how does this not entirely bring to light and establish the truth

of the facts and the sincerity of the authors of the Gospels? This most certainly highlights the fact that they wrote in different times and places: for Matthew was asked to write in Palestine, Mark certainly in Rome, John in Ephesus, and Luke somewhere else. And they were far removed from artifice and deceit in their words inasmuch as they were resolved to speak the truth. And not only did they not focus on elegance of style, which others were accustomed to employ for persuasion in preparing their stories, but they were not even able to do so since they were uneducated.

But let us go back to the succession of the narrative. After Mary said what she did to the disciples and the first day had ended, the next day was beginning [. . .].[31]

While the doors were closed because of their fear of the Jews, Jesus suddenly came in and greeted his disciples. Since their minds were troubled by this astonishing sight, he calmed them with the word [20:21] *peace*. And, in order to resolve their doubts because they thought they were seeing a ghost, he showed them his hands and his side. They could sufficiently recognize from the wounds that the nails had inflicted in his body that he was the one who had been crucified, who died and had risen again, since their touch also confirmed the sight and testified that a real body had appeared to them and was present. On the basis of all these things, the disciples firmly and certainly believed that Christ had risen and that he was the one who was speaking with them, and so they rejoiced in seeing this new and extraordinary miracle. He then employed his words to confirm them in faith and joy, adding, [20:21] *As the Father has sent me, so I send you*, meaning, "You are the witnesses of my resurrection because you did not learn about it from someone else, but you saw with your own eyes and touched with your own hands. Therefore I tell you: Just as I did

---

[31]The editor J.-M. Vosté indicates a lacuna in the text here. See above [1:19] and CSCO 4 3:i-iv and 353.

everything before you as witnesses in order to benefit the salvation of the human race—even to the extent, at the end, of accepting suffering on their behalf and destroying the kingdom of death with my resurrection, as you have seen—so it is also necessary for you, whom I have sent with goodwill and with constancy, to traverse the world, announcing all these blessings to everyone. Be confident because, even if afflictions come upon you from your enemies, you will rise too because you have sustained these things because of me."

After telling his disciples this in order to teach them about their future resurrection and how they were to receive the virtue of patience in their toils and afflictions, he first breathed on them and then said, [20:22] *Receive the Holy Spirit.* [20:23] *If you forgive the sins of any, they are forgiven them; if you retain the sins of any, they are retained.* With these words he taught them who gives and distributes all these blessings. By breathing [on them] he convinced them not to doubt this argument because the body was created in the beginning as immobile and inanimate but then received life, which it did not have in itself, through the entry of the soul that was created through breathing, as the blessed Moses said.[32] After Jesus breathed for the first time, he mentioned the Spirit in order to show that just as [at creation] nothing prevented the body from living—even though it did not possess by nature that which the soul by entering gave it according to the will of the Creator of natures—so now they should believe that the human body had been made imperishable through resurrection because the Spirit has the power to give this [life] to it. Therefore he said to them, "You must believe everything that has been said to you. You must have no doubts about the resurrection, nor should you reject the honor of the apostolate because you are afraid of being sent into the

world as messengers of a new teaching. For you will indeed receive the effectual working of the Spirit which, at the right time, will confer upon you resurrection and immortality. Even in this life you will receive amazing, supernatural power through the Spirit so that you may perform unheard-of miracles by a single word and even be able easily to confront the afflictions that befall you because of those who oppose your preaching." And even though there were many other things to be accomplished in them through the Spirit, without mentioning them, he enunciated the most important argument of all. "Here," he says, "is what will clearly demonstrate to you the power of the Spirit. Indeed, as soon as you receive it, you will be able to absolve the sins of whomever you desire, as well as to pronounce a sentence of condemnation against anyone else. If after receiving the gift of the Spirit you who are human will be able to do all these things that belong to God—indeed his is the power to judge—I leave it to you to consider what the efficacy of the Spirit is. Once you have received it, you must no longer have any doubt."

He says, *Receive*, meaning, "you will receive." For if he had given the Spirit to the disciples when he breathed on them, as some have thought, it would have been superfluous to tell them that they should not leave Jerusalem but wait for the promise of the Spirit after his ascension into heaven. And then he says, "But you will receive power when the Holy Spirit has come upon you."[33] And Luke openly asserts that the advent of the Holy Spirit upon the disciples happened on the fiftieth day after the resurrection, and after the ascension.[34] In addition it must be noticed that if they had received the Spirit from this breathing here, he would not have said, *Receive*, [but "because you have received." His expression, *Receive*][35] fits

---

[32]See Gen 2:7. [33]Acts 1:8. [34]See Acts 1:8; 2:1-4. [35]The passage in square bracket is missing from the Syriac text and has been taken from the Greek fragment. See PG 66:784; R. Devreesse, *Essai sur Théodore de Mopsueste,* Studi e Testi 141 (Vatican City: Biblioteca Apostolica Vaticana, 1948), p. 417 (fr. 138); Theodore of Mopsuestia, *Commentary on the Gospel of John,* introduction and commen-

those who still have not received it.

Above we have already noted what this breathing was. After the body was created inanimate, God, by breathing, created the soul that he infused into it and made it so that the body might live through it. Evidently the blessed Moses was suggesting that the breathing was something different of one kind or another. For God did not breathe, because his nature is incorporeal; rather, people at that time had this opinion, especially those who had been instructed in the law.

When after his resurrection the Lord appeared to the disciples and proved to them that he was the one who had spoken to them, was crucified, died and was raised again beyond all expectation, he wanted to teach them as well to have no doubt about the resurrection and to believe firmly that the resurrection would be certain for them as well. And when he revealed to them from where this new and extraordinary thing would come, he indicated [the Spirit] as their defender. Since[36] <he prepared them as preachers—and struggles, persecutions, tribulations of all kinds are perpetrated by demons and sinful people against preachers—he clothed them with a supernatural power, "with which they would be able to quench all the flaming arrows of the evil one."[37] Therefore he gave them this gift through breathing in order to be recognized as one and the same Creator who had infused into Adam the breath of life—and so Adam became a living soul[38]—and who now [breathed] on the disciples. And if that first breathing extended and flowed throughout five thousand years and more, and still flows, this second one also necessarily will last and flow through infinite times and centuries.

These words, *Receive the Holy Spirit*, were said in place of, "you will receive," in the upper room. Therefore the gift, conferred through breathing, pertains only to the power of binding and absolving, as will be seen. This is the fulfillment of what was said to Peter, "I will give you the keys of the kingdom."[39] It was necessary that he granted these gifts so that they might know that he was of the same nature and substance of the Spirit who would give them an overabundance of gifts. This is why he said, "He will take what is mine and declare it to you."[40] Consider, however, how far this breathing extends, [20:23] *If you forgive the sins of any, they are forgiven them; if you retain the sins of any, they are retained.* What truly wonderful gifts! Indeed [the Spirit] not only gives power over the elements and the ability to perform signs and wonders, but even concedes that God has called them by name, and that which is only appropriate to himself is given to his servants. The prerogative to absolve and retain sins only belongs to God. The Jews sometimes raised this objection to the Savior, saying, "Who can forgive sins but God alone?"[41] And yet the Lord generously gave this power to those who feared him.

[20:26] *A week later his disciples were again in the house, and Thomas was with them. Although the doors were shut, Jesus came and stood among them and said, "Peace be with you."* [20:27] *Then he said to Thomas, "Put your finger here and see my hands. Reach out your hand and put it in my side. Do not doubt but believe."* [20:28] *Thomas answered him, "My Lord and my God!"* [20:29] *Jesus said to him, "Have you believed because you have seen me? Blessed are*

tary by G. Kalantzis, Early Christian Studies 7 (Sydney: Saint Paul's Publications, 2004), pp. 143-44. [36]The section of text included within angle brackets (< >), ending on p. 166 is missing from the Syriac text and has been taken from the so-called Syriac catena Gannat Bussāmē: see J.-M. Vosté, "Le Gannat Bussāmē," RB 37 (1928): 221-32, 386-419 (394-96). Unfortunately the original Syriac text of the catena is not included by J.-M. Vosté in his article. Instead there is only a reference to the pages of the manuscript (Vat. Syr. 494, 321b-323b), and to Ishoʿdad of Merv, who quotes this same section of the *Gannat Bussāmē* with a few unimportant variants (see *The Commentaries of Ishoʿdad in Syriac: Luke and John*, Syriac text edited by M. Dunlop Gibson, HSem 7 [Cambridge: Cambridge University Press, 1911], pp. 222-23); CSCO 4 3:356. [37]Eph 6:16. [38]See Gen 2:7. [39]Mt 16:19. [40]Jn 16:15. [41]Mk 2:7.

those who have not seen and yet have come to believe." The narrator counts eight days from the first day of the week when Jesus was resurrected to the time when he then appeared to those who did not know where he came from or how he had gotten there. And since he rose from the tomb as a spiritual being, luminous, thin and agile, he easily passed through closed doors and whatever else he wanted to without any difficulty—although it was no one else who had risen other than that same person who was dead but nevertheless, in the glory of immortality, was in a state incomprehensible to us. And when [Thomas] ever so carefully touched him and accurately ascertained the truth, he confessed his fault saying, *My Lord and my God!* But what does this mean? While Thomas did not previously believe that the Savior had risen from the dead, does he now call him Lord and God? This is not likely. Thomas, the doubting disciple, does not call the person whom he touched Lord and God. The knowledge of the resurrection had, in fact, not taught him that he who had risen was God. Rather, it was as though he was praising God for the miracle that had been performed, astonished at the miracles he saw. Three times grace was given to the disciples who believed: in the mission to the Gentiles, after the resurrection and at Pentecost.

"*Blessed are those who have not seen and yet have believed,* namely, your ten brothers and companions in ministry." I am certain, as the Scripture also testifies, that these also believed after they saw him, but by no means before seeing him. However, since they were not as open in their resistance, nor did they say, like Thomas, "If we do not see the spots of the nails," and so on, they did not deserve the reproach he received. And yet this expression must surely extend to the entire multitude of believers who did not see the Savior and yet truly believed in him because of what they heard.

[20:30] *Now Jesus did many other signs in the presence of his disciples, which are not written in this book.* [20:31] *But these are written so that you may come to believe that Jesus is the Messiah, the Son of God, and that through believing you may have life in his name.* The Evangelist shows by these words that the signs which the Savior did in the presence of the disciples were innumerable. Beyond this, he testifies that the words of the Gospels are true, namely, those words that were written independently and accurately by the other [Evangelists] and were omitted by him. There is no hint of polemics in John not reporting what they said; rather, he makes it clear that their words are authentic and that they suffice for those who come to them with faith as they ponder them, read them, and come to understand them. The blessed John refers to the Gospel written by him as, *this book.*>[42]

Our Lord had said, *Have you believed because you have now seen me? Blessed are those who have not seen and yet have believed in me,* indicating those whose strength was such that they believed in him without seeing him. On the other hand, the Evangelist adds something even greater than this by saying, *Jesus did many other signs in the presence of his disciples, which are not written in this book.* In other words, "Even those things that *were* written hardly reveal the extent of his power; no one indeed can perfectly perceive its magnitude; but [these were written] so that, through them all people might know, insofar as is possible [for them to know]."

Thus he spoke to his disciples.

[21:15] *When they had finished breakfast, Jesus said to Simon Peter, "Simon son of John, do you love me more that these?" He said to him, "Yes, Lord; you know that I love you."* [Simon] does not dare simply to believe in his own word but entrusts this to the knowledge of our Lord. For he thought about the fact that he had

---

[42]This concludes the missing section from the Syriac text referenced in n. 36.

previously said he would lay down his life for him, but the Messiah had reproved him for his pride, saying, "You will deny me three times."[43] Therefore, because Simon remembered this, he responded correctly when he said, *You know*, that is, "you fully know. For I previously thought otherwise[44] about myself;[45] <but your words turned out to be true. Therefore I am more careful now." Jesus replied to him, *Feed my lambs.* Peter had answered modestly and with humility as to one who is all-knowing and able to inspect the deep things of the heart and the inner thoughts of the mind. Therefore [Jesus] promoted him and placed him as the head of the lambs of his flock and said, "*Feed my lambs*, that is, all those who by their words believe in me who are weaker because they have only recently received instruction. This is why you must carry their burden and protect them and comfort them in their weakness and nourish them with the grace that was given to you." [21:16] *A second time he said to him, "Simon son of John, do you love me?" He said to him, "Yes, Lord; you know that I love you." Jesus said to him, "Tend my sheep,"* that is, those perfected men of consumate wisdom who obey you in the ordained orders of the church, in the apostolate, in the priesthood and in the pastoral office. [21:17] *He said to him the third time, "Do you love me?" Peter felt hurt because he said to him the third time, "Do you Love me?" And he said to him, "Lord, you know everything; you know that I love you." Jesus said to him, "Feed my sheep,"* that is, all the rational souls, the holy virgins, the righteous nuns, the pure and modest wives, the cleansed penitents, the entire group of women of proven spirit, together with all the men who are decent and simple. The Savior does not say to him, "fast" or "keep watch for me." Instead, he entrusts him with the pastoral care of souls, since this

is more worthy and more useful to the community. "I," he says, "need nothing. Feed my sheep, and return to me the love with which I have loved you, because I will receive your care for them as though it were devoted to me."

Therefore Simon was not so bold as to simply answer him, "I love you," but said, *Lord, you know everything; you know that I love you.* He thought about the fact that before he had not only said, "I will never deny you," but also that he would lay down his life for him. So the Lord, in a reproach to his pride, said to him, "You will deny me three times."[46] This is why Simon now says, "You know, Lord—and know better than I." *Peter felt hurt because he said to him the third time, "do you love me?"* Simon was upset by this third question and felt hurt because he thought that the Lord, perhaps foreknowing another denial, wanted to mock his affirmations of love. Thus, after being wounded by the sting of the third question, he recognized the Lord's just knowledge of the future. "You," he says, "know I have been shown incapable of predicting the future; I am ignorant of such things. You are the spring of wisdom; you are the principle of knowledge." But the Lord, in consideration of his wound, dispelled his fear and sealed his love with the seal of his testimony, and confirmed his confession by offering the remedy of confession to the wound of the denial. Thus he demanded a triple confession in order to apply the remedy of a triple confession to the triple wound of denial, and in order to display before the disciples the ardor of Peter's love. But at the same time, he also wanted to show that Peter's denial was providential and not simply happenstance. Through these three [questions] [Christ] also removed from Peter's soul those three struggles in which Satan tempted Simon, and he sanctified him. At the same time, he

---

[43]See Jn 13:38. [44]In other words, Peter previously thought he could withstand temptation, but he has since seen the error of his ways. [45]The section of text included within angle brackets (< >), ending on p. 169 is missing from the commentary of Theodore, and has been taken from the so-called Syriac catena Gannat Bussāmē. This section of the catena, however, is not included in the commentary by Ishoʿdad like the previous one. See above n. 36; Vosté, "Le Gannat Bussāmē," pp. 221-32, 386-419 (394-96); CSCO 4 3:359. [46]Jn 13:38.

suggested to Peter that those three categories of his flock should be baptized in the threefold name of the confession of the Trinity and should be sanctified and led into his kingdom.

[21:18] *Truly, truly, I say to you, when you were younger, you used to fasten your own belt and to go wherever you wished. But when you grow old, you will stretch out your hands, and someone else will fasten a belt around you and take you where you do not wish to go.* [21:19] *He said this to indicate the kind of death by which he would glorify God.* Since the Lord saw that Peter was tortured by the memory of the past and that he was heavily burdened and full of grief because of the memory of his denial, he revealed to him what he would suffer for his denial. Peter himself committed everything to the knowledge of our Lord. Once the Lord had taught him that a great change would occur in him, from what he was before to what he would become later, he said to Peter, "Do not fear the future. In fact, I know that your love for me is so strong that you will even be crucified for me upside down." And since what the Lord said here was not clear, it was explained by the Evangelist, *He said this to indicate the kind of death by which he would glorify God.*

Someone else will fasten a belt, because those who die the death of the cross are fastened to the wood. When Nero ordered him to be executed on the cross, [Peter] asked his executioners to crucify him upside down, that is, with his head down and his feet up, so that an identical passion like that [of Christ] might not cause him to be venerated by the more simple people. Therefore, since he was teaching people to worship the cross of the Lord, he did not want to provide, to those who like to argue, the pretext for objecting, "In what does the cross of the Lord differ from that of Simon? Both of them were nailed to the cross in the same manner." And so Peter changed his own cross.

Someone else will fasten a belt, because the one who is crucified with his head down and his feet up hangs suspended from the cross with his feet and loins well bound. But the hands of the one who is crucified with his head up are tightly bound to the cross so that by dying he may not slide and fall from the cross. The words, *and take you where you do not wish to go,* are said because the crucified must necessarily be bound by others where he does not wish. *After this he said to him, "Follow me."* The Savior said to Simon, "Follow me in the same way of the passion in which I suffered, by carrying your cross with all patience and forbearance."

[21:20] *Peter turned and saw the disciple whom Jesus loved following them; he was the one who had reclined next to Jesus at the supper and had said, "Lord who is it that is going to betray you?"* Peter turned, thanks to a secret decision of providence, and saw from a distance the disciple John, son of thunder, who was slowly following behind, admiring the great and sublime promise made by our Lord to Peter. [21:21] *When Peter saw him, he said to Jesus, "What about him?"* That is, "What death will he suffer for you, and through what path of good works will he come to you?" [21:22] *Jesus said to him, "If it is my will that he remain until I come, what is that to you? Follow me!"* [21:23] *So the rumor spread in the community that this disciple would not die. Yet Jesus did not say to him that he would not die, but, "If it is my will that he remain until I come, what is that to you?"* John lived a long time, that is, seventy-three years after the ascension of the Lord to the time of Trajan, and died a natural death in peace and serenity after all the other apostles. The Lord then alludes to this by saying, "If I want him to live long enough so that he remains until my return, there is no need for you to pry into this. Be concerned with what pertains to you; in other words, look after your own work and follow me."

[21:24] *This is the disciple who is testifying to these things and has written them, and we know that his testimony is true.* [21:25] *But there are also many other things that Jesus did; if every* one of them were written down, I suppose that the world itself could not contain the books that would be written. The Interpreter[47] says that the words, *But there are also,* and so on, are not by John, but by someone else.>[48]

And here we conclude the seventh treatise, which finishes and completes this commentary on the harp of the Spirit, on the heavenly theologian and apostle, the friend of the glory of the Lord, the holy John the younger. And the universal Interpreter and perfect doctor, the holy Theodore, light of the Christian church, composed this commentary in the good order of the chapters and various articles, and in a logical manner, and with precise examination.

May their prayers be a wall [of defense] for the entire universe. Amen.

---

[47]This is the name usually given to Theodore of Mopsuestia by the Syriac Nestorian Church.   [48]This concludes the missing section of text supplied by the Syriac catena referenced in n. 45 (p. 167).

Scripture Index